In loving memory of my mother
Alice Eugenia Cleland Clagett

Acknowledgments

My gratitude to my mother is never-ending, for all that she gave me in her life and in her death. Heartfelt thanks to my mother's sister Rita, my last mother, for her continuing unconditional love; and to Elizabeth and her mother, Ruth, for their support in sharing their coterminous journey. Thanks to the Society for PSP and all the members on its online Forum at the time for practical and emotional support. I relied on a network of friends, back home in Colorado and where I grew up in Virginia, as well as states in between, to keep me grounded in my own essence as I felt myself spread too thin. Their love and support, their emails and dinners, helped me face every day with some semblance of grace and courage: special thanks to Amy for Tuesday dinners and to Wayne for being there, to Beth for showing up, to my cousin Melinda, and to Gaytha; and to all my friends away from there too numerous to name, you know you lifted me and held me up. I am deeply grateful to Suzi and to Salon for helping me weave my way back into life at home when I returned after a difficult year away. Thanks to Marion, Auntie, Connie, Chris, and Melody, who were kind and helpful readers as I sorted out how to present this material, and to Diane, whose editing was an inspiration. Thanks to the staff at Johns Hopkins University Hospital and at the Mayo Clinic for their compassion and competence. And finally, thanks to my father, the Colonel, for enabling me to make the journey, and for doing the best that he could.

Preface

Progressive Supranuclear Palsy is a rare brain disease affecting only a few thousand people in the U.S. each year. When my mother, my best friend, was diagnosed with PSP, I knew my life would change radically, and I began to journal the undertaking as I helped her cope with her diagnosis, her decline, and her death. Being a caregiver for a parent is a challenge that can be full of contradiction: devastating and uplifting at the same time. I hope that these excerpts from my journal and selected correspondence during my mother's last year will help other caregivers in their own journeys to find support, humor and compassion during a deeply difficult time.

Introduction:

Killing Mother

*T*he year I turned forty-five I was forced to seriously consider killing my mother. In the end, despite my best intentions, I did not do it. I did move from the ragged interior of the country to the urban East Coast that year to help her die.

When I drove away from my sanctuary hidden in the high desert, I believed that if she asked me to, I'd be able to end her life. I also believed, even more strongly, that if I had the disease she'd been diagnosed with, I would wait as long as I could, drive to the edge of the Black Canyon, videotape a short goodbye, including apologies to those who'd have to clean up my remains, and take a flying leap off the rim of the two thousand foot chasm. I'd fly. I'd soar as I plummeted to the bottom. Theoretically, I'd be dead of a heart attack long before I hit ground, but I'd try to stay conscious as the jagged boulders holding the river rushed to meet me. I'd spread my arms, try some freefall spins, and cry out to god all the while offering thanks for the splendor of the life I was ending.

I never thought, when I was growing up in Virginia, that I could live farther than an hour from an ocean. I thought I'd die of claustrophobia stuck inside the middle of the continent. I couldn't imagine then that I would end up finding peace of mind in the rural West. But here, I'm within a day's drive of anything I could ever need in life: the deserts, red and pink, apricot, sand and rock, of Utah and Arizona; the ghostly hills of New Mexico and O'Keefe's paintings of them in Santa Fe; any number of rushing untamed rivers, wild in all or in part, accessible by foot or raft or canoe; the wild terrain of puma and bear, elk and mule deer, badger, coyote, bobcat; the most cold and barren peaks stateside, alive with alpenglow, and lower, the miracle of tundra; all these places a reliable vehicle and my feet can carry me and my longing within half a day's journey. So I do not miss the sea.

I love the sea, but I do not need it in the way that I need the spare wildness of the desert, or the sight of mountains, or the embrace of slickrock canyons. My mother helped me purchase land here, near the edge of a cliff overlooking a small canyon. She encouraged me while I built an adobe house on the land. She watched from the balcony as I laid flagstone for a patio, then drank her tea on the patio while watching birds at the feeder. She taught me as a child to feed the birds, to love the wild, and her support allowed me to build a life within it. I drove away from that life back to the coast, intending to give back to my mother all the love and nurturing she'd given me, confident that I could help her end her life if she asked it of me.

However, after several months with my dear mother and her rapidly degenerating brain stem, I had no certainties left. None at all. Not about my ability to assist her suicide, not about my own conviction to end my life if I end up with the same disease. Only after she finally did die, did I realize I'd lost my faith as well, somewhere during the long, quick ordeal of her demise.

The intensity of her will to live is part of what kept me from being able to end her life when she asked me to. Despite egregious bodily discomfort, and a lifetime of rage at one circumstance after another, still she managed to laugh, and to dress, to do her ablutions and go through the motions, day after day. Until, one day, her desire to die finally overcame her will to live.

Three years before she was correctly diagnosed with PSP, my mother Ali was misdiagnosed with Parkinson's Disease. That summer, we took a trip to Alaska, to fulfill her long-held dream of a cruise down the Inside Passage. She'd already fallen once or twice by then, but nobody thought anything of it. You get old, you fall. Our first night out we were walking back from cocktails on deck, staggering in the ocean air along the narrow corridor between the deck railing and the ship's wall, giggling and laughing at how we staggered, swearing it was the rolling ship and not the cocktails that made us weave like weathered drunks back to our cabin. Possibly, in her case, it was partly the PSP. I blame my staggers on being seasick.

She fell on a shore walk in Ketchikan, though it seemed clear at the time that she'd tripped. We were walking over driftwood and smooth boulders and seaweed to see some petroglyphs along the shore. She had passed on several of the proffered shore tours but, ever the art appreciator, not this one. She was bruised and sore afterwards, yet undaunted. In the end, we were so glad we'd gone to Alaska when we did. She knew at the time it would be her last trip. She didn't even come visit me again. And she began to fall more often.

When she fell, she fell straight back. Just dropped, no blackout, no light-headed warning, she just fell back. Once she hit her hip on the corner of a granite table in the lobby of the Home where she lived with my father, the Colonel; twice she hit her head on the apartment floor and required stitches. While falling was her most dramatic symptom, the most insidious might have been her double vision. I'd visited three years earlier when the Colonel had an appendectomy, to help her with his recovery. I flew in and met her at Walter Reed Army Hospital in D.C., the hospital where her grandfather the General had finished out his life. After I'd visited with the Colonel in his room, she and I went down to the car in the parking garage. I offered to drive but she said she was fine, and so she drove into the bright light of the ramp leading into the heart of downtown traffic. I glanced over and noticed she had one eye closed.

"You're driving with one eye closed!" I shrieked. "Why are you driving with one eye closed?!"

"Double vision," she replied. "I only see one if I close one eye. It comes and goes." By then the light was green and let us out and I couldn't insist that she pull over. The hotel was only two blocks away, but after we arrived I took the car keys. Eventually her eye doctor prescribed special glasses to try to help the double vision. Prisms, she said. It didn't occur to me to ask any questions, as long as Dr. Schefkind was doing something to fix it; after all, he was the doctor.

She'd also been seeing Dr. Williams, a neurologist who'd diagnosed the Parkinson's. Where did he come from? How did she end up in his hands? I think he was on some list the Home published for their residents. Dr. Williams recommended that Ali read a book about Parkinson's, and so she recommended it to me. I ordered it from Amazon and a few days later began to read. On page 11, chapter 1, What Is Parkinsonism? I found this description of one of several diseases often mistaken for Parkinson's:

Progressive Supranuclear Palsy is the most common of the 'Parkinson Plus' syndromes. The initial clinical presentations may be like Parkinson's disease. For this reason, it is often first diagnosed as Parkinson's disease. The correct diagnosis is usually made several years after the first symptoms appear or not until after the patient dies and the brain is examined at autopsy. Patients with PSP complain of falls, gait disorder, visual problems, speech difficulties and swallowing abnormalities.... Tremor is usually absent, and there may be a rigidity of the neck muscles that keep the head in extension. Patients have a wide-eyed 'astonished' stare that sometimes can be differentiated from the masked face of typical Parkinson's disease. The diagnostic criterion by which PSP may be recognized during life is the inability to look down voluntarily.... As the disease progresses, other eye movement abnormalities may occur.

I read a few more pages, but I kept coming back to that paragraph. It described Ali's symptoms to the letter. The first symptoms I had noticed, not knowing they were symptoms, were her slump and her slowness, years before Alaska. She was sitting at my table sipping a drink. Her shoulders were hunched forward and her head hung so that she was looking at the table rather than at me. She held her glass in one hand and raised it in slow motion to her lips. I told her to sit up straight, open her heart, lift her eyes. When she was reminded, she was able to square her shoulders somewhat, and hold her head up, but very shortly she'd forget and droop again. She also had that astonished stare. There's no other way to describe it.

I made it to page 33 before I determined that Ali had PSP so why bother reading about Parkinson's. This was in July 2003. I suggested she bring up the possibility to Dr. Williams. So she told him, at her next appointment, opening the book to page 11, "My daughter thinks I may have this disease." Naturally, being a highly trained neurologist, Dr. Williams said, "I'm the doctor!" and that was the end of that discussion. I suppose I wanted it to be Parkinson's and so I let his opinion stand. By that time I'd read more about PSP, and definitely didn't want her to have that.

But we started then trying to get her an appointment for a second opinion at Johns Hopkins University Hospital, and could not get one scheduled until January 14. That November, I visited for a couple of weeks, and I knew it was bad. I returned from my travels just before Christmas, and after the holidays I found myself at loose ends, wondering about my purpose and value in life. I felt so lost and down that I prayed fervently for some work more meaningful than the job I was doing. And I had thought I was doing what I wanted to do. But it felt empty.

My brother called from his cell phone on the way back to the hotel after Mom's visit to Hopkins and said, "You were right." An hour and a half in the hands of a stellar young neurologist who knew what to look for and knew, above all, that the disease existed, and my mother had her answer. It turns out that many neurologists don't even know enough about PSP to diagnose it. That day I looked online for Dr. Katherine Widnell at Hopkins, and found a photo of a woman young enough to be my daughter. I also telephoned the Society for PSP, which I found listed in the back of that infamous book I stopped reading on page 33. I told the nice woman there about the diagnosis and the symptoms I'd noticed for years, then said, "I guess I'll finish up some work here and then move out there, maybe in the fall."

"That may be too late," said this unknown woman on the other end of the phone line, and so I resolved to move in spring. It was that simple.

I told Mom on the phone a few days later that I was going to start winding things up at home so I could move out there in spring. "Oh honey, I don't want you to do that," said my mother, "I want you to come when I'm *dying* dying, you know—I don't want you to give up your life and come out here now." I thought, but you *are* dying dying now, don't you know, don't you see? So I finished up the projects I was working on, and prepared to move back East at the end of March.

During the course of those two months I often visited the PSP Forum online. When I'd spoken with the Society in January, the woman had told me about the Forum and suggested I visit it, but "maybe not just yet," as she feared its content would be too intense for me to handle right away. Within two weeks after diagnosis I visited the Forum and became a regular reader. Every night that I logged on and read the threads of accounts of various wives, daughters, husbands, sons, and a very few parents struggling with PSP's ravages on a loved one, I ended up bawling before I logged off.

PSP is fatal and usually kills between one and ten years after diagnosis. PSP gradually takes away all a body's motor functions, voluntary and involuntary, while leaving the mind's awareness virtually intact. Many PSP patients die of aspiration pneumonia after inhaling their own saliva or their dinner.

PSP is about 1% as common as Parkinson's disease. Estimates suggest that perhaps as many as 20,000 people in the U.S. actually manifest symptoms of PSP, but only about 4,000 are diagnosed correctly; most are misdiagnosed with Parkinson's. However, about 25% of people diagnosed with PSP end up, upon autopsy, having had something else, either Parkinson's or one of the other rare, weird brain diseases that kill these days. I have to wonder if the human brain simply has not evolved as fast as our human strategies to outrun death far into old age.

What research there is suggests that there is a genetic component to PSP and there is also some kind of environmental trigger or triggers. The genetic component has been identified as the H1H1 haplotype on a particular gene, but nobody can figure out what the environmental triggers are. On the PSP Forum, family members are trying to link it to exposure to certain chemicals, or to some sort of physical trauma preceding the first symptom, or to any tangible source they can identify. Yet the cause of PSP remains a mystery, while the effects ravage thousands yearly, one family at a time.

I began to write about my mother's, and my, journey with Progressive Supranuclear Palsy, knowing only where it would ultimately lead, but unaware of how we would get there.

In her first few visits to me in Colorado, Ali was able to walk to the edge of Buck Canyon in my back yard. Here she sits on the rim with Dia, the calico cat, looking east toward the mountains.

Part 1: *Before*

January

This deep sense that I'll have to leave here for a long time has today been verified when Jock called with our mother's diagnosis. I answered the phone. "You were right," he said simply. It looks like I'll go within a couple of months. Yes. I feel as clear and driven to follow this path as I ever have about any big decision.

I've led a selfish life. I've never done all I could for her—or for anyone, really. I've always held back something for myself, no small portion, either, but a whole lot of myself. Or perhaps, and this is the problem, isn't it, I've not been whole. Not for a long time. I've seen myself as broken—split—fractured. I have clung to my privacy, my space, led "my" life for years, hoarding and protecting myself. I need to give everything to this mission.

But getting caught up in "good" rushes is just as "bad" in a Buddhist sense as getting caught up in "bad" rushes is in any ethic. Being attached to being a hero is no better on a certain level that being attached to watching violent crime shows on TV. Pursuing a benevolent or heroic path motivated by ego is as spiritually ignorant as a life addicted to fear.

Saturday, January 24

Mother called awhile ago. She was trying to comb the scab off the back of her skull while standing at the bathroom mirror while talking to me on the portable phone. I begged her to sit down, and suggested that, say you have five years, what you want to do immediately is start reducing risks, so you can make it that five years and don't kill yourself in a fall before then. She said, "I don't think I'm as far-gone as you think I am." Jesus. I scolded her.

I finally called Jock tonight. I should have called much sooner. I guess I expected he'd call me. Or I was giving him time to decompress and process all that he'd been through when he came up to take Mom to Johns Hopkins.

He told me two stories. One, while they were in Baltimore, Jock was letting Dad pay for things and then quietly tipping people for their extra help. Neither Dad nor Mom seemed to notice that Jock was tipping. But afterwards, when they were home, Mom asked him how much money he had paid those people in tips. Though she had seemed to notice nothing, she was in fact paying attention. Then he told me of checking out after taking her to the hairdresser. The lady told her it would be forty-seven dollars, and Mom turned to Jock and asked him if he wanted "one of those brochures."

"No," he said. The lady behind the counter asked, "How do you want to pay for this?"

"It's for men," Mom said, indicating the advertised product. Finally, though, she caught up and proffered her wallet to pay.

I tried to tell him about things like that happening when I was there in November. Different from him seeing it for himself, though. I remember she asked Dad a question, and he interrupted her with the answer before she was halfway through—she continued on and completed asking the question, and he yelled at her, "I just told you!" Later I suggested to him that this lag in her reaction time might be a function of the disease, that she can't process quickly enough to interrupt herself once she's started the sentence. Hence, I must learn patience and curb my impulse to interject. Until such time as she has more trouble with words—oh the poor little woman. I want to pour love back into her.

Sunday, January 25

Dearest Mother,

I'm sorry if you felt I was picking on you last night. I do worry about you now that I know more about PSP. I don't know how much of the literature you've managed to read, or how much Dr. Widnell told you about it. Why don't you tell me what you know, and then I'll tell you what I know, so we'll both be on the same page.

Based on what I know, no matter how long you have to live with it, the best way I can imagine to manage the rest of your life is to minimize risk and to enhance enjoyment. I have lots of ideas about how to enhance enjoyment, also, and that's why I want to come back there to be with you. Meanwhile, I'm simply offering suggestions of how to minimize your risks of both falling and choking.

"I just want what's best for you." Now it's your turn to hear that from me, and you have to trust me, because I've always trusted you when you said that to me. I love you and I hate that you're suffering with this ailment. I have to try to do something. Love, your Night Rainbow.

Monday, January 26

Dearest Mother,

What you have done for me is support my efforts to create for myself a nurturing space, a fulfilling life, a deep yearning to be good. You've helped me to set myself up to bear your absence when you are one day gone.

Did you ever think, ahead of time, about your mother dying? It's said that what makes us human is our awareness of our own impending deaths. What really makes us human, makes us soft, forgiving, wise, is our awareness of the inevitable deaths of everyone we love.

I have struggled all my conscious life with the fear that one day you would die and I would be truly alone in the world. For no other person has ever meant as much to me. You're my "more-than-I-can-say-friend," as you say I told you when I was two or three. You've *made* me, by letting me become—and someday I will create something great—or at least simply live a good and quiet life. Only you have given me so much of what is me.

So I have feared all my conscious life, losing you—and been steeling myself for it by examining my fear of death and its role in defining my life.

In light of death all life shines more brightly. My other fear has been that I would die before you—and how could you have borne that?

It is an honor, a rare gift, to even contemplate being able to walk with you toward death. You have given me, truly, the gift of life in so many ways. I will miss you terribly but you will be always with me. Because of your generous love, and appreciation of who I am (for you have always known) I arrive at the age of forty-five almost knowing myself, and well-prepared to thrive where I have planted myself. I am deeply grateful for your financial support over the years that has ultimately enabled my fondest dream to come true—this peaceful home on the canyon.

But more, it's the emotional support behind those gifts. Emotional is too narrow a word. I believe it's what's the same in you as in me that offers this unconditional love. Your half of my genes, or god, or both—what's the difference? I have had you to depend on long enough that I am strong enough now to depend on me and the god that links us.

In Baguio, the Philippines, where the family often drove to escape the heat of Manila, while her father was stationed as an aide to her grandfather.

February

She was burned when she was five. I have a small, hand-colored photograph of her from before the scar. Her shoulder and the side of her face are in shadow, her hair is pulled back from all across her forehead and tied with a wide satin ribbon. It's a precious, little-girl hairdo, as though her mother parted a circle around the top of her head and pulled back the curls. Her unblemished forehead is framed with baby blonde wisps. She wears a white sleeveless dress. Where the scar would be on her right shoulder is clean baby skin.

She is clearly healthy in this photo, so she must be about three, for she had been ill quite awhile before her grandparents took her to Jacksonville to stay with Aunt Julie, away from her parents and siblings. The climate in Florida was thought to be better for her croup than the climate in Nebraska. Every night she had a croup-kettle steaming at her bedside. Apparently, one night she pulled it over on herself. The whole family was downstairs at dinner and heard her screaming. She never was fond of Aunt Julie after that.

In the picture, she smiles and those smooth cheeks nearly dimple. Her eyes gleam with wonder and delight. She was the darling of the family, the youngest, and her sister Rita says she was everyone's favorite because she was so adorable and sweet. She was especially Grandfather's favorite, and he felt awful when she got burned, for he was the one who had insisted on taking her to Florida to recover. He regretted it until the day he died.

As she grew up, even as the trauma of separation and the horror of the burn dissipated during her charmed childhood, she began to see herself as disfigured. It must have been especially hard for her as a teen. At some point, she began to wear her hair always parted on the left and swooped down near her right eyebrow to cover the scar on her forehead. As I was growing up, she always kept her shoulder covered.

For all that, which she incorporated somehow as her due, she did manage to have fun as a girl. She and her sister dated brothers, best friends, the boys next door; they smoked cigarettes, spied on each other, and, her brother says, pretended to be good when he came home on leave from the war.

The sweet golden child in this photograph has not yet met a single disappointment, betrayal, or threat. Her hands are clasped in front of her chest, elbows bent, knuckles of her left hand just visible below the curve of her right fingers. I look at it now and try to replicate the exact amount of tension in her bent arms, her taut knuckles, and the bright expectation in her eyes; she is excited about something, a prize at the end of the portrait, or just being there, being photographed all by her beautiful self.

That was before the scar. She wore her hair over her right forehead all her life until very near the end, when all her skin had gone so pale and fragile that the scar disappeared into it.

Thursday, February 5

So emotional, life. This life. Today, talking with Mom, realizing that she doesn't really understand the progression of the disease. If she'd read all or even any of the material she's gotten, wouldn't she know? Maybe not. And maybe it's a function of the disease minimizing her comprehension.

On the PSP Forum a note from a woman named Elizabeth saying if I need a place to crash on my way from Colorado to Virginia I'm welcome to stay with her in St. Louis—made me blurt out laughter and tears at the same time. Such kindness always does. The voices on the Forum are so very kind, so loving, tender, fraught. I really worry that Mom doesn't realize how bad this is going to get. The selfish thing was not getting on an airplane in January and flying out right then to discuss the diagnosis with her.

I need to get her antioxidants that she can swallow. What are the antioxidants? I can't remember. I see it everywhere and I don't know what they are.

Snow coming down strong now, after a partly sunny, partly hazy, soft, and very cold day. I skied the dogs for nearly an hour this morning, did a bit of yoga in the tower, and snowshoed up the driveway to get the mail. Feeling quite good now, after a brief lapse into fatigue.

Am awaiting a call from Mom and her new speech therapist. Her voice is deteriorating noticeably since I was there three months ago. When I asked her if she'd like to talk with someone else who has PSP, I brought up the possibility that this woman on the Forum may not be able to speak much longer. I said, "I don't know if you know this, and I hate to tell you, but some of these people are writing about ways they've figured out to communicate with their parents when they can no longer speak at all." She said, "Gaaawd! I hope they're not *deaf*!"

How will it go for her, I wonder. Oh I am just hating this. I need to get there. The snow is flowing up as much as down, swirling above the ground. Kind of how I feel.

Tuesday's yoga session with Nancy was helpful. When I mentioned my fears about living in Our Nation's Capital, she said, "You have to remember you are there to do light work. You can't even go to the dark places in your thoughts." She also cautioned me, "Don't get caught up in the suffering of the one." Hmmm.

Saturday, February 7

There's another plus. There must be great coffee shops around there somewhere. I found myself telling Linda, "I'm really looking forward to this move." I am, when I do not let myself think of the blistering prospect of leaving here, my soul's home, with deep snow and clear sun and stars beyond compare. With deer and elk and lion, eagle coyote bear... with my poets and my sisters, my friends, my canyon. Oh well. If I don't think about what I'm leaving 'til I get there and can reminisce productively, I'll be better off. And really, I do believe my energy is returning.

Monday, February 9

I got to laughing tonight thinking about the chicken foot. Will I tell Mom when I see her?

She's come to see me almost every year I've lived out West. The first year I lived in Colorado we took a road trip. We drove into the vast unknown (to her) of the red and yellow Utah rockscape. We visited Capitol Reef, the Moki Dugway, the Burr Trail, where she squealed when I got too close to the edge of the sheer drop off the red clay road. We visited Calf Creek Falls, south of Torrey on Utah 12, one of the finest drives a road-tripper can take. We camped high up in the aspens and firs of the Boulder National Forest off that two-lane road, where she painted watercolors of the trees and I photographed her doing it. We crossed Lake Powell on the ferry at Bullfrog Marina, and marveled together at the reflection of orange rock in blue water lapped with silver waves. We stayed in lodges, inns, and tents, and she loved Monument Valley, where we stayed at Gouldings' and took the native jeep tour of the escarpments.

On the way home, we stayed at the Best Western in Blanding and ate dinner next door at a greasy café. She ordered fried chicken. She always made the best fried chicken in her electric skillet. I can see her standing at the counter next to the sink in an apron, dipping chicken pieces in flour and laying them in an inch of saved bacon fat in the green electric skillet, then putting the lid on. God, that was good fried chicken. It was Granny's recipe, from Tennessee, and she—well, they both—loved that they were famous for it.

So here we were in Blanding, Utah, far from the deep South, and she ordered fried chicken in this little greasy diner on Main Street. I remember the seriously cooked green beans, just like down South, and really enjoying my pork chops. She really enjoyed her chicken, too, but she couldn't eat it all. There were several large families nearby, and quite a lot of noise in the white-light glare. There was a salad bar back in the shadows, and we sat on the threshold of dark and light, near the front door.

I don't remember exactly when I saw the chicken claw. I just remember seeing it peeking out from underneath another piece of fried chicken, gray and scaly, clenched but not completely closed, with bits of browned batter stuck around the toes. It was awful and hilarious at the same time. If I'd been eating fried chicken too I'm sure I would have lost it. I gasped, but she didn't notice. I turned her plate a bit, pretending to look at her vegetables, teasing her about not eating them, and then moved on to discuss dessert. Like the elephant in the room, the chicken foot loomed. Eventually, she'd eaten all she wanted, all the while missing this chicken foot with every mouthful she reached for.

I never said a word. I found myself overcome with giggles now and then the rest of the night, but managed to succumb only when she was not around, when she had gone into the bathroom for her evening ablutions, after she'd gone to sleep. I couldn't stop grinning from the awfulness of it, and I wanted to protect her from the knowledge.

It seems silly in retrospect. So what if there was a chicken foot on her plate? To many people in the world a chicken foot might be a real delicacy, a tiny bite of protein in an otherwise bleak diet of starch. But this was Ali the proper, Ali the protected. She would have been revolted. Or, maybe she would have laughed out loud.

I still have the card she sent me after she got home: "I think our trip was the most fun I ever had," she wrote, "Love, Mother."

Saturday, February 14

Mom's aide Joan said last night several things: one, "You don't need to worry about your parents with me there, Rita," and two, "She move too fass for her feet!" She says she's thought about saying something to Mom when she careens around on her walker, but decided better of it, and so she just hangs on, but she gave the impression that Mom totters, and it makes her nervous. I need to go online and order her a wheelchair now, so we have it when we need it.

Tuesday, February 17

This afternoon I called Mary, whom I met on the PSP Forum. She lives in Little Rock, and wanted to speak with someone else with PSP, so I responded to her note on the Forum and offered to connect her with Mom. They haven't spoken yet, but she and I had a good conversation. A strong, brave woman. She's applying for a trial with a brain-surgery research project that will put two tubes from her stomach to her brain, and so on.

If the process works, she will get some relief from the awkwardness of the balance problem, and some of her other symptoms. She suffers from rigid fingers, and had gone through carpal tunnel surgery before the PSP diagnosis revealed the true cause. Mary is sixty-one years old. God, how awful. At her age, I understand why she's willing to get tubes in her brain.

I can't believe when Mom was here in 2000 for her birthday, and she was moving so slowly, that I passively sat there and thought, It must be COPD (Chronic Obstructive Pulmonary Disease). That, of course, was her diagnosis at the time, her first misdiagnosis. Probably even her lung problems are related to PSP. Ah well. At least I'm on the right track now, and moving toward efficacy.

I am appalled at the significance of every little thing in my own solitary life. I am floored by the total insignificance of my one life among the billions of lives of all sentient beings.

How to reconcile that insignificance with the flux of benefits that come to me from being born when and where I was. Who could I have been if anywhere else? I am so glad for who I am at this moment, though still I know that I don't do enough, don't live with enough integrity. Am not sufficiently vigilant.

Nothing lasts. The uplifting music on the radio fades into DJ gibberish. A crater rim of snow around the circular drive melts.

Saturday, February 21

Mother says she thinks her first symptom was in 2000 when she was visiting me, at the Delta Pow-Wow, when she couldn't get up from her seat on the ground. Later she says double vision was the first symptom. Clearly she is trying to understand: Why did I or did I not notice? As though, poor dear, she might think she could have headed it off.

As far as striking the perfect balance between making me and letting me become the person I am today, you did perfectly. I am so delighted with myself. I like myself as well as anyone else I know. I love life. Life. I revel in every day, its dramatic adventure no farther than the next breath.

What will I do when you're gone? Who will remember that I like peanut soup?

Ali's grandfather, General John L. Hines, a celebrated son of White Sulphur Springs, West Virginia, owned a home nearby called Rocky Gap, where Ali and her siblings spent summers growing up. Here at around age twelve she poses on the swing.

March

She says her saliva is stringy. She doesn't like soy milk because she says it "enhances" that stringy saliva. I advised her to get Joan to rent her a wheelchair for trips to the commissary, doctors, etc.

She wants me to "find Samuel Pepys Diary," to see if that's where the Lady from Philadelphia is. She says, "I can't find—in my memory—where she is." I find her, finally, in *The Peterkin Papers*, and order a copy from Amazon.

Thursday, March 4

Something is at work in me that I have not yet acknowledged or articulated. I find myself alone, deeply craving company—lonesome this night as I survey the chaos of impending departure. I went with Marion and Marla to Delta today, shopping, lunch in Cedaredge—I was not myself—solemn, quiet, sad. Marla and Marion both said what fun it was. Thank god Marla came for she and Marion did have fun. As did I, but on a different plane, or from a different place. I am so sad to be leaving my friends. More than my home I will surely miss their fine company.

15

There is a void waiting. Nobody to trust. (Ha! There is everybody to trust. There is god. There is the power way you have innocently been walking. Trust Our Mother, who has given me the gift of being able to nurture one of her own, a woman who was mainly a mother, who gave her entire life after my birth to protecting and nurturing me. That is how I see it now, how I will recall it.)

Saturday, March 6

I've been working on death since our cat Mittens died when I was nine. Her death, and my role in her last days, gave me a premature awareness of impermanence—of death, the finality of the end; which may have seemed like a curse through some years but ultimately I always knew to be a gift. Yet it gave me another gift I've only just realized: validation of my powers of observation and communication. I didn't realize that gift at the time, just resented that no one took me seriously for three days, ignoring my insight that the cat was very sick.

Knobbydog's death gave me another gift. Awareness of the essential nature of compassion, what lies at the core of compassion, as well as how essential it is to a good life, to Right Being.

Sunday, March 7

In Hospice training five years ago we did a guided visualization exercise. This thirty-minute exercise literally changed my life, in several ways. Before we began the journey from diagnosis of terminal disease to moment of death, we were asked to cut fifteen slips of paper, and to write three answers to each of five questions.

The first, name three people you love. Easy. Mom, Steve, Julia... well, not so easy after all. How to stop at three?

The second, name three things you enjoy doing. Your three favorite things, or three of your favorite things, to do. Equally easy. Garden. Read. Walk with a camera. Not necessarily in that order.

Three qualities in yourself that you value, qualities you aspire to or appreciate in yourself. Honesty, compassion, kindness.

Three things you want. Things maybe you want to achieve: clarity, long life, community. I can't remember the exact question, but at last I have again the answers. I had lost these little slips of paper for years, and tried to recreate the exercise for others whom I thought might benefit from it, but I could never remember all five of the categories. All I remembered, with eternally shocking clarity, was the moment of truth in the exercise, and how the room heaved a collective gasp, and nearly everyone began to weep at the same moment. Those who weren't already weeping quietly to themselves.

The answers to the fifth question are "close connection with people," "appreciation of Nature," and "spiritual exploration." What do you suppose the question was? In any case, I remember what I had left at the end.

Through twenty minutes we volunteers-in-training listened to Pati describe our decline. At first, she said, you get the diagnosis. You haven't been feeling well, you're a little weaker than usual. You're told you have six months to live. You're shocked. Your life fills with doctors' appointments, discussions about your prognosis, lab tests, chemotherapy perhaps. All this takes time. Tear up one of your slips of paper. Any one. You choose.

The illusion of control. One month goes by. You understand your diagnosis, and you're determined to do some of the things you've always wanted to do. Do you take a trip to Paris? Do you hike down the Grand Canyon? What do you intend to do with your remaining five months, while you still have the energy? (Me, I am thinking about swinging in a hammock on the edge of my canyon, writing a book, but that's neither here nor there.) Tear up two of your slips. Any two.

Well, the first one wasn't that hard. Long Life was a no-brainer, no pun intended. But the next two? Now we're talking attachment. Mom? No. Community? Nature? Clarity? I think not. Steve? Julia? Well, Steve, anyway. That came as kind of a surprise, as we had once intended to marry. But he'd been such a shit when my knees blew out that I knew I didn't want to spend the last five months of my life being tended to by him. That left Julia in. I probably let go of Community next, clinging to a few loved ones.

Then she says, two months go by. You more or less settle into your routine of doctors, therapies, you make a certain measure of peace with your diagnosis, you still have strength to go out to dinner, still have an appetite, still have some energy in your day. But not as much as you used to. You tire more quickly. Some days you don't feel too well in the mornings. Or in the evenings. Tear up three of your slips. Any three.

It gets harder. She goes on like this, until you're lying on the couch with one month to live and you have about six chips remaining. At this point, I've already planted myself in my living room, not in a Tuscan villa or a Cancun thatch resort. And I'm looking out my beloved big window I chose myself, with the view I selected myself, and the hummingbirds someone is feeding for me. I'm looking up at the vines wrapped around the juniper post holding up the loft, the tree trunk I peeled by hand and oiled to a golden shine, now in late afternoon slanting green and golden light.

Oh well. It could have certainly been worse. Then she takes us down, down to the last week, the last day, the last minute of life. We have three chips apiece. She asks us to rip one and place the other two face down at the front edge of the table. I have long ago lost track of the people around me, the twenty-nine other students in this end-of-life workshop. I have been engrossed in imagining my imminent mortality. But here I sense that most of us take a long time to choose. I feel the struggle of the souls in the room. Some of us are already sniffling or openly weeping at what we have already lost. I have kept my cool, but now am shaken. I remember the last two standing on my platform are appreciation of Nature and spiritual exploration.

Then the goddess of death makes her move. She sweeps around the room tearing in half one of each pair of someone's dreams. It happens so fast. Then she stands before us and says, "Turn over your last slip. Take a good look." And we do. And I, for one, feel a surge of attachment and relief. This is all I have left in all the world and in myself. And then she says, "Rip it up."

The room heaves a collective gasp of recognition and dismay. A palpable silence follows. Then the thin sound of lives shredding dissolves into sobs and sniffles. We release tears of loss and longing, release regrets, release, at least for a moment, what is rigid inside that has been holding us back all these years. In this moment we have all confronted the inimitable finality: this *all* one day ends.

All week long there have been boxes of tissues on the tables, and these are passed around now. Pati tells us to take a break. I don't remember what happens next. I don't remember much about the rest of the workshop, but I know I was never the same again. I dumped my callous boyfriend then and there, and softened for good inside. I would give and give after this, and try not to cling. What mattered became more clear: the here and now, the moment, the love and comfort and help we can give each other. As much, too, the voice inside that insists on integrity and peace of mind. Choices became easier.

Tuesday, March 9

This is going to require a tremendous opening to the world. I have felt this coming, but it has come in a way that is so different than what I had anticipated, expected. Much sooner and much differently than I had expected.

I thought I'd turn fifty having found my voice, become a columnist, and have a small loyal following. I'd have to speak out, of course, all the time. Like Hightower, Molly Ivins, Arundhati Roi, Amy Goodman. That would be how I would open to the world, as a voice for justice, peace, and love in the world.

Instead, I open to the world as I move to my anathema, mythical city shrouded in fears. Pushing all my buttons. And I move there to tend my dying parents. I never thought it would end this way. I thought he would die suddenly somehow (it still could happen that way, today, any moment, don't forget), and she would eventually move out here to live with me. While she could enjoy it, or after she needed full time care. I would bring her here, that's the way it always played out in my projections.

I did ask for this mission. I prayed at the end of the year for more fulfilling work. Unbelievably, then this family crisis presented a move with meaning, a work worthy of total dedication.

And I go with a heart both joyful and afraid. Yes, as much as I believe I've let go of fear, now I find I must face it again. But I face it differently this time, with more trust, I guess. I have seen the work of my god both in me and through me. I have evidence, yet still I wallow in sadness and despair as though I had the luxury of time. Life is short, infinitely rich in qualities that defy description, an endless ongoing of lessons, opportunities, leaps of faith. I keep leaping. I keep leaping and I keep landing deeper into joy with each fearful leap.

What drives me? Is it an engine of fear and regret always lumbering behind? Or is it a carrot of peace held out before my quivering nose by the lure of enlightenment? Is it a furnace of tenderness for the besieged life forms on the planet? A fiery love for all that lives, for all that live?

Keep a notebook always handy in this new life. Have one at your apartment, one in your bag, one in your parents' apartment. Go there and love them, and come from love in every choice you make, every word you speak, every minute you are there.

Thursday, March 11

Mother said tonight on the phone that Dad is in denial. She illustrated this by saying, "I asked him the other night if he wanted to pull a wishbone, and he got the wish. When I asked what he'd wished for, he said 'I wished that you would get well.' I told him, I am not going to get well."

She said two of her friends are giving her a hard time, saying, "Well you have a helper now, you can do whatever you want all the time, why are you not doing this or that?" My fake friends, she called them. Luli, she said, is wonderful, always asking her how she's feeling. Bess too, and Nell.

Oh my god. The dogs barked, the phone rang—and I had an anxiety attack. Second or third time in a week, like nothing before. Painful constriction in my throat, going down into my belly and somewhere turning into a cramp along the way, shortness of breath, rapid pulse. Had to call John and Ellie and say I'll be late for dinner. Repressing my departure? My mother's imminent death? Not, she says, within a year, but imminent nonetheless.

Wednesday, March 17

Mom didn't go to her swallow test yesterday because she had diarrhea the day before and felt so awful and weak.

Thank god I am not attached to things the way I used to be. All the things to leave behind! The Skilsaw; cleaning and tidying, I see the Skilsaw out on the patio. So what if they burn it out or something? It won't matter. Skis, boots, the TV, VCR, dishes, it won't matter. The garden, houseplants, reptiles, the cat, I'm still attached to them. But the pure *stuff*, if the housesitters wreck it, so what.

Friday, March 19

What a whirlwind of social excitement it's been since last Friday. Connie's epic party that night, tonight an intimate dinner with Julia, Larry, and Michael, then a neighborly fire out back with the addition of Suzi and Geoff, and neighbor Fred, my new surrogate steward of the field. In between, so many small meals and visits, so many precious moments. Nan making cacciatore with Fandango the parakeet singing between Julia and me, then giving me that bracelet, a silver bangle with the inscription, "Life is a journey, not a destination." The girls at Bee Yard making a gourmet potluck lunch for me this noon, all so kind and natural, Liz orchestrating it, Donna encouraging, and asking the amazing question: Do I think there is any other reason for me to be going back to D.C. besides to care for my parents? She gave me some lucid parting words like, "You go follow your life." And was grateful that I'd nagged her about her nose, when she discovered last fall she had a malignancy, and had to have Mohs surgery.

I've probably forgotten too many of those precious moments throughout the week. But by far one of the most precious was when Michael finally took his leave tonight from the fire, and realized he wouldn't see me again before I leave, and he cried. I hugged him close and said, "You know how much I love you." Poor dear. "I'll miss you," he said. And dear Larry saying he admires me, and getting a wee bit teary himself. Promising to "stage a visit" to Our Nation's Capital.

Friday, March 26

Nevada, Missouri.

You no longer have to shop for bargain hotels. You have known this now for some time, it's not worth the money saved. I feel anxious here, the industrial side of town. Desmond The Problem Turtle, who seems somewhat humbled, sits in the tub. The proprietress gave me quite a warm smile once I'd paid—and I gave her one in return, after we'd sized each other up. It was an authentic exchange, if not entirely honest. I did not tell her about the turtle. Or the snake. I guaranteed the dogs, and said if she wasn't comfortable with that, I would not be comfortable and I'd as soon go elsewhere. I said I understood she had no reason to take my word. "No, it isn't that," she said, "just some people, their dogs pee and everything on

21

the floor. We had a cat in here two weeks ago and it took eight days for the smell to go away."

So I got a little anxious about the turtle on the carpet, and put him in the tub—only to find the bed linens are stained! The pillowcase looks like little black grease stains, the sheet—it could be anything. But I remember fleabags like this traveling with Sally on our cross-country trip after college—with sparkles in the ceiling—along the Gulf Coast and the Atlantic, with phosphorescence in the ocean sparkling all around our naked bodies in the night. So. And with Marion and Tara in Salida, in fact, where they even provided dog beds. And even alone, in that Wild West trailer motel in northern Nevada. There have been pleasant fleabags all along.

Tomorrow I head to St. Louis to meet Elizabeth, whose ninety-two-year-old mother has PSP. She wrote, "I must say you'll be seeing what you will be facing with your mom. That should give you plenty to think about on the rest of your trip east."

I am imagining meeting her mother, and praying for the presence of heart to be how I need to be, to make this an authentic exchange. Plenty to think about on the drive tomorrow.

The anxiety has all but gone. With the TV sound off, the fan on, the air in here refreshed, the dogs passed out on their blanket, the car just outside the door so I can repack easily. Holding the snake will also ease the anxiety.

Saturday, March 27

At the home of Elizabeth and Ruth, in the old University part of town. Two remarkable women. I am floored by the courage of both of them. Elizabeth greeted me at the door so warmly that I wept instantly. I left the animals in the car at first, and she led me through the old wooden foyer and hallway straight through to the back porch, screened and shaded, where she introduced me to her mother. I gasped when I saw the little woman covered in blankets, her mouth hanging open, eyes glassy. I thought, She looks just like my mother!

But of course, she doesn't. Not yet. It is as though I see in Ruth's completion what in Ali is foreshadowed. Ruth grasped my hand as I knelt down to be on eye level with her, and she growled.

22

"She says she's glad you're here," Elizabeth said. I arrived later than I meant to, after lunch, and we sat on the porch all afternoon. Elizabeth's little dog Molly was good with Mocha and Brick when I brought them in, and didn't fuss with the turtle. Ruth loved the turtle. Her eyes are very expressive as she turns her head slowly to take in things. She loved the snake. I took some great shots of her with the snake around her neck, holding the turtle. At five sharp we had cocktails, thank god. I was so relieved and pleased when Elizabeth offered me a gin and tonic. She and Ruth had one also, and Ruth got to give Molly some treats at cocktail hour. "It's the highlight of her day," Elizabeth said.

Elizabeth and I talked all afternoon, and now and then Ruth would growl slowly some words I could nearly understand but not quite. Sometimes she tried to write with a pencil, but mostly made little squiggles. Fortunately Elizabeth understood what she meant, and translated. I imagine the gradual decline of Ruth's speech allowed Elizabeth to adapt her listening as needed.

At some point in the afternoon Ruth growled or signaled, and Elizabeth transferred her to her wheelchair to take her around the corner to the bathroom, a small cubicle filled with a dozen versions of Noah's Ark. A small space to maneuver a wheelchair, an invalid, and a caregiver. Elizabeth showed me how she transferred her mother to the toilet and back using a gait belt, while I watched discreetly from the hall.

For dinner she had made a delicious casserole, all soft so Ruth could eat it too. A wonderful Easter Egg collection decorated the center of the dining table, reminding me of the season. We sat at the table a long time, while Ruth moved one bite at a time slowly to her mouth. Elizabeth had to stop her many times and cut the portion smaller. "That's too big, Mom," she'd say, and cut it smaller. I was on the verge of tears through the whole meal, alternately sad and admiring.

At bedtime, Elizabeth showed me the suction machine next to Ruth's hospital bed in the living room, showed me the egg carton foam under the sheets, and various other adaptations. Then she showed me to my own bedroom, where I am too exhausted to write any more. But I remember Ruth's grip on my hand as we said goodnight.

Tuesday, March 30

Passing the same Super 8 I stayed in last fall on the same trip, only this time I know where cousin Melinda lives and I stayed with her instead of a hotel. Meeting family again after more than twenty years! In the green hills of Kentucky, of all places. Melinda gave me a lovely bookmark, Fred took me and the dogs for a walk down the lane. Her brother Gary and his fiancé Lorraine were there too, remarkably; they are all leaving tomorrow for a reunion with their Tennessee cousins on their Dad's side, that they haven't seen for almost thirty years! So it was good timing, and how easy, how safe and fun and lovely it was to be grown up with them after all these years. Lorraine insisted I put their wedding on my calendar in September, and try to make it up to Syracuse.

The last time I saw Melinda was more than twenty years ago, when we met to camp in the mountains in southwest Virginia. We hadn't known each other well even then, not having seen each other more than a time or two growing up, she ten years older. But we'd met at her wedding a few years before, and for some reason we just decided to get together. We camped for two nights, took some hikes, and then as we were leaving the park stopped by a ranger station to use the bathroom.

The station was closed, but while we were trying the door a ranger pulled up and let us in for a few minutes. In the course of chatting about our visit I mentioned that I had come, in part, to visit the place where my dear friend and college roommate had died. I asked if he remembered when a young woman had died of hypothermia there a couple of years earlier. He blanched. "I found her," he said. We all teared up instantly.

Tomorrow I will see Mom and Dad. Tomorrow I will see my new life.

Ali sits with her two children beside her grandfather, the primary father figure in her life. He lived to be one hundred, surviving his wife, the original Rita in the portrait above, by just over a decade

Part 2: *During*

April

Thursday, April 1

First full day of my new life. Woke up in our "permanent hotel room" as I told the dogs—one week ago tonight, that first hotel, Best Western in Garden City, Kansas, the one by the highway. One week ago this morning I woke for the last time to my incredible view east.

Desmond Turtu has explored the living room and arrived, curious, at the stained-glass tortoise lamp Marion gave me. It sits on the floor just inside the front door, and plugs into the wall switch, to welcome me home by lighting up. Desmond has sufficiently sniffed to try to bite its shell, and now sniffs around, rubbing his neck over the top. He alternately postures and caresses—now he moves behind it preparing to mount. I should go unplug it, or see how hot it is. He nips at the back edge of the shell—now he has sidled up alongside, the right shoulder of his shell supported by the edge of the other's left side—his interest unreciprocated, he finally turns and plods away.

Friday, April 2

I have been asking for this challenge since I finished building Mirador. I could live in an apartment in the city, I realized, once ensconced in the magnificence of my new home, which seemed far grander than I deserved. I could live anywhere, I told myself. It's not the dwelling—it's who you are inside of it.

Now who could ask for more? Here I live, an apartment in the city—close enough, traffic enough, for two cities. Yet a tall pine tree guards my bedroom window and a gorgeous flowering tower of a cherry peeks over my balcony. More pines screen the next building, and a stream runs through the remaining old woods that once covered these slopes. As I sit for just a couple of minutes outside, a flock of gulls pours overhead, then a triangle of pointy-winged ducks crosses the gulls. Yes indeed, a fine place, a hummingbird feeder and a few geranium pots will make it truly home. There is god in the city.

And that I should land next to a sewage treatment plant, I who have proclaimed that I haven't got a grip on how to deal with my own waste. Here it is all condensed and expanded—overflowing dumpsters, careless tosses of garbage bags over the fence by tawny Asian businesswomen, litter blowing among the mayapples at the edge of the swampy woods—and then across the narrow woods and over the hill, the county's human waste is processed. How? By whom? Not far to the southwest, as I see when I drive here from Mom's, a giant plume of white smoke billows. Which way does it blow? What kinds of toxins does it spout? Whose is it? Learning to deal with waste—minimize it, simplify.

This morning I struggled to set loose an upwelling of joy at the recognition: this is just fine. I am the same person, and I like me. Look at how lovely I can make my space. Like Diane with her attic, her sitting room, her pots and pans hanging under the new stairs—like Marion with her writing shack. I can see how it will be: the green carpet on the deck, the row of geraniums of all color blossoms, a true patio garden six by eight feet, a basket birdhouse at the top of the wall, a hummingbird feeder, hanging plants... oh yes. And do the same on Mom's porch. And oh, a cardinal alights in the top thin limbs of the pine and I am giddy for an instant with delight.

Two instances of total strangers helping: Yesterday a tired white man, gray really, about my age, offered to help me carry the Korean chest upstairs. I introduced myself, he said his name was John, he lives on the first floor, adding grayly, "Just what I want after a nice long day at work."

It was obvious from his shoulders askew that the man needs a massage—he was generous and kind in helping but gave me an eerie vibe.

As we were leaving Target today after a comedy of errors getting there, a young black man offered to help with the packages while Mom sat in the cart and my car waited in the rain. We got them all in one load—at first glance I thought he was a Target employee but grasped fast that he wasn't—then I came back for Mom and said, "It's OK, I can get her from here." He smiled down at her with a wide, warm, angelic smile and asked, "You sure?" to Mom, with love and compassion and awareness pouring from his eyes and his smile. "You are too kind," I said.

Saturday, April 3

I think about everybody dying: Amy's parents, Amy, me. Just that they might, that they will some unexpected day, and it breaks my heart. Amy and her folks have been such a godsend. My solid dear friend from when we were twelve, how she has grounded me since I've been here. Across the country, back in my home town, people are dying: Diane's mother, after a long and awful illness; and a neighbor, at sixty-four, of a sudden heart attack, while driving. Who's next? Any one of us at any moment—how can we love? How *can* we not?

What I know of human weakness is this: the gods have seen enough of it before me that I know I'm not judged by them for frailty. They just laugh and nudge me forward.

Worries: parking, dogs, Mom's allergies, Mom falling. Me still being, somehow, too late. Not finding time for reading to her, or doing her exercises with her, before it's too late. Clearly eight hours a day isn't long enough—and what of my poor good dogs? But what am I worrying about? Eight hours or ten, I can't be there full time—let her have her independence—if she falls what's the worst that could happen? Just be sure she knows how much you love her, how you've enjoyed being her daughter, you like her, you enjoy her, who she is. Just have fun! That, after all, is what you're here for: to brighten what's left of her life, however much that is.

Monday, April 5

"I'm so stiff," she said today after physical therapy, as she strained to straighten her spine. Massage therapist! Quick, get on this, she really doesn't have long.

What shocked me at first was my sense that it wasn't imminent, and my surprising reaction. And now, a week later, what shocks me is the sense that we have no time to lose. We need to begin talking, but where? I almost brought up Hospice today but I was driving and it seemed like too casual a place to discuss her dying. It's time for a sit-down talk.

Wednesday, April 7

It's "Geriatric Month" at the vet. I saved 10 percent and still paid five hundred and ten dollars for intake for two dogs. At home that visit would have cost about fifty dollars, at most.

A pair of osprey soared in the sky above a line of traffic. Was I the only human to see them?

A car honks as someone locks it, and Desmond ducks his head, which is sticking under the balcony railing into the sun. He sits basking at the end of a line of potted geraniums. The door and the bedroom window are open. A lovely breeze between balmy and cool blows through the apartment. Petals float from the flowering cherry. June Stewart would have loved it. She always recalled the rain of petals in April in Paonia when she came to visit me—now that blossom rain always brings her to mind. She died just over a year ago, eighty-five, from sudden cancer.

Outside, brakes squeal down the highway, sirens screech by—inside *Mahabaradha* plays—outside, too, chorus frogs tickle their combs, a monarch floats against the screen, cardinals court in the pines. I am practicing contentment. Now the petals are floating up, I must go sit out there. I love being in the treetops. Wasps, bees, moths, butterflies, birds, blossoms, breeze through pine needles. Scent and whispers. I am in love with these geraniums. Eight different colors. A chorus frog. And the locusts to look forward to!

Desmond and Brick lie together stretched out in the sun. Together might be an overstatement. Side by side. Desmond has an interest in Brick but Brick shies away when Desmond gets too close.

Thursday, April 8

Dear Marion,

Shall I describe my new space? But it's awkward to type, I have a split fingertip. I thought I had left those behind in my garden. But this apartment air is so dry, how could it be drier than the arid homeland, yet it seems to be sucking the sap out of me. I've only used the heat a couple of times, have kept the screen door open when I could, but it's been so cold and windy.

It rained the first five days I was here, and then it turned sunny with a bitter chilly wind. Yesterday, though, the afternoon topped out at seventy-five degrees, and this big tree outside my balcony rained white blossoms down and up and all around. Still there are plenty left on the tree this morning, but it's been cold and gray again all day. Yesterday all of us sat out on the balcony, marveling at the eight different colors of geraniums in their pots, laughing at the petal rain, enjoying the various mixes of feet, paws, and heads as we all shifted in the warm sun. Brick, Desmond, Mochi, and I.

Then Mom had an awful day and evening, and I tucked her in before ten p.m. Today I watched myself micromanage her about medication, swallowing technique, talking with her mouth full. Tonight I kept the TV on the right channel and picked up Dad's dropped, popped-apart remote, knitted two rows, thickened her water for the night and the next morning. We buy this thickener to help her swallow, and put three plastic-capped cups out each night, with an inch of thickened water in each, one by the toilet, one by the sink, one by the bed. Making the water thick herself, adding four little packets of gel to a sixteen-ounce jar, had been taking her an hour each night. Now I do it, one less thing for her to struggle with.

She had a much better day today, and a better evening. My main job right now is making sure she eats and gets her meds on time.

Friday, April 9

Posted a query about her mouth sores on the Forum, and got a few replies. One suggests swabbing the sores with a dilute solution of hydrogen peroxide with a sponge-tip toothette. Someone else said to be sure to let the doctor know in case it's related to her medication, and that there could be sores in the rest of her digestive system. Mom thinks they are from the Atrovent she takes for asthma.

She has a catastrophic inability to focus on what's relevant, say, food, swallowing, a serious conversation—any line of conversation—and an uncanny ability to avoid logic with slithering agility. And then she homes right in:

"How many weeks have I been going to physical therapy?" she asks. "What's the point, if in six months I won't be able to get around anymore anyway? What's the point in getting so tired out?"

Maybe I need to ask her if she would rather lie in bed, have every day be Saturday and never have to get dressed? For years she has been telling me how she loves Saturday because it's her day of rest, she doesn't get dressed, doesn't have to go out, doesn't have company, doesn't feel she has to accomplish anything on Saturday.

I wonder if my insistence on helping her makes her feel demoralized? Makes her feel she can't get along?

If you don't want to live, then set about the business of dying. The journey of dying? The business of dying has nothing to do with shuffling through piles of paper, or ordering from catalogs, or counting how many weeks or dollars—the journey of dying has to do with looking death in the face and welcoming it as a restful adventure, a friend at the end—it has to do with slowing down, letting go, simplifying, dwelling upon, contemplating what matters. Who matters. Let somebody else worry about the timing of medication and what food you eat when.

Sunday, April 11

OK, first off I'll concede it's hardly the city. But compared to where I came from, it's downright urban. Driveway less than a quarter mile? Neighbors visible from the back porch? Urban. And with a density of twelve families per building, and a strip mall less than a quarter-mile away, it feels urban to me.

Just twenty miles outside Our Nation's Capital, and surrounded on two sides by woods, Woodside Apartments earns its name. The third side is a major U.S. highway, and the fourth a sewage treatment plant for the Lower Potomac Region. The Potomac River flows past several lovely county and state parks just fifteen minutes away. So it's an anomaly, in a way, in our society: densely packed humans from all over the world in such proximity to actual open space.

Killing Mother

Where I come from, I haven't spoken to more than half a dozen black people in years, and I've spoken to every one who lives there or has come through town. Here, in the Woodside Apartments, African Americans outnumber Asians, who outnumber white folks. The woman across the hall from me is half Asian and half Australian married to a black man, the family on the first floor whose father drives a Diamond cab is from Africa, the boyz on the balcony last midnight were from some other 'hood, the men on the radio last night speaking French were from Haiti, and the joyful celebration across the parking lot this Sunday afternoon spoke a language I couldn't identify but would place in some lush land in tropical Africa.

I heard the party start mid-afternoon as I watered the geraniums on my new little balcony, and saw flits of brightly colored clothing between the leafing limbs of the cherry tree between us. I envied them. They were drinking and eating and laughing with all their friends and families. They were young and carefree and it was a hot summer afternoon in mid-April. I was tired and content and resting briefly between excursions to my mother.

Since I have moved here I have been blessed with the music of African voices around me every day. Whether in the dining room of the Home, or wafting up from the parking lot at Woodside Apartments, or in Target or Nall's Nursery. Everywhere I go here I hear the cadences of other nations, other peoples, from the Caribbean, from Africa, India, China, from places whose names I don't even know. And I feel a long forgotten stirring of a wish to know—who are you? How do you live? How does friendship happen? What matters to you?

I think that I have seen enough of life, seen deeply enough into the lives of many I have known or simply met, to know the answers to many of these questions will be the same no matter of whom they're asked. Children, parents, love, food, home, slowly, magic... these are the answers that all fall under one umbrella no matter the name, that refers to the song of life pulsing under everybody's skin and in every flower.

To be so gently deposited in this microcosm, transported from my rather ethereal existence wandering the gardens of the gods for decades to this solid sector of humanity; to be given the opportunity to observe with relative anonymity the patterns of my species living at this density, and to feel fairly safe, strong. Ah! 'tis all an illusion.

"Eet ees oll yust an illusion!" as the magician Jean-Claude used to say. Little did I know at the age of twelve how much he meant by "oll." All. It really is *all* an illusion. At any second this illusion could collapse:

The phone rings. One of my parents has died, or fallen. I am always waiting for the call.

A shot rings out. Those crazy boys with panties on their heads have gotten into a scrap with a pistol.

Anyway, midst all this family dynamic, dealing with the terminal nature of Mom's decline, to step anywhere outside the center of the storm and hear the music of African languages dancing through conversations lifts my spirits and keeps my private drama in perspective. The world is vast and full of people. Every one of them suffers and grieves, many so much worse than we. *Don't get caught up in the suffering of the one.*

Thursday, April 15

I walked in the big woods behind the buildings again today, for the first time in sunshine. Low, thin concrete foundations abandoned and buried under thick oak leaves and moss. Tangles underfeet of little-leaved vines, creeping tendrils of things reaching up beyond my shoes grasping, growing visibly every day more dense, taller, trees overhead are leafing out, beginning to green the canopy.

Rhythms of the World every night at eleven on WPFW, Tony is on Thursday, real Caribbean. Oh, and Senegal. The light show flashes from the cheesy delightful stereo, I write under the festive colored globe lights. I breathe. The young woman at the health food store reminded me with a smile to breathe. "Yeah," I laughed, "breathe, right." She'd said, "How are you today?" and I'd sighed and said, "Flustered," and she smiled and said she appreciated the honesty.

It's been a rough week with Mother. But we've grown closer, come to a more shared understanding of my mission. Today was a good day. We laughed a lot today, and had fun. Ate lunch at Chili's because someone had told her of something delicious they'd eaten there. I thought, Not Chili's! and caught my lips from disparaging, and smiled and took her to Chili's. She didn't like the food too much, she didn't mind too much the noise. But I did, and I minded that the toilet seats were all splattered and needed to be wiped off first, but I cheerfully wiped off the big-stall seat for her, truly only irritated at the restaurant for the grossness more than the inconvenience, but not too revolted nor at all put out. Unconsciously walking the walk of a recent insight: Patience only begins when patience comes to an end.

Anyway, Chili's was fun because it was new and different for her. What else can we do, where else can we go, new and fun and different? Small French restaurants, bistros, nice places… like Mike's Italian, now why not just the two of us go there for lunch on the way home from physical therapy some time next week? Like the lunch at the crab house, that was fun too, last week. Today we shopped for a bed for her, and I forgot to order the one I picked out for Dad. Tomorrow I must order beds for both of them.

Driving home tonight, three fire engines and flood lights down by the creek. Under the power lines, all lit up like a big event. And a couple of nights ago, turning into Woodside Lane, three cop cars flashing one behind another behind a small black sports car with several occupants, weird, guy in a suit approaching with a cop, two backup cars arrived just before me, so I drove around the wrong side of the island. Sirens every day, oodles of them, yet I've not yet encountered them in my short forays up or down Route 1.

Looking into these expensive aids, like the foam bed, like the CCTV, a machine to magnify reading material. She wants to take the time to research and ponder, and I guess I just need to find the energy and focus to do that, even though I believe she doesn't have *time*. The opposite of how I used to look at film: she has more money than she has *time*. She can afford to spend the money and spend it fast, so she gets the maximum benefit of the product no matter the cost. She *can* afford, both of them can, but they have this poverty consciousness, no, frugality consciousness, that they no longer need, and don't have time for!

It's only been two weeks, and I'm exhausted. Twelve hours today of nonstop service. And I enjoyed most of it, all but the last forty minutes or so, bedtime seemed to drag on without needing me there. For the first time since I've been tucking them in (nearly a week?) I wasn't back there helping her, but watching TV, waiting. Which was good in a way, means she had the energy and focus to do her things for herself. It was fine, but I'm afraid I betrayed my tiredness as I was leaving. I so do not want to make either one of them feel that I resent being there, for I do treasure the time with them.

I love that Mom and I laughed today, and that I've made Dad laugh a couple of times a day for days. These are the things that give me peace of heart.

Mom and I, and Dad and I, had conversations about death and dying last week. Separately, of course. Mom said she was not afraid to die. Dad said, another day in his den while we sat together with whiskeys while Mom was in the bathroom, that he was beginning to think about death.

"Beginning?" I asked astonished. He said he never thought about death, never, until recently as he watches all his friends die. Even while he was fighting in World War II he did not think about dying. While I have thought of little else since I was nine years old.

Friday, April 16

I took the morning off to finally get the dogs out to some of the local parks, and I drove the few miles along fairly rural roads to Pohick Bay Regional Park. We walked along the river awhile, then up into the woods, then back along the shore, and I saw ahead of me what looked like a whole litter of puppies frolicking on one of the boat ramps. I snapped my dogs on their leashes, and walked closer, and to my astonishment found that they were big dogs, all the size of mine, all different colors, and by then they were tied in front of the restroom. I waited. A man came out and gathered all their different colored leashes into his hands, and while we talked he did this finger thing whereby he kept them all untangled as they mingled about him.

I said, "Are you a trainer?" He said, "No, I'm just a walker." We talked about where he walks them (they all live in downtown Alexandria, half an hour from here, and they all rode in his little station wagon). I said, "I don't want to keep you from your walk," and he said, "That's okay, I'm already late today. I should be getting these dogs home about now and I'm just starting. I'll be late for my afternoon dogs, I have another group of nine, and then some solos."

Saturday, April 17

I'm just so tired right now I don't think I can think or write about it. Each day deepens her awareness of her condition, and increases my patience, compassion, and ability to be of service. It's becoming increasingly clear that I really don't have time to do most of the other things I thought I would (like a class, my quilt project, work…) and can barely manage to take care of my parents, of my dogs, and of me. Once all of our needs have been met for the day it's midnight. This may change once I've taken care of more of the one-time needs like getting her an adjustable bed, wheelchair, etc., because I'm doing a lot of comparison shopping in my "free" time.

There are good days and bad days. Today was a good day. I also saw several osprey, one of them diving in the pond at the Home, and one bald eagle over the river, and Mom was in good spirits and had pretty good energy. Yesterday was an exceptionally bad day. I have this killer stiff neck so I've been eating Advils like candy for two days, and I woke yesterday morning to two puke spots on the carpet and one huge poop smear. Damn! Must have fed Brick something too oily. But he didn't wake me up! He's only ever had accidents in the house when I've been gone. I guess I was knocked out from the Advils so I didn't notice him get out of bed. We had a long talk about it last night, and I think he understands now that he needs to wake me up. But I just this afternoon finally got the stains mellowed out a bit.

So I'm still eating Advils, and still hurting, but I've learned that if you buy yourself a fuzzy red toilet seat cover you are more likely to keep the lid down, and I like that. Also, don't ever feed your dog or dogs beef bones in a confined space like a balcony floored with indoor-outdoor carpet, because then your balcony will smell like rotten meat even if you scrub it by hand with stain and smell remover. I'll be removing the indoor-outdoor carpet soon and replacing it, a mere twenty dollar mistake.

Oh, and I discovered chocolate croissants at the Whole Foods store, and that's a good thing. And all the neighbors are all different colors, too, and they all seem to get along, and that's nice. I've seen all different colors of people of big and little sizes all coming in and out of the same apartment, and I like that.

Some of the bumblebees here are very big, there are lots of mosses, and lots of different kinds of trees, with all different colors of green leaves sprouting out of them. And of course, the different colors of the light show on my stereo. It's colorful here. And loud. And that's it for tonight.

Monday, April 19

Whoa. That's all I can think of to say. Whoa. Whoever thought it would feel this wild. I'm reading Dad's durable medical power of attorney, and I'm watching my mother disappear. Dad is coming to the realization that he'll be moving to the Third Floor eventually. He took another spill today, this time missing the desk chair as he was hobbling from his computer chair. I had seen him when mom and I left, sitting there at the computer, and consoled myself with the thought that he'd be moving back to his chair before Joan left, so even if he fell—when what to my astonishment, though not surprise, does he tell us when we've all returned to home base after lunch? While we were out he missed the chair, and sat on the floor and couldn't reach the phone to dial for help. However the phone rang, he grabbed the cord, and it happened to be Dr. Wise calling about a prescription of Mom's, so Dad asked him to call the clinic to send help. He told us this story as we sat around a cluster of mail-order packages. Five arrived today. We've gotten almost everything we ordered. Time to head out to Target tomorrow.

Therapeutic shopping? To some extent. For me at least, and possibly for her. But there are many things she either needs or that can make her life easier, more pleasurable, more comfortable. I need to say to her, "Put your money into a really high-quality wheelchair or scooter, a permanent seat that you can spend time in, so you can go from one task to another without having to get up and walk. You'll save time and be safer. You're wobbling more than when I arrived, more than last fall, and moving much slower. You see less, and bump into edges more often. I believe the walker is becoming more of a hazard than a help."

I need to say to them both, "I worry that if we fail to address the issue of either or both of you moving to the Third Floor, that one of you will suffer needless trauma, that if we don't address the question of *when*, sooner rather than later, one of you will fall and break a hip or something worse and be in pain and even more discomfort, have to go through hospitalization, or surgery, which are always risky, and end up at the Third Floor anyway, only less capable and less well."

Maybe ask them separately (or together), "Do you feel that you will eventually end up living in the Health Center? If so, don't you think it would be a good idea to address the question of when before the decision has to be made as a result of a medical crisis? I mean would you rather move there with a broken bone or without one?" Jeez. How does a person ever make that decision for him or herself?

Daryl called in the midst of that thought, and we talked for nearly an hour, and laughed and shared an understanding of each other that we enjoy every time we connect. Shared our feelings of fear and disgust with the human race, questioning our reactions of rage and walking a fine line. Now I'm down for the count.

Tuesday, April 27

Dearest Pa,

I don't mean to harp on you about your relationship with Ali. I know very little of what's transpired between the two of you over the past fifty years. I'm sorry if my being so frank with my thoughts has bothered you, and I won't bring it up again.

I know from personal experience how uncomfortable it can be to examine some aspects of my behaviors, not to mention trying to modify them. So I feel for Mom needing to realize her increasing limitations and learn new habits, and I feel for you with your sense of having "outlived your usefulness" and having to see your anger come out at your wife.

Maybe the most useful thing you can do right now is the kind of internal work that you've labeled (under the heading of psychology) "bullshit." I mean, the most useful thing you could do might be to simply learn how to deal with your feelings of anger. (It's never too late to learn to meditate.)

Or you could just ponder like you do, and continue to mellow out. You said to me a couple of years ago that more and more you just want to sit quietly. You seem to want peace, or peace of mind, or something like that.

Lord knows I've been uncomfortable enough having to look at my own way of being. By that I mean my judgments, reactions, angers, emotional attachments, over the past few years. I certainly want peace. I want peace of mind and peace of heart. I want to die knowing that I've done the best I could. I'm sure you want that for yourself too.

Our "bests" are different, I understand that. Doing my best entails simply living as close to god as I can, and that means giving as much love as I humanly can wherever I can find to give it. Your lucky day! I'm right where I need to be to fulfill my highest good. Now I just need to live up to myself.

To this end I offer this tender apology for meddling in your private feelings. Know that I'm here to support you in the challenges we all face these days, and I'm always available to talk. Also know that I depend on my certainty that you support me too.

Wednesday, April 28

I react with rage to the shooting of purple martins with a BB gun by the white boys across the pond from the Home. I call the cops. How involved I got so instantaneously. I did consider walking up the hillside to stand right below them and demand, "What the fuck are you doing? There are old people out there! Those birds are eating mosquitoes." Fucking ignorant rednecks.

So maybe it was better that I simply called the cops. Meanwhile I met old Claude Turner, ninety-two, from down the hall. He and his daughter were sitting out on one of the observation decks on the close side of the pond. I heard the first splash when I was walking past them, and wondered if they'd heard it, but I didn't see any reaction. A little farther along the path I stopped to listen, and search out the source of the sound. Then I heard the first couple of pops. I felt my blood begin to boil. I yelled, "Knock it off! You in the red shirt, knock it off. I see you! One more time and I'm calling the cops!"

Then I turned, and for some reason walked back toward the old man and his daughter. I was shaken, I guess, and wanted company. They hailed me before I even got there and thanked me for doing it. We sat and visited for awhile. Of course they wanted to know who I was visiting, and when I told them, Claude said, "I know Bob and Ali. She's really been going downhill fast." And before I knew it, he was asking me why I wasn't married, and saying he guessed my mother and dad don't talk very much to each other, for which he got roundly scolded by his daughter after I left.

I know this because I did call the cops, and while I sat out front of the building waiting for them, I saw Claude on his patio and went and joined him.

Finally the cops came to the front circle. I met them and rode in the back of one of the cars to the pond. With the good cop. At the pond the bad cop joined us, he was older and more officious, kept demanding if I'd actually seen anybody fire anything, which of course, through the leafing trees, I hadn't.

The relief of course is that once the trees all leaf out those idiots won't be able to see to shoot at the purple martins. But that won't necessarily stop them from shooting, which might be even worse. (See how I worry about the worst-case scenario: that they'll take a shot at me or my dogs, that they'll one day get enraged and use a bigger gun on someone walking along the pond.)

Later I called Auntie, and when she asked how Mom was I took the phone out on the patio to answer. In a few minutes Mom came out asking me for help with something, made me give her the phone, said "Bye" and hung up while her sister was still talking to her. Actually hung up on her sister, to demand I help her restring her gold cross on a different chain. Right now.

I suspect it was more than that. Because I was out on the patio she probably feared we were talking about her and couldn't bear it, so she got a pretext to interrupt. No, it wasn't only a pretext. She had gotten sidetracked at her jewelry box and really didn't care about talking to her sister anymore? How complicated we are.

Thursday, April 29

Water water everywhere and I'm paying nearly two bucks a gallon for distilled water to drink. It rains here five or six times a week, sometimes for days at a time. The ground never dries out. Any old lawn has patches of bog. The storm sewers hiss on a dry sunny day with runoff seeping through them. Some places the ground smells rank. Creeks and rivers run all around for miles up and down the highway, the river, the bays.

Dead snail shells wash up on the beach of Pohick Bay, and today we saw a whole catfish, one catfish head, and one nearly two-foot gar, I think, dead, which bit me when I picked its head up by the snout.

Does she really understand that this is terminal? This afternoon, driving back from a physical therapy appointment, I finally said, "Mom, you do understand that this disease is terminal, don't you? You are going to die." She said, "You know that, and I know that, but nobody else will admit it. Your father certainly won't."

She has seemed more easy in mind since then. It helps her to have it out in the open.

A studio portrait of Ali at eighteen, shortly before her first wedding.

May

Saturday, May 1

I called an old friend who lives three hours south, in the foothills of the Blue Ridge Mountains, to let her know I'm in the neighborhood. She was delighted to hear from me, and called back shortly to say her husband had offered me his ticket to the Indigo Girls concert this weekend so we could have a girls' night out.

Mom has been doing pretty well the past week, and I felt fine leaving her and Dad alone for a night, knowing she had Joan's phone number to call if she needed help with anything.

I arrived at Gaytha's house and sat for a couple of minutes, then called to remind Mom to take her pills. Ironically, at that moment she was in ER at Fort Belvoir, having fallen during the afternoon, hit her head on the floor and cut it open. Dad said she was in the CT scan room at the time of my call. Amazingly, I managed to go ahead and enjoy the concert and the visit with my friend anyway. That's what I call some good work on detachment. There was nothing I could do but what I had already done, instructed Dad to call Joan and have her pick Mom up at the hospital and come spend the evening and get them both to bed. Besides, I have to admit I was thoroughly glad that I hadn't been available to go sit at the hospital for hours. I get the willies in hospitals.

I had begun to lose my patience, and after that twenty-four-hour R-and-R I was able to go over there this afternoon and get through the evening scene with plenty of TLC, patience, humor, and efficiency for everyone. I really begin to see what everybody meant when they told me that if I didn't be sure and take time to take care of myself I wouldn't be any help to anyone else.

This morning, the new helper, Rita A, came early and got everybody breakfast, and did a great job with Mom. When I arrived after my leisurely drive back through the green Virginia spring country, Rita A was still there, waiting 'til Dad got back from lunch. I said she could go on and leave for the day, and I watched as she went over to my mother with a warm smile and told her something to do and gave her a big hug goodbye. I came this close to weeping, and when Rita A turned to me I'm sure she saw the tears welling up, and I reached out and hugged her too.

I had been so worried that she wouldn't work out, and I think she's going to be great. Just seeing her be so caring with my mother, seeing that they'd obviously achieved some rapport during the course of the morning, gave me such joy and relief. Rita A is from Ghana, and Mom and Dad had a hard time understanding her during the interview, and she seemed possessed of a certain lassitude. But I suppose she just has that relaxed way of some tropical women. I get the feeling she's been through some shit in her life in Africa.

I need to get myself some kind of lover some day soon for one reason and one reason only: I've got to get somebody to check me for ticks every few days! I just scratched my back and knocked off *two* ticks. I thought if I stayed on groomed trails I wouldn't get the ticks I was getting from bushwhacking. Go figure.

Also, I need bifocals. It's raining again, I'm writing at the computer, and I need to be able to look up without adjusting my head, raise my gaze, to see the rain, and lower my eyes but not my head to read the page. Think about it. The practice in raising my gaze could become extremely useful habit should I ever come to suffer from PSP.

Desmond Turtu pads across the dog bed toward the patio door. Outside, eight colors of geraniums grace the balcony. Desmond believes he'll venture down the step. Birds light in treetops at eye level. When I lie on my bed, I am inside a tall pine tree abuzz with thumb-size bumblebees in pollen coats.

It is sufficient. A breath of orchid fragrance from the windowsill, a statue of Ganesh, a small Jizo Bodhisattva, tender links to what is real for me. All this within the cushioned embrace of a living pine, its limey candles growing green and scaly in the flush of spring.

It guards my window like god and gives me a sense of protection and belonging I can't imagine being this content without. I may not be exactly happy, but I certainly am content. Yes, Mother, it is harder than I thought, as you told your brother on the phone the other night, but only in the sense of not having enough time or energy to get to so many of the things I had envisioned doing for you. Harder only in that it's taking longer to accomplish things and I'm not getting to the fun things I had hoped to do with you, like run an exercise group for a handful of people with difficulties like yours, using that Movement book.

I guess it's harder than I thought because I had to dive into it so deeply right away, without really any time to settle in. Here it is a month to the day of moving in, the first of the month, a Saturday. I've been out most of the day with Amy, first to her mom's to pick up some hay for Desmond, then to Dulles Expo for the Sugarloaf Crafts fair, and plenty of retail therapy.

Nature is so fragile here. I walked with Amy through some acreage a friend of hers is developing. We walked along the fresh gravel road then off into the slash of all the down trees cleared for one of the houses. This may have been to her a walk in the woods. I felt a little nauseous at the carnage, but the dogs sure enjoyed running free and poking about all the roots and logs.

Then I exercised refrigerator rights in Amy's kitchen and made a turkey sandwich, then home via the thronged parkway, to catch my breath before heading off to the Home for the evening.

No, I barely took any time to set up and settle in. I snatched evenings and mornings the first week, then right away into an intense level of meeting needs and demands constantly. All of which I knew it would come to, but I'm understanding burnout and I've barely started. I'm not even close to burnout, but I definitely get the concept. It's not a matter of stealing more time to myself, but of being more engaged in external activities, more involved, in what free time I do have.

There was a nasty little episode with some geese on the six-lane highway, but I won't go into that. Nor anything else unpleasant. I've been working on a list of good things about being here, including balmy nights, good Brie, international news, and the locusts are coming soon.

Sunday, May 2

Dear Elizabeth,

What a relief (in many ways) to get your email. Not only are you there and okay, but I really needed to hear from you and talk to you tonight. After just over a month, the shock of my arrival has worn off and the challenges are rising big time. There are no real specific surprises, except overall her seeming refusal to receive advice and suggestions about how to "self-protect." I learned that phrase from Tape One of the Proceedings of the Society for PSP conference in 2002, which I ordered from the society on videotape before I left Colorado. They finally caught up with me last week, and today Mom and I watched the first one.

One of the speakers mentioned, as a characteristic of the disease, this very inability of the patient to respond to training efforts. That was an interesting slant, and made her resistance easier for me to accept and for her to understand. I think showing her the videos is really going to help us make some progress in whatever work I think I'm doing with her. She seems easier with the disease the more she knows, which is helpful for me.

I certainly understand your comment that it's easier now that your mother's unable to get out of her chair than it was when you couldn't trust her not to try. I've thought a number of times, and dared to articulate it once but not again, that I thought it would get easier when she could no longer move about on her own. Whoever I said it to didn't take to that idea, I could tell. Mom is always pulling herself up and walking away somewhere. Even a step or two. Tonight I was reading to her and she grabbed her walker and got up to reach across the table to get her water! I was right there. All she had to do was ask. She said she hadn't wanted to interrupt me. And of course what she did was ten times the interruption her asking would have been.

Another thing that emerged in this video was more information about the psychological aspects of the disease, chiefly, impaired insight and judgment. Unfortunately, nobody went into detail about these aspects, but most every speaker mentioned a different type of intellectual failure. I had thought any kind of dementia component was much less significant than it apparently is. And, I guess the one surprise is that my experience this month has borne this out.

Monday, May 3

Dear Elizabeth,

So, who did you bet on in the Kentucky Derby? And who did your mom bet on? I put my money on Pollard's Vision, #17, how could I not? A one-eyed horse in the Kentucky Derby! He was second most of the way, then came in second-to-last. I thought as I was driving to their apartment, I should stop at the grocery and try to find some mint. But the grocery near here is not gourmet, and I wasn't sure I had time, so I had to make do with a gin and tonic, though julep was on my mind!

Yes, I agree with you "that while the mind is generally alert, especially memory, there is indeed a failure to see consequences from one's behavior, a critical part of learning." This is why I think they have such trouble being "trained." Mom has also become more self-involved, and I've actually encouraged this, as I think it's about time she put herself first.

Stopping at your place on my journey was a very key piece of the cosmic way this whole mission has panned out. It was so helpful to me to meet your mother, and to watch how you are with her, that it continues to inspire me. And now being in email touch with you, I look forward to many virtual chats and mutual support. I've found, oddly for me, that I really don't want to talk on the phone much. Most of the day there's nothing I want to say or hear, but when I want to communicate there is email on my time and in my size dose.

Please let me know how the Birthday Party goes! Ninety-three, and probably her last, what a very important party it is. I'll be thinking of you all.

Wednesday, May 5

Dear Michael,

Would you please define for me "haplotype?" It turns out, people with H1H1 haplotype are predisposed to get PSP. People with H1H2 haplotype have a much lower incidence of PSP. People with H2H2 haplotype, none of them get PSP.

Naturally I have a vested interest in finding out my haplotype. PSP also has defibrillary tangles, much like Alzheimers, in addition to its Parkinson-like neural traits. Yippee. R

Dear Rita,

Haplotype refers to genotype at certain immune system loci (genes). H1H2 would be a heterozygote; H1H1 and H2H2 would be homozygotes for the "bad" and "good" genes, respectively. If your Mom is a homozygote H1H1, you are probably a heterozygote. But I'm just guessing. You should talk to a medical geneticist who specializes in this disease. Love, M

Thursday, May 6
Hi Marybeth!

It was so good to see you and the children the other day. It's been forever since I've seen you and Bill and any of my cousins on Mom's side. She always tells me when you've been by to visit them, and it means so much to them both that you come when you're in town. I've always appreciated you for being so attentive to my parents. I'm glad I was here for your recent visit, and I thoroughly enjoyed you, your sense of humor, your quickness, and your beautiful children.

Thanks for your observations. I agree, one of the most dramatic differences in her is her inability to stay focused on any one thing for any length of time. The restlessness. And she's getting very frustrated with her rapidly deteriorating speech and most recently with her inability to call to mind the word she wants. We started watching a video of a conference focusing on PSP, and that's been enlightening for both of us. I've tried to get in touch with a PSP support group and it's not panning out. We also talked with Hospice, her doctor says she's not ready, so I asked about pre-Hospice emotional support. This local Hospice doesn't deal in that realm yet, and had no leads, so I'm still casting about.

Dad keeps pretty much to himself. He pedals a little stationary bike every night. He seems pretty depressed.

I agree, I am definitely getting to the point where I could use some advice and help. It has seemed like I'd be able to handle it all, and in a way

I'm doing fine, it just seems to take so long to make each decision, to find the right match on every kind of aid device, etc.

It turns out PSP has changes in the brain that resemble Parkinson's, which we knew, and some that resemble Alzheimer's as well, which we didn't know. Now the dementia is not as bad as with AD, but the brain gets defibrillary tangles, clusters of certain types of cells, that is a pathology similar to AD. In any case, judgment often becomes impaired, and I see that for sure.

Also her memory is getting dramatically worse. We watch *Friends* nearly every night, and have been sure not to miss the last three "last" episodes. Last night they reran both of the previous two episodes in preparation for tonight's big finale, and Mom did not remember seeing the first one. I told her we had watched it together the other night, but she remains convinced she did not see it and got upset with me for saying she had, so of course I dropped it. But she did not, kept referring up 'til bedtime, wondering when it was I might have seen it that she didn't.

OK, enough darkness. On the bright side, we both got massages the other night, and Mom slept really well and felt great yesterday, and my neck is nearly restored to full mobility. It was wonderful. I have a handful of friends left here from high school, and have been in touch with all of them. Am planning this weekend to see my grown goddaughter, who will be down from New York for Mother's Day, and her mother who lives in Bethesda also. I hope they'll come over for a slumber party and dye my hair red. That ought to take care of me! Thanks for your concern about that. The pets help. Walking in the woods. I know I need to do more for myself, though, find a yoga class at least. I am buying myself an orchid for every month I'm here! That fills a small hole.

I like thinking of your happy beautiful family frolicking among tropical flowers in the Mexican sun. That brings a smile to my face. Take care. Hope all is well with you all.

Sunday, May 9

Hi Elizabeth!

Thank you so much for telling me all about the ninety-third birthday party. I can just imagine the serenity of the pre-party days, with all the cakes and flowers, on the lovely porch, and lovely Ruth taking it all in. Honestly, that is one thing I don't think I realized at the time I was there, but I recall my visit there and I recall an overall sense of serenity.

Your mother seems so peaceful compared to my mother. But I do glimpse moments of peace in her, and I see so clearly now that that is the feeling to cultivate in her apartment. Inadvertently to this end, I have been sorting through piles and throwing stuff away, simplifying, and also bringing lots of plants onto the patio, and getting her to sit out there for a little bit each day. Your porch was such an inspiration.

Watching the PSP videos has put us both in a "dawning" phase, her especially. I think she has fluctuated between believing and not believing that this is terminal. Certainly she's coming to know her disease, and this makes both of us very tender at bedtime, which is especially sweet, no matter the frustrations of the day. I too am learning deeper surrender, and am learning to let go of my reactions to my frustration. Not the frustration itself, but I can name it and get on with things without letting it seep out, most of the time.

Even to the point, that when I went to get in bed at one o'clock this morning, and found that the heavy rains earlier had leaked through my ceiling and soaked my bed, I didn't blow up. I just slept on the couch, and handled all the maintenance and office stuff calmly in the morning, and resigned myself to the fact that I won't be able to sleep in my new bed that I love for god knows how many nights 'til the roof is fixed and the ceiling replaced. Oh well. About time to hit the couch now.

You help me plenty simply by being someone I can really communicate with about this—maybe the only person who can truly understand. Just email me from time to time and don't mind if I ramble on at you, that's a big help from afar!

Monday, May 10

Debbie brought dear Melody over last night and we celebrated Mother's Day and Deb's birthday and seeing each other again after all these years. Melody was visiting for the weekend from New York. She fed Desmond an ear of corn and fell in love with him as he chomped the kernels off the cob. Deb tried to teach me to salsa in the tiny kitchen. I burned the bottom out of the coffee percolator thinking I had turned on the burner under the soup to warm up. We drank wine and ate the feast they had brought and laughed 'til after midnight. As always, told stories with Melody about those good old days when she was two and three and we all lived in Charlottesville. Talked about our men or lack of them. The evening will go down as one of the brightest in my stay here, I am sure. Too happily exhausted to write down more. Though I can't shake the image of Debbie wielding that carving knife as she gestured.

Monday, May 17

Knowing the names of plants teaches you ecological stories that, as they accumulate, bring you perspective, weave a richer picture of the world.

Knowing the stories of *things* can weave a different kind of picture. The Korean Chest, for example. I cherish these things because these are the things I was raised with, and they taught me to value craftsmanship, artistry, skill, beauty, and story. These ancestrally collected objects range from gorgeous to insane, from useful to frivolous.

Take the Family Opium Pipe. I have actually coveted this treasure in my mother's glass display cabinet for more than twenty years, since I smoked my first hash and bought a first edition of *Confessions of an English Opium Eater*. At last she gave it to me when I traveled out here last fall, along with a box full of other small treasures: the silver cigarette case of Aunt Alice's, her tortoiseshell and silver cigarette holder, Grandmother's rosary, the Orthodox Madonna icon… the list goes on.

When I moved into this apartment, a part of my inevitable trajectory, my mother gave me many furnishings. Amy lent me an antique bedroom suite, some tables, lamps and things. We drove in her truck to her parents' house in the country, and raided Judy's antique barn. My small suburban apartment is furnished with many lovingly crafted pieces of wooden furniture.

In the course of ceiling repairs much plaster dust covered the Korean Chest, the dresser, the bed frame, the fancy rocking chair that squeaked me and my brother to sleep as infants. I took a cloth and a bottle of furniture polish to them, and lovingly cleaned them. The first time they'd been paid attention to in years, all of them. I watched their glow unfold as I wiped and polished them, rubbing the soft white cotton over citrus oils until cloth glided smoothly over surfaces.

The detail of the beading along the footboard of the bed, the turnings of the mirror hanging posts, the two tones of the rocker, emerge under cleaning. The intricate friezes depicting scenes from Korean life, or perhaps mythology, on the dark wood of the Korean Chest, revitalize beneath the cloth. Within the story of the Korean Chest I find a thread of history, in the rituals enacted in the friezes, in the time and world of the carver, in the history of the piece. This is the appeal of antique heirlooms. What was Korea like when this piece was carved? Having recently read something about the wars that forged North Korea I have much more curiosity about the provenance of the Korean Chest, and how it came to live with my family. I want my mother to come over here Wednesday and go from room to room and tell me about each object.

And by the way, what an ego-awakening weekend I spent, pondering the conflict with Management here at Woodside Apartments. Over the ceiling affair. My impatience rose up within me all self-righteously, and I thought if I simply demanded, controlled, endeavored to dominate the situation, I could get what I wanted. All I got was a heavy conscience and a bad name with Management. Then I got paranoid that my illegal turtle could get me evicted, which, when I finally read the lease, was confirmed; so last night I moved both reptiles over to Mom's and erased all trace of their presence—in a week or two, once the ceiling leak fiasco has faded from memory, I'll tell them I'm getting a turtle, and it will be okay to bring him back.

It's interesting how that whole scenario panned out. When it all came down to it, what I saw most clearly was my own arrogance, selfishness, and sense of entitlement. It didn't take much to turn me around after I lost it with the nice maintenance man, Jeff. He seemed truly concerned that I was so upset, and he tried to tell me, "It's not the end of the world." Well, another person, that might have pissed her off. Me, it made me think of the war in Iraq, and of Nick Berg who was beheaded there, and of the gang boy up the road who had his hands macheted off the other day, and of the whole rest of the suffering world, and caused a complete ego crash within. Which was a good thing. So it shouldn't take ten days for a ceiling leak to get fixed. Big deal.

56

The thought of losing this fabulous walk-up, this veritable arboretum apartment, made me quail and quake. I found myself grasping, gasping, for a pious way out of the quagmire of my own deceitful nature. I had once again gotten myself into a pickle with my particular combination of assumptions, reactions, and hedges. I could have taken it anywhere from there last Friday. I could have stayed pissed off instead of falling into the soft relief of humility, could have stayed angry with the maintenance man and the manager instead of heaving a sigh of apology; could have fretted and fumed all weekend and ruined my visit with my lovely aunt.

I have really needed time with me. I'm deepening the feeling of connection with me, and oddly, with my faraway friends—hmmm. With my closer friends here, too, Amy, Gaytha, Wayne, I'm treasuring my conversations more, with them, with my mother. Within my circle my bonds are strengthening. Arrrg! Attachments are strengthening, but detachments are increasing as well.

Tonight, Auntie Rita is with Mom, so I got to come home early at nine, and have a couple of hours to finally fix up the bedroom, vacuum my bed, make it up, and get to bed before midnight. Yippee! And today was such a good day. Clouds in the sky.

"Cumulonimbus," Mom said today. She said it again and again, laughing. She loves to say it.

Her beloved grandfather walking Ali out of the family home in Washington, D.C., on the way to her first wedding.

Wednesday, May 19

I brought Mom over today for lunch, and to record her telling me the stories of some of these *things,* these treasures she is passing on to me. Rita A brought her over, and when I got downstairs to meet them, Mom was ten feet ahead of Rita A without her walker, leaning on my car and stepping up onto the curb. I yowled at both of them, and then Rita A reacted as if she hadn't noticed what Mom was doing—I thought, this is getting off on a bad foot (so to speak), and lucky for me, my Buddhist practice (again) kicked in, and once the situation was in hand I *let it go.*

We all came upstairs, I finished the tuna casserole and asparagus I was preparing, Mom and I quizzed Rita A about Ghana, and we had a really nice time. Then we discussed what needs to be done for Mom daily, and gosh, if Rita A picks up the ball now that she has clear directives, life just might get a little easier.

I asked Mom first about the Korean Chest. A week before she turned nineteen, my mother married her mother's best friend's son, Perrin. She had completed a year of college, studying art; she was gorgeous and naïve, he was handsome and, as it turned out, schizophrenic. I hope they had some good times together, but she rarely speaks of him so I don't know. She worked as a medical secretary to put him through college. She told me one story about him several times, and this one, about the Korean Chest, just this once:

Her brother brought it back from a tour of duty and gave it to her as a wedding present. She treasured it. She always kept her linens in it. Perrin scorned it. Her voice cracked as she told me, "It was our first argument. He said, 'What do you want me to do, put it on the floor and piss on it?' So I never have liked the word piss since then. He was not very nice to say that, do you think? He was really an S.O.B, and I thought he was so great. That's the first time I realized that he was not. I won't tell you about all the other times."

I knew that she did not like the word piss. One night when I was home from college and we were sitting up late on the yellow leather couch, she told me how she broke the Colonel from saying it. For some reason as yet undiscovered, he was not fond of the word fuck. But he did say piss, a lot, apparently. When he'd said piss one too many times for her taste, she retorted, "Fuck! Fuck! Fuck!" Every time after that that he said piss, she reiterated fuck! three times. As she told the story we both dissolved into laughter, and cussed and laughed our way down the hallway to our bedrooms. Ever after, if one of us cusses we both end up laughing. The Colonel had stopped saying piss in short order.

She met the Colonel when he was a Captain and she was living with her brother and his wife at Fort Benning, Georgia. She had fled Perrin in the night after six years of marriage. This is the story she told me several times: He stood over her as she lay in bed and threatened her with a butcher knife. He took the knife into bed with him and turned out the lights. Hours after she was sure he was asleep, she slipped from under the covers, grabbed her purse, left everything else she owned, ran in her nightgown to the train station downtown, and caught a midnight train back to D.C. where her mother lived with Grandfather and Grandmother.

It must have been awkward between the mothers at first, but her mother and Perrin's remained close friends until decades later when Perrin's mother died. Meanwhile, his twin sister was diagnosed as schizophrenic and later killed herself. Mom never saw or heard from Perrin again, but learned of his diagnosis years later through his mother. Ironically, he outlived them all.

So after fleeing in the night she lived with her brother and his wife, helping with their baby while they both worked for the Army. John introduced his sister Ali to his pal Bob. Bob was a great dancer, he listened to classical music, he loved to read good books, he quickly won her wounded heart. Their honeymoon movies show them laughing and wading along the Gulf Coast, floating in the Great Salt Lake, and ogling the Grand Canyon. They lived happily for some years. Their son was born in Japan, where Ali learned the fine art of flower arranging and was featured in a Japanese magazine article about Ichibana. Their daughter was born two years later in Washington, D.C. That was me.

Thursday, May 20

Every time I've gone to Mason Neck State Park to walk the dogs, I've seen some kind of wonderful wildlife, osprey, bald eagle, gorgeous box turtles with bright yellow patterns, black snakes.... This morning as I was driving in on the beautifully wooded lane, an owl flew across right in front

60

of my windshield. As if that weren't exciting enough, a little farther down the road I saw a snapping turtle just sticking her head out over the road. I stopped to look more closely, and intended to try to herd her around and back into the woods, but realized she was digging and laying a nest! Right under the edge of the tarmac. So as I stood there scratching my head and wondering what to do, a biologist from the adjacent National Wildlife Refuge pulled up, and we stood there quite awhile chatting, and waving a few vehicles around her. The fellow invited me to go bird-banding tomorrow.

Unfortunately there is some road construction going on in the park, and these giant trucks keep screaming up and down the road, and we feared that they being oblivious would crush the turtle. The chief ranger of the Park stopped by, we all searched our vehicles for some kind of flagging, fruitlessly, then both men left, saying to me, "I guess if you want to make sure she's okay you'll just have to stay there and watch her."

Not more than two minutes after that, a maintenance truck rolled up, and this young fellow with technicolor arms from the wrists to the shoulders got out with some pink tape. We flagged a couple of sticks and laid them in the road in front of her, then he said, "Hell, I might as well just drive back and get some cones, can you hang for awhile?" So I took the dogs out and strolled up and down the road, and got plenty of exercise for my triceps by waving my arms alternately over my head nonstop to chase off the incredible density of swarming deerflies. Then the tattooed man came back and set up some cones. I drove on to try to walk the dogs, but the flies were too bad, so we came home.

This is what I do: Go over midday to make sure Mom eats lunch and gets her early afternoon pills. If we have any shopping or errands we do them in the middle of the day, sometimes eating lunch out. Then I come home and steal a couple of hours napping or walking dogs again, then head back over about five or six to make sure she gets dinner, to help her tidy, sort, go through piles, all these never-ending tasks, because she won't get rid of anything—we just move stuff around mostly, but sometimes look at pictures, take a walk around the lake, watch TV.

Then we begin bedtime, which starts around nine thirty and ends about eleven. This mostly involves me keeping her on track with what to do next, then making sure both of them are in bed. At this point I read them a story, currently from *The Peterkin Papers*, a children's book she loved as a kid. Then I turn out the lights and come home.

Soon I will take her to speech therapy down in Woodbridge two or three days a week. I go grocery shopping a couple of times a week, and take her to various doctor appointments.

I've been setting up a container garden on her patio, where I keep the dogs at night when I'm there, and sometimes we sit out there for awhile in the evening, or I go out to water, deadhead or just talk to the plants. I drink several gin and tonics each evening to keep my cool. The last three days have been difficult, but before that she had a great week with lots of energy and alertness.

I had it out a bit with the Colonel tonight after a tension that began last night. As soon as I walked in he'd said, with that tight-lipped, stern demeanor, "Your mother and I are not seeing you around here as much as we expected to!" I fell for it, hook, line, and sinker, bit right on. I calmed myself outwardly but inside I seethed, raged the rest of the night, and it bubbled along quietly under the surface all day.

I hadn't realized what stress I was under until the ceiling leak caused me to lose my temper with certain Woodside Lane employees, and I guess I hadn't realized until Dad said that, how much of a toll it's taking on me. Some of it is simply being here in Our Nation's Capital, in dense humanity, away from my wide open spaces and tortoise-paced life at home.

A couple of weeks ago, the day before the bad guys beheaded the American in Iraq, a sixteen year-old boy in Alexandria, just a few miles up the road, had both his hands cut off by rival gang members with a machete. Doctors did manage to reattach them, though he was left minus four fingers. This story really hit me hard. Dad saw me burst into tears when he told me about it, and he offered compassion, his brand of it anyway. Tonight as we fought he said, "Boy, you sure *are* hypersensitive." In the end, he said, "I'm sorry," and I forgave, but it left me shaky. Who is he to determine whether I am overly sensitive? Who is anyone to judge that? Failing to feel that boy's pain—or anyone's—seems a little under-sensitive to me.

As I drove out the road from their complex, I had this recollection of saying to him, "It would be good if you could hold her once in awhile, kiss her some before she's gone." And of his saying, "I can't sit anywhere where I can hold her" (because he can really only get up out of one or two chairs, neither of them wide enough to hold a wife). Then I pictured them sitting side by side on the edge of his bed, where they can both get onto and up from—but they won't—and I just burst into tears. I cried through both traffic lights, and by the time I got to my parking lot I was sobbing.

I pulled into a space across the lot from my building, because over there just up against the woods the honeysuckle grows so thick and lush it perfumes the whole parking lot. I've been parking there at night so I can walk the dogs along under it for their midnight whiz, and I've been inhaling the nectar deeply. Tonight, I sat and sobbed with my head on the steering wheel, windows open, dogs sitting quietly in the back. When I finally pulled myself together, I couldn't smell the honeysuckle because my nose was full of snot and I couldn't find a damn Kleenex! What a sad story!

Anyway, I'm laughing now, because I feel better having written, and while I've been doing it, Brick has been trying to decide if he wants to lie in the bed or guard his chewbone in the living room. When we came in tonight he got very possessive of this rawhide he has ignored since I got it for him a month ago. As I've been sitting in here, he's gone to bed twice, and twice come back out to grrrr at Mocha, who is sleeping happily by my feet and couldn't be less interested in his bone. He can't make up his mind, and now he's just grrrr'd at Mocha and taken the bone back into the bedroom and—hey! Get that thing off the bed!

Well, I'd better buck up because it's not going to get any easier. And really, none of it was such a big deal. Not in the big picture. I'm still a really lucky brat.

Friday, May 21

Having "a little smoke" sometimes when I get home at night takes the edge off the difficult days. She knows I smoke grass. I told her one day on her annual visit a decade ago, because I was determined not to hide it anymore. "I'm thirty-four years old, and damned if I'm going to sneak around my own home to smoke, when she drinks three Scotches a night," I told a friend. When I told her, she didn't bat an eye. She asked a few questions: "What is it like?" "Where do you get it?" Then she said, "Everyone needs something."

A few days after that revelation, I came home from work late, and she had already poured her first drink. "Sorry I'm late," I said, "Work was crazy." She said with a soft smile, "Wouldn't you like to have a little smoke?" So that secret lost its power over both of us.

Saturday, May 22

Dear Dad,

I know you want to forgive and forget and so do I, but despite my best efforts to get over our encounter the other night I can't shake it. I remain deeply stunned by your insistence, for you repeated it last night, that I'm not there as much as you expected. After much thought, I don't even want to know what you expect from me. I came here to give what I can and I am giving to the max of my ability. I hope with time my ability will increase.

Please recall that I have been here now just six weeks, and have not gone one entire day without being there at least some hours. I am already stressed to the point of tears nearly every night and have a stiff neck that just won't go away. I will not get an ulcer for you or anyone.

When I came here I intended to devote myself to Mom's care and to your relief (and care as you needed it), but I thought I'd have a little while to ease into it and begin to build a life for myself outside your apartment. It has not happened quite like this. Since I arrived I've dived into a situation more desperate than I realized and have had little time to do anything for myself other that settle into my apartment and reconnect with a few friends. When I'm not with Mom or running errands for her or you, or walking the dogs, I am at my apartment catching my breath and a little rest. I don't know what you think I do when I'm not on duty, but I can assure you it isn't much.

Your stunning announcement Tuesday night sapped what little energy and enthusiasm I had for going bird-banding right out of me. Granted, my reaction, my choice not to go, is entirely my responsibility, not yours. But your criticism took the joy out of it for me, and has left me feeling desolate about being here and trying to pursue any of my own interests.

Do you understand that I'm here for a marathon, not a sprint? I'm here for the long haul. I need to have a life of my own, however slight, in which I can find comfort and diversion and renewal from the very sad and draining work that I am doing for you. I'm struggling to manage the emotional weight of the changes in all our circumstances—Mom's, yours, mine—and in fact, the world's at large. By the way, to say "it has always been thus" is to have your head in the sand.

Now don't get me wrong. I also find deep joy in being able to serve and love my parents, to whom I am grateful beyond words for the life you've enabled me to live. But I need time alone. I'm doing my best to take care of things for you and Mom, and I will strive for my best to keep up as your and her needs increase. I know I'll be needed more in the future than I am now. Please don't make me feel guilty or burn out this early on. And please try not to talk to me with that vicious Colonel tone and glare you have. Let's both try to be more tender with each other, please? I'll try not to react the way I learned from you. Love, Rita

Sunday, May 23

Dear Linda,

You made my day. I loved hearing about my garden from you, and you are here with me telling, and I am there with you in my garden as I read it. Thank you! My desert willow! Wait until she blooms! And I'm so happy to hear about my kitty, that her spirit is good and her face is healing. I'm not surprised the irises didn't bloom this year. But as long as they grew good green leaves I feel quite certain they will bloom once I arrive home— whenever that is.

Yes, there are some emotionally challenging times. There haven't been many, in terms of events, but there's a steady state of anxiety that requires all my spiritual training to live calmly within. My shoulders are in permanent spasm, despite a couple of massages. This really is *so much* an exercise in being in the present moment, in accepting and being grateful for the way it is in every moment, every breath. If only I could remember this with every breath.

I wonder how the emus along the driveway are doing, and how Paul and Ramona are. How is Paul's health? I should call them. I can slip so easily into envisioning life on Fruitland Mesa. The reality is setting in, now that the shock of deciding, packing, travel, has worn off. Yes, I am indeed in the belly of the beast here in Our Nation's Capital. And I am small and white and preoccupied. Scandal bubbles toward eruption across the river, while I am absorbed in the gradual decline of a single human being. But as the body declines—which is inevitable—can I possibly help the spirit to expand? I hope so. For sure my spirit is undergoing all sorts of gyrations, which will no doubt result in its getting a good stretch.

Having such vivid recollections of my friends and their homes and lives gives me great joy. My time there was well-spent. I cherish my life there even as I delve into my new life here, finding joy in the beauty of my mother's face when she smiles as I tuck her into bed. Bedtime shifted everything for me early on, gave me a ground, a specific place in the day where peace is certain. We all look forward to it. It took me a couple of weeks to get Mom's bedtime from eleven or midnight down to ten, which is when Dad has been starting to bed for many years. Now Mom starts to bed at nine thirty, sometimes as late as ten, and they both end up in bed at roughly the same time, around eleven. Then I read to them! I know they enjoy it, because it's what gets Mom to go to bed that early, she knows if she goes too late I'll tuck her in but won't read as long—and last night, Mom was really tired, and started to bed at nine. Dad came along at nine thirty, so he wouldn't miss the story! Oh, he didn't say so, but I knew. So at the end of every day, all my frustrations, challenges, sadnesses melt away in this sweet time of the three of us together. I am so *lucky* that I get to do this with my parents!

Also, Mom and I are learning to really relax with each other. We spend more and more time out on the screened patio, where the dogs have beds, and I've filled the space with potted plants. I snagged a potted hibiscus that had been abandoned behind the dumpsters and left to die. True, it was largely leafless, and dry as a bone despite last night's rain, but bursting with new growth just waiting for some TLC. So I brought it up and soaked it in the tub this morning, and tomorrow I'll prune it back and set it out on my balcony! It's lovely, it has a braided trunk. I'm excited to see what color its flowers will be! Excitable me!

Sunday, May 30

Dear Elizabeth,

I'm always so glad to hear from you. I understand what you mean about sitting on the porch in a storm. It's a wonderful feeling. The dogs come with me in the evenings, and stay out on the porch because of Mom's allergies. I usually get them a good walk in the mornings, and can leave them in my apartment during the heat of the day. Then I take them to Mom's porch for the evening.

Today was gorgeously cool, and I took Mom out to the Bay to sit on a bluff and watch great blue herons flying over, and sailboarders, skiers, kayakers playing on the water. I did not know about National Turtle Day, but I did buy Desmond some organic dandelion greens at the health food store yesterday.

I'm sad to hear about your mother's increasing difficulties, and her lack of interest. The more time I spend with my parents, the more I simply cannot get over your stamina. Granted, I think it would be easier for me with just my mother, but still, I get so frustrated even with her, *every day*, and it's sometimes such a struggle to not snap at her. Though we do manage now at least once a day to share a sweet hug, and we've talked more about death.

Last night she talked a little about feeling that sometimes it would be a relief to surrender to PSP and other times wanting to fight the disease and hope for a cure. That just broke my heart—I mean *what* are the chances? Here again, you and your mother are an inspirational example to me. I just want to care for her and love her while she's here, helping her eat while she can eat—and then what? Have you made a decision about a PEG tube? I can't remember if we talked about this when I was there. I have this sense that as your mother eats less and less you two have agreed to let her go. I don't know why I think that—maybe I'm projecting?

Mom and I have talked about it a few times. I think it's important for me to discuss it with her 'til she's comfortable with the thought and can evaluate her feelings about it with a fuller palette. So to speak. Her life is so difficult even now, for her, that I can't imagine her wanting to prolong it, especially later. I guess this is what they mean on the Forum about getting the tube while it can "prolong a good quality of life," rather than waiting and trying to "regain" a good quality. That's the real question: Is her current quality of life one she wants to prolong?

Her speech is rapidly deteriorating, not dramatically, but evidently. It is worse now than it was two weeks ago. We start speech therapy next week, and have some mouth-strengthening exercises to do this week in preparation. I keep forgetting, which is how bad I am at this job.

My dad is another story. Ever since he told me he and Mom weren't "seeing as much of you around here as we expected to" I have been angry with him. It's like he uncapped the well of decades of anger I thought I had flushed out—but I realize now, only in the past few years did I really think I was over it. Clearly I'm not! I simply refuse to tolerate his disdainful, controlling behavior. I wrote "nature" at first, but I hate to go that far. He can be very sweet, so maybe it's not his nature but just a bad habit he picked up in the military.

Speaking of which, there was a lot of hoopla in Our Nation's Capital for Memorial Day. Even I got a little teary watching some of it on TV, just from the touching stories of individuals, and from the fact that my father survived WWII and must have some deep-down scars. But honestly, the festivities seem like a giant pageant to glorify war and thus bring the current regime back into favor with the populace. It's a convenient and joyful distraction for the people, it's patriotic, and it's not a calamity, so they are milking it for all its diversionary potential. Oh well. The monument looks quite lovely. I wonder if I'll get the nerve to drive in there some day and see it. I've sworn never to drive on a road with 95 in it again.

Well my good, strong friend. You enjoy your evening out, and remember you're my hero.

Monday, May 31

In March, when my mother realized that I was really coming to live, she got excited about getting things for my apartment, so she went to a tag sale and bought me a toaster. The ladies who run the tag sale have an apartment downstairs in the Madison, the farthest away of the buildings, crammed full of stuff they've acquired from donations and estates, and they trot it all out to the auditorium once a year in October and sell dishes, hats, tools, old phonographs, ugly furniture, jewelry, baskets, chachkis, all manner of things you'd find at any tag sale, and some of it quite nice. If you want to buy something from the tag sale and it isn't October, you can call the women who run it and meet them down in the apartment full of stuff, and peruse at your leisure. So when she realized that I was coming to live, Mom called Mickey and met her downstairs, and bought me a toaster for five dollars.

She was so happy to have provided me with a toaster that she called and told me about it before I even left home. She gave me the toaster the day I arrived. It's a brown-paneled thing in pretty good shape, thirty years old at least. It has been toasted in for many years. It doesn't have bagel-size slots.

I had been thinking before I left home, I can't wait to get a new toaster. I couldn't take much with me when I moved. I packed only one box full of treasures to make my new apartment feel like home, comfort items like the little turtle lamp, a few scarves, a precious bowl. Endeavoring to find whatever bright spots I could in this move, I was looking forward to it as an excuse to get all kinds of new things I wanted but couldn't bring myself to buy at home: new sheets, a standing lamp, a boombox, and a brand new state-of-the-art toaster that could hold bagel halves. I couldn't take my household with me when I moved here, but I figured I could ship back what few things I'd buy for myself along with everything else when I leave. I knew I'd be bringing home most of Mom's belongings.

So she gave me the toaster, and, though disappointed, I thanked her kindly, and took it home and plugged it in. No new toaster for me; I couldn't hurt her feelings. However, this morning, she was nagging me about something, and the toaster came up, and I blurted, "I wanted to get a new toaster! I didn't even want that toaster!"

The minute the words were out of my mouth I froze. I quickly said, "I'm sorry. It's a fine toaster, it was very sweet of you to think of getting it for me—" I tried to undo the hurt I'd done, but it was too late. It was as though I'd stuck a pin in her, all the excitement she'd felt about my coming and her preparation for my arrival escaped through the wound and she deflated.

Somehow, though, the moment passed. Perhaps she forgot about it quickly. One possible benefit of a brain disease.

While Bob was stationed in Japan, Ali turned her artistic appetite to the traditional Japanese art of flower arranging, Ichibana.

June

Tuesday, June 1

Door to door from my apartment to the Wilson Spring Trail in Mason Neck State Park takes only twenty minutes. There are other trails, the Great Marsh Trail in the Wildlife Refuge, and some trails in the county park a little closer to home, and the dogs and I enjoy walking on all of them, but Wilson Spring was the first we tried and remains, perhaps because of being first, the most comforting. I discovered the trail in mid-April, finally finding time to explore dog-walking options in the area. Here my pavement-tired feet walk on soft, moss-covered earth run through with roots, bathed in moss and carpets of leaves. Having lived without soil, topsoil, moist soil, for a decade and a half it is a pleasure of astonishing newness to walk a clean, manicured trail through old thick deciduous trees and their inevitable seasonal debris.

I find I'm falling in love with my old home ground, the land that taught me to love Nature. Fallen trees, oak leaves piled, moist air throbbing with birdsong. I hear the symphony of birds. What I've been hearing at home have been quartets, the chamber orchestra of the desert—here it is a full-fledged symphony. And here is *Acer rubrum*, the red maple, and sycamore, with their gorgeous leaves of early spring. I am learning to listen in the forest, with dogs, following their gaze with my ears, following their

71

noses with my eyes. We flushed a pair of white-tail does, yearlings—or are they just so much smaller than the mule deer back home?

Here is a dying tree—what's the natural rate of decay here? Are these trees dying at a natural rate or from some event or condition? Many are rotting at the base. What's that about? I know enough to ask these questions, enough to care, but not enough to figure it out. Huge root systems, incredibly shallow, these old trees down from last year, old brown leaves still clinging to the limbs.

These woods were my first love, but they were never safe for me as a child, they were fraught with dangers of human denomination. I remember seeing my brother's friends out there, later, smoking grass or shooting up, and when they were younger, pouring salt on slugs. How could they not? How could a child hear that pouring salt on a living creature dissolves it and not want to try it? I know that I watched once, in fascinated horror, but I heard the slug screaming. Even now, the soft moist earth under my feet springing with hollies, deep in the park along the river, I hear the grunting thrust of progress from some "improvement" being inflicted nearby, and the scream of overhead jets.

But here is a discreet improvement, also: a blind at the edge of the marsh with a bench to sit and watch the bald eagle in the tree across the water, to watch the redwing blackbirds, the Canada geese, at their daily business. I would personally like to thank Scott M. Jones of Annandale Boy Scout Troop 50 (my brother's old troop) for his Eagle Scout project at Mason Neck, the blind he built. There is a little plaque weathering with the wood of the blind. I come here and sit many days, walk down Wilson Spring Trail to the Bay View Loop Trail, and come to the blind on the marsh.

I've only seen the marsh at low tide, and in early summer it looks a little mucky. Still, I see the ecological richness spread out before me and how this cycles through the seasons, a still place, though not quiet, raucous with frogs, birds, and insects.

I find rivers a great comfort. I have not lived around rivers for years, have not lived in the moist East for decades, and all this time I've missed the unmistakable aroma of low tide. The slow insistence of rivers soothes, their steady inexorable letting go reminds me to flow. And river people are the same, the state, the country over, perhaps the world over. They have a different time, an awareness of the world, their natural world, deeper perhaps than that of landlubbers. This marsh, this refuge, opens to the Potomac River just south of Our Nation's Capital.

And the forests themselves, deciduous hardwoods with lots of maples, tulip poplars, oaks of different colors, sycamores, ashes, sweetgums, and many kinds of flowering trees, so different from the evergreens at home. And *in* the forests themselves, topping the list of good things and finally emerging, Brood X, their true official name. Ever since I arrived, I have been waiting for the cicadas.

These are the seventeen-year cicadas that I last experienced thirty-four years ago, when I was eleven. Even then I was impressed, not grossed out like so many people around here this time. However, the prevailing attitude seems to be one of mildly interested tolerance. Tolerance? For this extraordinary manifestation of Nature? These people should be feeling awe. We should all be down on our knees in the woods joyfully tossing handfuls of copulating cicadas into the air.

That's another good thing about being right here, in Fairfax County. They have an amazing regional park system. In addition to Mason Neck State Park and National Wildlife Refuge, which protect the largest freshwater marsh in Northern Virginia, we've explored Burke Lake County Park, the South Run Dogpark, Pohick Bay Regional Park, and Huntley Meadows Regional Park. At this last park I took my dogs and my mother to walk along the paved path through yet another second-growth, mature hardwood hammock. The other day, I drove past with the windows up, and, stopped at the traffic light at Telegraph Road, I heard the first cicadas of the season. Through the closed windows. An audible roar. So the next day I took Mom and the dogs to the Huntley Meadows Trail, a paved path easy on her walker.

She was delighted with the cicadas. They perched on trail posts, crawled across the trail, clung to trees. We paused so I could record the fifty thousand or so cicadas in audible proximity. These thumb-sized creatures with orange bug-eyes and translucent orange-veined wings crawl up out of the ground every seventeen years like clockwork, and have for millions of years. They nibble on tree roots while they scrabble up from their one-foot-deep dens, then climb to the tops of the trees and pump a membrane in their abdomens to make this lovely sound which, in northwest D.C., has been measured at 85 decibels. They are reputed to measure up to 110 decibels, well above the range where hearing protection is recommended by our federal government.

Their populations sweep through much of the Northeast and mid-Atlantic regions from mid-May into June. People sweep mounds of them off their porches. Roads can become slick with their carcasses. They emerge, they climb, they fly about, they breed, and that's it. Then they die. Piles of dead cicadas at the bottoms of trees begin to stink in the heat of a D.C. summer.

They are odd and primal and beautiful, and they come by the millions only once every seventeen years for only a few weeks, only out of undisturbed ground. Consequently, there are far fewer cicadas here than when I was eleven.

The blades of progress I hear everywhere, behind my apartment complex, across the street, next door to the Home, even out in the woods of the state park, have been scraping relentlessly for decades, tearing down these old deciduous forests and digging up sleeping cicadas, disturbing ground at an abominable rate. In the weeks they are here, the cicadas manage to drown out the drone of the earth-moving machines in some places, casting a fleeting auditory illusion that Nature can survive our thoughtless onslaught after all.

Wednesday, June 2

I feel sort of pathetic for feeling so much better when I finally hit upon a "me project," like rearranging the furniture. I've finally conceived the perfect place for everything in the living room—something permanent! And I feel a rush of energy to accomplish it, and I laugh and feel like dancing. And now the living room is lovely. Just perfect. After three hours with a vacuum, a vision, and a little strength it is transformed to a peaceful corridor. I can take some pictures. Cool summer breeze stirs the pine trees outside, wafts in to soothe.

The Colonel has a great sense of humor when it comes to being a conduit for dumb internet or lunch table jokes—all so cliché with rarely an original thought or punchline—and telling them three or four times to the same people. But no sense of humor about the whereabouts of the three-hole punch, or the screwdriver, or whatever he is looking for that is missing from its place. It's up to me to inject humor into whatever scene is going down at the Home. It's been so awful there the past week. He's being such a grump. Maybe he just wants more attention, but he's setting up a vicious cycle for himself. When he feels neglected he's mean, he acts out, which makes everyone want to neglect him even more. Which makes him madder.

Oh well, it's nice to have that clear at last. I need to first be polite, second cultivate compassion for him, too, maybe about this WWII memorial—how nobody in his family seemed to appreciate it or share it with him. He turns up afterward wounded that we didn't watch the dedication of the memorial on TV, but he never said a word ahead of time about wanting to share it with us, or even about watching it. That's probably the root of this week's conflicts. He feels disrespected and alone in an emotional time for him. (As if he had any emotions. When I once accused him of having feelings about something, he said I was nuts.)

Friday, June 4

So many insights flying at me so fast. I can hardly keep up with them. Not the least important of which is: it is so much easier to focus on one's own needs, wants, unhappiness, suffering, than it is to open one's eyes and see the suffering of others. I mean not just read in the paper, watch on TV, commiserate with a friend who's lost a loved one, but really see the suffering of others authentically. Nursing a terminal parent comes to mind readily, of course, but that's relatively easy compared to being a journalist covering a war, massacre, or famine. To be there and see that with the eyes is all most people can do, but to see with heart the depth and magnitude, the bottomlessness of suffering in the world as it is today, is very difficult. So much simpler to fret that I have too much of one thing and not enough of another. To watch Mother each day declining; the stages of this illness as they overtake her are stunning, and her quiet misery discomfiting.

As far as Dad, I think I have that one figured out. Money isn't gratitude. Money doesn't even mean gratitude. Money means function. I could handle everything so much better if I didn't feel that by his behavior he is beginning to show himself an ingrate for my being here.

As far as the mission: It's one thing to understand intellectually about the need for time for oneself, and the all-consuming nature of the work. It's quite another to begin to feel the magnitude in one's body and soul. That getting to bed by eleven thirty, and stealing a quiet shower in the afternoon could be considered luxuries—moments, in fact for which to be grateful, when just last week you thought you might be able to grow a life for yourself here to bolster you through the process. Now the process has become all. Can it be it's getting this close this fast?

How I long for the help and guidance of Hospice.

Saturday, June 5

Dear Dad,

I want to ask you to do a couple of things for me but I don't want to talk about them around Mom, so am trying this way to communicate.

Both have to do with Dr. Wise. Could you please ask him what it would take for him to give me a prescription for an anti-anxiety medication? I am about out of the one which I have taken sparingly since before I moved out here. Nothing too strong.

Second, could you please have a frank discussion with Dr. Wise about Mom and her alarming rate of deterioration? The reason Hospice did not agree to accept her six weeks ago was that Dr. Wise told them she's not ready for Hospice care, i.e., that she has a certainty of at least six months more to live. That may still be true, though I believe it is equally likely she won't survive that long.

You do the math: weigh the decline you've seen in her since I arrived two months ago, and her rate of decline in the six months prior to that. Do you think it's getting worse faster than it was? I do. Dr. Wise hasn't seen her in at least a month. I believe we would all benefit from the types of help Hospice can provide. Where I am forced to discuss with Mom the possibility of surgical insertion of a feeding tube to keep her sufficiently nourished, as recommended just today by her neurologist over the phone, Hospice could provide counseling and perhaps acceptance and assistance that would preclude that very traumatic decision.

Ali wants to sleep all the time, and she can't even sleep at night. She is very very tired. From discussions with her I know that part of her really wants to surrender to the disease, give up and let herself die, and another part of her wants to fight the disease and "hope there will be a cure." Sadly, there is no cure in sight for PSP. I believe she and I could both benefit from the comfort of Hospice care rather than continue carrying on as though there is some hope she'll have anything other than a continuous decline in her quality of life.

Just some food for thought. Please feel free to email me back rather than try to discuss any of this in the apartment.

I'm sorry I appear so thin-skinned to you, by the way. It is painful to me to see how much both of you suffer in so many ways, particularly the ghastly nature of her discomforts. Handling all this is difficult enough, but feeling, as I do on the occasions when you snap or glare or scoff at me, that you are not grateful for my being here makes being cheerful infinitely more difficult. 'Nuff said about that.

Maybe you'd come out and watch the horse race with us tomorrow afternoon and have a mint julep with me. Just a small one.

Saturday, June 5

My dearest Diane,

Thank you for your timely and encouraging note. It offered a much needed perspective about how our (my family's) suffering is just a drop in the bucket. Not that I don't get that kind of reminder every single day by reading one or two headlines in the Post, or by catching a minute or two of Fox news. The things that people do to each other in this metro-sprawl make my skin crawl.

Today was the roughest day yet with Mom. I took her to a lung specialist to try to get an alternative to an asthma medication she takes which gives her mouth sores, which make it even more difficult for her to eat. She coughed and gagged her way through the very long appointment on this dreadful stringy saliva, one of the effects of the PSP. It has been intermittent until today but went on all morning and afternoon. Fortunately, the doctor gave her some other medication, and set her straight about her cocktail of allergy medications she was mixing with abandon.

Then we stopped at Fort Belvoir to pick up my permit to drive on post—that took an hour of paperwork in a double-wide that smelled of port-o-lets that were being cleaned, while Mom waited in the car in the rain. A somewhat calm evening after that, though Mom and I both felt we'd been beat up by the day, with all her retching and gurgling. Then I got home at eleven fifteen after tucking them in and reading part of a chapter of *Alice in Wonderland*, to find that my boy dog had shit a foot-long streak of diarrhea across my bedroom carpet. I cussed and cussed until I had it cleaned up, then walked them in the rain until we were all soaked. Of all days for him to have that AGAIN.

So you see how refreshing it was to then—after lying still for awhile—read your email and get things back in focus. Now I can climb into bed and hug the poor terrified dogs and sleep. I cherish your kind and wise words and your loving thoughts of us, and I am so frustrated for you with your surgeries and broken wrist and nailguns, but I bet your remodel is finished before I get back, and then we can sit up there and drink sherry and read and laugh and I can't wait for that.

Sunday, June 6

We are down in White Stone, Virginia, visiting Rita and Ford for a few days. It's been only mildly challenging. Mom handled the three-hour drive well, and the new house is lovely, and very accessible. Her sister, as usual, gives and does and gives and does. It is respite care for me, not having to lift a finger to help myself. Rita makes wonderful meals, and the drinks flow freely before each meal. Except breakfast, but no one would object then, either, I suspect. Though Ford has diabetes he *will* not surrender his sugar, so there is homemade cake for dessert. It feels very safe in this nest of love, for both Mom and me. Knowing her sister loves her as much as I do, and is *here* for her, gives me a sense of relief I haven't had since arriving in Virginia.

Rita makes cards using cancelled postage stamps. People who receive them are reluctant to throw them away they are so beautiful. In her sunroom she set up a table with all her supplies so that we could all make cards this afternoon. We sat in the sun amid blooming orchids, and made cards with colorful shreds of paper, glue, stickers, and stamps. Though Mom can't really see the details on the stamps, she loved playing with the colors.

She has been craving bright colors. About a month ago she asked me to paint the outside wall on the porch bright red. She wanted me to paint the whole porch, in primary colors, but the Colonel pitched a fit and refused us

Rita and Ali, Irish twins at eighteen months apart, on a double date at a nightclub on Connecticut Avenue in Washington, D.C., in 1945.

permission. "We're responsible for those walls! They'll charge us to repaint them!" We blew him off, and painted the one wall bright red. The day I was priming it white, he busted me in the hallway carrying a paintbrush to the bathroom sink to wash. "You're not painting that wall, are you?!" he yelled. "You told me not to," I replied with a sweet smile. He seemed satisfied.

I don't think he's noticed. We snicker in mock fright from time to time when it looks as if he'll join us out there, but he hasn't brought his scooter across the threshold, so he can't see the other side of the wall between him and us. As we left to come down here, the Colonel accompanied us out to the car. He couldn't have missed the red wall when he turned around and headed back to the building, but he hasn't said anything on the phone. We have a little trepidation about whether his wrath will welcome us home, but there's nothing we can do about it now!

I'm sure he wonders what is happening to his docile wife. I'd only been here a few weeks when Mom told me she was tired of sleeping on white sheets. She said, "I've slept on white sheets all my life and I want something else!" We went out for a little retail therapy. I bought new sheets, she bought new sheets. She picked out a raspberry red set, which she alternates now with the mail-order set of gold satin sheets I had shipped overnight when she said she wanted them. I ordered her silk pajamas with red dragons crawling all over them, and an orange silk nightshirt. She delights in the luxury of color and texture she has denied herself until now. What misguided sense of frugality or obedience or timidity or *what* caused her to deny herself the glory of wild color in her bed all these years?

Or maybe she has simply transferred her passion for color and fabric from her studio full of paints, her closet full of shawls, dresses, pants, blouses, shoes and coats, to her new domain as an invalid: bedclothes and linens, the wall.

In White Stone, Dick and June came over for drinks last night, and a high school friend of Rita's and Ali's came over from Richmond for lunch today. She handled the shock of Ali's appearance with good cheer. My dear mother sitting in the high-backed blue chair, disappearing into it, smiling without saying much, as we all sat around the living room with our rum and cokes.

Monday, June 7

I realize that I'm subtly agitating for her not to opt for a feeding tube, i.e., not to prolong her life. I have this intuition that death is racing up behind her and I need to help her prepare for it. She has to make a decision soon about getting a PEG tube or not—not will hasten her demise. Getting one will prolong it, but at what quality of life? No guarantees that it will keep her even at the level she is now for long, and then will it keep her nourished possibly far beyond where she would like to have died? I guess we cross that bridge when we come to it. *This* is why I'd like to have Hospice involved now, to help discuss the difficult questions.

Wednesday, June 9

Dr. Widnell, the Johns Hopkins neurologist who diagnosed Mom, recommended her to Dr. Calvert, a neuro-opthalmologist with an office nearby in Alexandria. Mom had been to him a time or two since her diagnosis. Though he was not accepting new patients, he did take her case because the disease is rare and he is doing research. I drove Mom to her appointment following her directions, avoiding major thoroughfares such as the beltway and I-95, following much the same route as she'd used to take us to the hospital the autumn before when the Colonel had been whisked away in an ambulance.

He'd been losing his lunch from both ends for two days before I called Dr. Wise, who suggested we get him to the hospital for hydration and evaluation. I could find no other way to transport him than by ambulance so I finally called 911. "What is your emergency?" the dispatcher asked. "It's not really an emergency," I explained, "my father is crippled, and he's heavy, and he's been throwing up, and I can't get him in my car, and his doctor wants him at the hospital." Those Fairfax County paramedics were there within seven minutes, got him on the gurney, started his vital signs. "I'll follow you," I told the ambulance driver.

"Oh no you won't!" he said. "I'll be driving through red lights and weaving around traffic. It isn't safe for you to follow me and you'll be breaking the law." Whoa. OK. So Mom and I slipped out the back door as they hauled the Colonel away out the front, and in the car I asked her how to get there. She led me all over Robin Hood's barn, turn left up there, right here, now left again, stay in this lane, veer right, I think you turn here. I kept saying, "Are you sure this is the right way?" thinking her disease could be confusing her.

Being an alien to the southern end of the county I had no choice but to follow her directions. Suddenly out of a residential neighborhood we emerged into the hospital parking lot, and I pulled up outside the ER door. Just as I was wondering which door we should enter, the ambulance carrying my father pulled up to the entrance. Despite the circuitous route, despite my mother's as yet misnamed brain disease, despite my unfamiliarity with the roads, we'd beaten the ambulance. We reveled in our smugness when the ambulance driver dropped his jaw to see us there first. I got Mom settled in the ER waiting room to wait for news of Dad, then I went outside and puked three times between naps in the front seat of the car. I'd gotten the bug too.

Six months later I found myself driving that circuitous route again on the way to Dr. Calvert's office, down Telegraph Road, left, right, left, onto Franconia Road, under I-95, right, left, right, and there we were at a twelve-story white building just inside the Beltway. The foyer was like all corporate foyers but smaller, the elevator claustrophobic, the hallway we emerged into a dingy blind white, lined with anonymous white doors.

Dr. Calvert's white door opened into a deep brown room dominated by an enormous fish tank. Fish tank? It was a serious aquarium, the key feature of which was a splendid assortment of living corals. A handful of fish swam among the coral, living accents, bright ornaments, a pair of clownfish to groom the anemones, a yellow drill-nosed dart, a bright blue circle with yellow tail, and a slender magenta bullet shooting through the arms and arches of the coral. I did not realize Mom's vision had gotten so bad until she told me she couldn't see much more than colors. I sat and gazed at the tank, smitten with the bright pink fish. It was the most gorgeous aquarium I've seen outside of a public spectacle.

When Dr. Calvert came out to lead us back into his office I nearly wept. Anyone who would keep such a difficult and gorgeous display in his waiting room had to be good. He seemed nice at first, until I asked about the possibility of getting Mom into Hospice care. "Are we trying to rush her along?" he asked, with a snotty looking sneer.

"I can see why you might think that," I said, amazing myself with my calm. "But it isn't the case. I've seen how fast this disease has progressed since I was here last fall. I'm just trying to get some help." In the next few minutes we explained that I'd moved here to care for my ailing mother, and bless her heart, she went into great detail describing what I'd left behind to come and be with her, so that by the end of the session Dr. Calvert apologized for his initial reaction and said, "I was abrupt and I didn't understand the context."

Only then did my knees go weak with rage at his presumption, but I said thanks, no big deal, and drove Mother home through the maze of suburbia. We decided not to see Dr. Calvert again. It's become clear that we were simply paying him to contribute to his research: there is nothing he can do for her.

He did say to her, though I'm not sure she heard him, "Everybody needs their own space, you have to have your life, and your caregiver has to have her life, and you need to understand that there might be anger, frustration, and even some resentment about what your daughter's given up to move here, even though she wanted to." It was a good speech on the need for caregiver respite, but again, I don't know if she heard it.

Friday, June 11

I think it's been two entire weeks that I have been with Mom between ten and twenty-four hours a day. I ran by this morning to help them—Mom, Dad, and Rita A—figure out how to run the new twenty dollar food processor. What could be simpler? I asked on the phone after some troubleshooting, "Well is it plugged in?" The Colonel laughed (for a change) and said, "That's the first question I asked myself." So I drive over there and of course it's not plugged in. It's the *old* food processor that is plugged in, the one Rita A broke the blade of by forcing it around with a knife.

I called in this afternoon to remind Mom that we were invited to a party tonight and she opened with, "I'm so confused!" I talked her down from that, I hope, and asked about the party, and left it that we'd decide later whether to go or not.

Dad called just now, one and a half hours later, to say Mom is having a hard time this afternoon and to ask when or if was I coming over today. I said, "I'll be there at five." He said, "Oh, there's your mother calling me, let me go see what she wants," and I said, "Call me if you need me," but what I should have said was, she just needs you to sit with her and pay her some attention. Tell her stories until she falls asleep. It's been ten minutes and I haven't heard back, so I'm optimistic.

In the past couple of days I brought up some of the difficult questions she must think about: Does she want to have a feeding tube installed soon to prolong her life? I said, "You need to evaluate your quality of life, and how you really feel about dying, and how you really feel about living." I said it rather matter-of-factly and also told her I personally thought I would choose not to have one, and later, that I would probably jump off the edge of the Black Canyon if I were in her shoes. I'm afraid she thinks I am trying to hurry her along, after Dr. Calvert planted that idea, when really I am trying to spur deep and painful reflection and advocate for having mercy on herself and just letting herself *go* without the added measures. I am evaluating her quality of life for her. That's a big no-no, I guess.

Another of the difficult things I brought up yesterday was that, in light of the fact that all her physicians think she has much longer to live than I thought when I arrived here (like years v. the six months to a year I've been thinking) that I really couldn't keep up the pace of the past couple of weeks. We discussed my need for space and time, and she said, "I thought you had a life of your own." I'm still thinking I need some big chunks of time to myself, so that I can be here for her completely in the coming marathon.

I have been invited to a party tomorrow night, and I've been very excited about going, getting together with some of the boys and one of the girls from my AP English class in high school. I barely remember a couple of them, and most have families who will be there too. So Mom has known all week how excited I am about going.

I had pointed out to her earlier that it has seemed to me that whenever I announce I am going to take an afternoon or an evening off, away from her, she immediately manifests some symptom of obvious decline. I can't remember how I phrased it, but pretty gently and not quite so articulately. She said, "I don't think that happens," and I said, "It's observable, and it makes me feel bad," and that was about all that was said.

I left her in bed resting and returned home for a couple of hours. When I got back, Dad had gotten her dinner and was sitting with her as she began to eat. She was drooling lentil soup with every mouthful. She continued to drool the chili. She could not bring herself to swallow. She ate very little. Then we went for a walk. We were sitting on a bench resting and I watched as she kept rolling this saliva around in the front of her mouth. I said, "You know you can just lean over and spit that out, that might be helpful, it's okay on the sidewalk." She said, "Oh, I can swallow it." I said, "I think it would be good if you'd swallow it then," so she did, and she did pretty well the rest of the night. I read from *Alice in Wonderland* and turned off their lights and came home. To be brought out of bed to plug in the food processor.

I feel just terrible for her. I know this has got to be living hell for her. I know I need some time off. Am I being just the tinsiest bit manipulated, however unconsciously, or am I being impatient and surly?

Sunday, June 13

I saw a woman lying in the middle of the road on my way to the party last night. I was in the left lane leading a pack of cars from the traffic light a few blocks back. I swerved into the right lane where the woman lay face down, her head at the white line. As I braked to stop the cars behind me, a middle-aged man came running from a gray car up ahead that sat stopped in the turn lane.

As I dial 911 and run toward her, he picks her up by the collar of her white shirt, arching her back like spaghetti she is so limp.

"Leave her down!" I yell, and see other people approaching—someone yells, "Has anyone got a cell phone?"

"I'm on it!" I call, then run to the scene where people are gathering. A young Hispanic man, a young white woman, an older white man. She needs a blanket—I turn back to grab one from the car. "She needs a pillow!" I call. The dispatcher asks, "What is your emergency?" Traffic stops and people run about, and I pace with the cell phone. I turn around and she has a pillow under her head, they've stopped turning her and she lies on her back.

Somebody else says, "3945!" and I see him pointing to the door of a house along the street—the address—duh—so I relay that, and say, "The traffic's really backing up," and the dispatcher says, "You don't have to worry about the traffic, the best thing you can do is talk to her in a normal tone of voice and tell her everything's going to be okay, help is on the way."

So I do that. I get down on the road with her, and I search her panicked eyes for consciousness. I get through. Her left cheekbone is a crimson weeping welt, her hands are skinned on every knuckle, the elbow of her shirt is torn. Her face has scrapes but her teeth are not bloody, and she manages to open her crying eyes enough to look at me. She stops crying and calms for a moment.

The young Hispanic man is kneeling over her, fanning her with a piece of paper and muttering a steady stream of fervent prayer, "Jésus, Maria…."

Someone asks the Korean man from the gray car, "Are you with her?" and the man says, "Yes. I was having a fight with her."

Whoa. Did she jump?

Sirens come from afar. The young white woman who may live on the street says to the bleeding, wailing woman on her back on the tarmac, "You did a really good job," and I say to *her* and then to the praying man, "So did you," and the sirens arrive. When I see the medic step to her side I step out of the scene, step back to my car beyond the fire engine.

This quotidian tragedy is in better hands than mine. She will live. This daily drama is not the most exciting thing in my day, as it no doubt is in the day of the woman in the road. My mother is slowly dying at home. This is my second night off since I arrived here two months ago.

I have a new haircut, a black dress, and I am on my way to a party. I'm late. I turn my four-wheel-drive mountain car onto the median and cross to a frontage road, and continue north on this new road in this new city, to meet old friends in new settings. A few blocks on I remember the soft flannel blanket I left on the woman in the road, and I start to shake. To calm myself, I focus on the gin and tonic I'm expecting at the party. You can shake when you get there, I promise myself. For a week I have been looking forward to this reunion of a handful of high school classmates.

Some of them are brokers, some attorneys, none can name the snake I catch in the yard, and none care for cicadas. We are all bright and eager and happy to catch up with each other however briefly, to make our happy impressions and go on our merry ways. We laugh and sigh and commiserate, drink beers and wine and gin, meet children and wives. Robin and I walk the dogs. She tells me she sees her cancer as a chronic disease, not terminal. Chris and I talk about compassion and granola. John remembers "that Halloween party." Some of us talk about death, some politics, one David makes drinks, the other David makes us laugh again and again.

It was truly astounding, maybe just for me, to feel so open. And grateful. And happy. And safe. And then the end of the evening came, we said our goodbyes, I got back in the car with the two dogs and drove south through the night.

It was then that the visions came. Her hands. Skin scraped away in patchwork, flesh too shocked to bleed yet. Her bleeding scarlet cheekbone swelling, her face scraped and wet from crying. Her terrified eyes.

"I was having a fight with her." The echo of the sentence whispers through the darkness of the night. Open windows let cool breeze wash through the moving car. Just as I think to myself, Now where exactly was it? I look to the left and see the very house number 3945.

Did he *push* her?

I know with certainty in that moment that he pushed her out of the moving vehicle. I see him again try to haul her up out of the road by the collar of her white shirt, her black-haired head hanging heavy.

When I get home I call dispatch. I tell them what I heard. I ask how she is, the woman in the road. He tells me Officer Neville will call me back if she has any questions. She leaves me a message. I leave her one. She leaves me another message.

She says some things I think no man cop would ever think to say, but maybe I'm wrong. She says she is not allowed to discuss details with me, and she doesn't need a statement from me. "Everyone who needed to be at the scene was at the scene," she says, "and yes, we got statements from the couple. I'm not at liberty to disclose information about her condition." But she hints that the woman is okay.

Only now, more than twenty-four hours after the incident, can I let it go. What remains of that evening is not the admiration of all those married fellows who said I'd weathered well the years, though that was certainly nice at the time. What stays in sight is the fragile, broken face of the woman in the road, and the shocking turn of her day.

Monday, June 14

Dear Elizabeth,

Wow. Mental vibes really do work. I was sorry to hear about your mother's fall and the paramedic escapade. That must have been intense. I'm glad she didn't break a hip. I hope she's doing okay again after what must have been traumatic for both of you.

I have some food questions for you. Is Ruth still taking Sinemet? Mom has to take hers on an empty stomach, so we can't spend the whole day eating, though it often feels like we do anyway. The hard part is getting her to eat half an hour after her pills, then getting her to finish one to two hours before the next pills, which are scheduled three hours apart!

And does your mom *want* to eat? Mine keeps saying she's not hungry. Do you notice thick mucous problems from the dairy in ice cream? Mom's lactose intolerant anyway, so that's out for her, but I would squeeze some in if I didn't think it would exacerbate the sticky mouth thing.

I'm blending most of Mom's food not to liquid but to mush, and that makes getting more food into her easier, but still…

Well, thanks for being there, glad you're both still hanging in. Hope you have a good outing Wednesday.

Monday, June 14

I got Mom an appointment six weeks earlier than scheduled to see her neurologist who recommended the feeding tube, so a week from tomorrow we go in for a long appointment—they have a special name for it when they actually take their time with you.

What I lack is discipline. But it's no surprise—the apple doesn't fall far from the tree. Mom has always had trouble with being aimless, just like me.

One thing that comforts me is Impermanence. I know this confusion will pass, this bad day will pass, it will gradually become more clear for me and for her. Getting this discussion and decision out of the way will be a big help, whichever way it comes down, because then I can settle down to whatever routine the ramifications deliver. I am definitely attached to a certain outcome here, a no-no for a budding Buddhist. You know, I guess I had not considered that it might be a "better" death for her if she chooses the PEG tube. Maybe she needs that time, maybe it will give her more clarity. I guess I really was trying to rush her. I can't say for sure what decision I'd make if I ever get her disease. I really was making it about me. And I knew this all along, maybe that's why I've been so crabby. I must remember that "Each must own her own death," and that no matter how well-intentioned, my values do not apply. I need to refine my mission statement.

Meanwhile, I had a quality walk in the woods this morning with a good meditation looking out over a large marsh. All alone for square miles, unbelievably, with all the life breathing all around me. I felt blessed. See, all I need is discipline, and everything I need and want is right here. Practice, practice, practice. Is anything ever not a lesson?

I continue to struggle with my role here, playing bad cop at the dinner table because she won't eat, facing down my inner demons about the feeding tube issue, trying to find ways to bring delight into her life.

I hope that Beth might be able to come visit sooner rather than later and talk with my dear mother about death and dying before she makes the choice about the tube. Give her an alternative to her fear that I think might drive her to choose the surgery. Help her to think about or see things I cannot articulate. I think she sees me as a bit of a servant, someone to do things for her, rather than a confidante or a spiritual guide or companion on this journey. I've told her I want her to talk to me about anything she is thinking or feeling but she rarely does. I don't know what questions to ask her to help her make this decision, I don't know how to bring the subject up in a way that opens discussion, I don't know what to ask or say.

Everyone thinks I'm doing such a wonderful thing being here, while I'm struggling to hold onto my good intentions and not just turn into Super Bitch. I am such a fake. Is it wrong of me to want *one day* all to myself some time? I don't even want it, I just feel like I need it to rest. This is not the toughest "job" I've had in any physical sense, but the constancy of attention and the emotional drain are stunning. And I see now that this Question has arisen, this really is just the beginning. Oh well. The good lord doesn't give us more than we can bear, eh? And really I'm doing fine, just trying to find my place here still.

Tuesday, June 15

Dearest Auntie,

You think much too well of me. You've no idea of the turmoil in my head sometimes, and how grumpy I can be. I'm sorry we didn't call you tonight, I meant to, but dinner was grumpy because she *wouldn't* eat and then she *would* try to read while she was putting food in her mouth—her doctors have said that she must focus on her food and have no distractions—and we have a running conversation going about whether or not she wants to get a feeding tube to enhance her nutrition. We've got an appointment next week with her neurologist who suggested it, and whatever she chooses will be a relief whenever she chooses.

I finally got her to eat tonight by pointing out that, "Here you are considering getting an invasive surgical procedure, which you've already signed a living will saying you don't want, and yet you won't eat while you can!" She was like a kid with Brussels sprouts! She choked it down (shrimp with lobster sauce over rice, all nicely pureed) but we were both pretty grumpy by then. I just feel awful about having to have this whole discussion, and having to be such a hard-ass with her sometimes. This after I came over at five to find her in excellent shape and spirits, talking well and seeming clear. I'm going to just have to clear that dining room table of everything except actual food-related items. Like most people's dining room tables.

Wednesday, June 16

We arrived for an appointment at her neurologist's office in Fairfax to find that it had been cancelled, so we drove down Route 50 and Gallows Road to our old house on Masonville Drive. There we marveled at the cedar tree my father planted that first winter forty years ago, now forty feet tall and eight feet in diameter at the base. All the trees were bigger; the neighborhood that had been new when we moved in had matured, reached its destination as a shady old-growth suburb.

We drove down to the park surrounded by woods where she'd supervised my play when I was in kindergarten, where we'd picnicked a few times as a family, where concrete turtles and dinosaurs provided climbing and swings overlooked the creek; the park where years later I'd walk my stray dog on the bike path and sneak a joint while I lived in the old home the summer before they sold it. This day, the swings and the old dinosaurs are gone. I help Mom on her walker down the asphalt path to the new bench beside the creek. We simply sit and watch it burble.

Friday, June 18

Dr. Wise saw Mom the other day, and finally someone besides me sees that she is ready for Hospice. He wasn't willing to sign her in six weeks ago, but he is now. He was very compassionate, I thought, during the discussion of her symptoms and the question of getting a feeding tube. He basically told her that she was dying and she had to choose now whether to prolong that or not. I think that calmed her some. She asked, "If I get the feeding tube now, can I have it taken out when I want to?"

He sighed. He said, "Once it is in, it's a very difficult decision for a person and her family to make to remove it. You don't strike me as the kind of person who would like to linger in bed for months, unable to speak. Then that puts the burden of deciding to remove the tube on your family. It's much easier to decide now either not to get it, or to commit to living with it until the end." He said, "It's never as easy as you'd like to think. You really have to come to terms with the fact that this is terminal."

He said, "From the moment we're born we're in a pre-terminal condition." She said, "My husband and my son don't understand that I'm dying. Only my daughter and I do." This was when he said he'd sign the papers for Hospice. It was quite touching. My father has been very sweet to both of us since then. Hospice nurse is coming Saturday. It sort of makes it all more real. And I'm going to see that doctor tomorrow morning (ack! This morning!) to ask for some anxiety drugs for me. Better get to bed. Don't want to look shadow-eyed and strung out in the morning. Or do I?

Saturday, June 19

Ali was admitted into Hospice home care this afternoon. The most amazing woman came to do it. Trish, an angel in her own right. I liked her immediately over the phone when she called to confirm the appointment an hour before. Just the laughter in her voice, I could hear the humor and warmth of her smile. When I came in through the patio about one forty-five she was already there, and opened the patio door for me, and fell all over the dogs. She was sturdy and loud and gorgeous, and laughed a lot. We were all smiling most of the time through this potentially difficult session. It was so easy. To converse with her about the disease, for all of us. I wanted to ask her after five minutes, "Will you be the nurse we get to see all the time?" but I refrained.

I feel like the minute we started to get more help, I began to think more creatively about how to spend our time together. I don't want to spend less time with her, I just want to spend it differently, maybe even more, just less *necessarily*—have more flexibility in when and how.

And now she's had her last appointment with Dr. Schefkind, her regular eye doctor who prescribed the prism lenses. "Did you realize," I asked him when he'd finished his exam of her, "that the double vision could indicate PSP?"

"Yes," he said.

"Why did you not say something to us?" His job, he said, was not to diagnose, but to address and fix symptoms.

"You could have saved us all a lot of pain, and saved her a couple of falls and stitches, if you'd said to her or to her neurologist, hey, this might be PSP," I insisted. He defended himself, saying the risk of alarming a person unnecessarily was just too great. Oh well, I thought, you're no good to us anymore, either.

And so it has panned out that the doctors, except for Dr. Widnell, the one who confirmed the PSP, and Dr. Wise, her longtime GP who got her into Hospice, seemed to be for the most part opportunistic leeches, keeping their appointments with Mom when there was nothing more they could do for her, so as to continue receiving the hundreds of dollars they charge per visit in their specialties.

The more safety I'm giving her, the more she's letting go into it.

Letting go. She's ready to let go. She's not quite ready, but she's ready to get ready. And in a way her brain is letting go, too. This recent confusion is so unexpected. No more "little gin drinkses" for her at night. But it seems like it's been increasing for longer than that. She is getting more happy again, too, though, after a couple of weeks of being angry; I think, from our discussions of the feeding tube and the final nature of her choice.

It seems likely she will choose not to get the tube, based on what Dr. Wise and Trish said. Trish mentioned all the complications from a medical angle: infections, peritonitis, hospital visits to clean and change the valve, etc. She said that it's not been proven to prolong living. And Dr. Wise said to me privately, "I don't know her a thousandth as well as you and your father know her, but I don't see her as having the kind of personality that would want to find herself unable to speak anymore, unable to get out of bed, and still wanting to go on living." I thought that was incredibly open and courageous of him. He is an old-fashioned doctor in that regard, as much a counselor perhaps as a medic. He sure works for Dad. I think Dad goes to see him so often as much for the conversation as for any pathology.

I'm glad I'm feeling better about Dad. As he was driving his scooter by her blue chair this evening on his way to get ready for bed, he pulled up close to her and leaned to kiss her, and she couldn't quite (or wouldn't) turn her head, so he kissed her cheek, lingering, then reached for her face and turned it so he could kiss her on the lips. How many years ago was the last time I saw them kiss on the lips?

I told him the other night he should pet Mom's new pajamas, and he said, "Oh no, I couldn't do that, I might get turned on," and I said, "Nothing wrong with that," and he said, "Except how do you turn yourself off?" and I still don't know what that meant.

A wicked two-day heat wave has passed in a cool breezy night. Ah, it's lovely. Leaves are blowing song and it might even be raining. I've opened the door and window as I like to do on cool enough nights. Four orchids bloom in the living room, and the fifth on the balcony is growing a pod of seeds. I must look up what to do with them! And look up the paperwork for Mom to donate her brain to PSP research.

Tuesday, June 22

We dropped that lady neurologist in Fairfax. After keeping us waiting in the exam room for half an hour, she burst in announcing cheerfully, "I have so many patients I can barely keep up!" Then she admitted there isn't anything more she can do except help us regulate the medications for as long as they are effective. She started this feeding tube discussion, which she thinks would be a breeze to install and live with. Nothing she said jibes with what the nurses, those hands-on witnesses to degeneration, say about the risks and downfalls of the PEG tube in elderly, terminal patients. It was a waste of time seeing her today, and with death at the door Mom has no time to waste.

Friday, June 25

All week she's waked at night and tried to do math. She called one morning and told me, urgently, "The formula is three."

"Okay," I said. Later, when I got there, I found on her bed an envelope on which she showed me a formula: If $80=a+b$ then what? There were all kinds of scribbled numbers with plus and minus and equal signs, and question marks.

Now, Mom has never been a math person. She understands nothing about numbers—or technology. She asks me every time I give her a long distance phone number, "Do I dial a 1 before that?" How many years has she been making long distance phone calls by dialing a 1 first? Every time, she asks me. Every time, until I took over dialing for her. I was stunned to find her doing nonsensical equations in the middle of the night.

Are these numbers, questions, symbols, the ramblings of the brain disease, or do they come from some deeper wisdom? Is this answer in a book somewhere? Is it in all the books? What is she trying to do?

We spend a week trying to figure out what this is about. Every day she shows me new numbers, tells me about new numerical contortions she has attempted.

"If I subtract it I get it back," she says, "but I can't do it. Say it says 3:04. I subtract 3:04, then I get it back, but I can't do it."

One evening I begin to discover the meaning of the calculations—after dinner she says, "If it says 20 then I subtract 20."

"If what says 20?" I ask. I try to understand, to think, What is the referent here? But I can not come up with any connection to reality, so I say, "You have a brain disease and there aren't any numbers and there's nothing you have to do."

"I'll show you, I'll have to show you what I mean."

"OK, you show me, and you have to trust me if I say this is your brain disease talking, this isn't real, OK?"

"OK."

We get her in to the bedroom, and she sits on the edge of the bed, and points to my father's digital clock on his bureau, which she can see from her bed, its big red numerals looming across the room.

"It says 10:03... and then it says 10:04, and then 10:05, and then I have to do something, I have to do 10:04, then 10:03—"

"No," I interrupt, and wrap my arms around her thin shoulders, rubbing the soft silk of her new pajamas and her frail arms beneath. "That is your brain disease talking. There is nothing you have to do. You don't have to think about numbers."

"That's such a relief," she says, her voice cracking.

She has been watching the two-inch-tall digits defining the minutes as they pass, and that has made her afraid to go to bed, afraid she will not sleep. I tell the Colonel that we have to unplug the clock for the night and see if that helps.

"Why not just turn it around?" he suggests with evident relief. I am touched by the simplicity of the solution, and I turn the clock around. The numbers will not trouble her this night.

Yet she continues her calculations.

Finally, today after breakfast she asked me, "Do you understand why I need to do it?"

"Do what?"

She furrows her brow. "What I do."

"Subtract time?" I suggest—her face lights up.

"Yes!"

I sadly shake my head. She sags a little. "To get it back," she explains.

"To get back time?"

"Yes!" again, smiling.

"No," I say.

"You don't understand why I want it back?"

"Time?" I ask, as it begins to dawn on me. I realize that at night she hopes to lengthen her numbered days. "Oh, well sure—you want time back. Of course! Anyone would. You want more time?"

"I want more time!"

"But we can't do that," I explain, "it's not the way the world works. Yeah, time is a man-made construct and all, but we can't make it go backwards in the real world."

She wants more time. She wants more time. I finally understand, after struggling with the mixed-up math for a week, as I sit here this afternoon and tumble it over, that she wants more time.

The feeding tube—will it buy her time? She has enough time. What will she choose to do with it?

I call to tell her I understand. "You want more time," I say. "You have enough time. You have enough time to do all that you need to do. It's okay. You have enough time."

She smiled, I could hear her smile over the phone, and she said, "I'm not going to do it tonight."

"You're not going to do it tonight? Why not?"

"I don't need to."

I heave a huge sigh, and tell her that I love her, and we hang up the telephones. It has taken me too long to understand. Outside, three hummingbirds at once have settled on the balcony feeder. I have reached a little epiphany as the little birds have reached a resting place. I need a little more time, too.

Sunday, June 27

John and Clara came to visit Ali for a few days, and it was quite touching to see how tender he is with his little sister. Nobody thought she'd be the first to go. Their granddaughter Amanda, a competent and cheerful twenty-something now, came with them to chauffeur, as they both suffer from macular degeneration. The Colonel got them two guest rooms downstairs. The first night they visited for cocktails and we had pizza delivered. Afterwards Mom, Clara, and John sat side by side on the couch and looked at some of the older photo albums with images of their mother, grandparents, themselves as children, and I took new photos of them together, with Dad's digital camera to go in new albums.

The second day we took a picnic to Mason Neck State Park, all gourmet goodies I bought at Whole Foods, including stuffed chicken breasts, olives, cookies. John got bit by some bug that crawled up his leg, and we had to swat mosquitoes a few times. Amanda and I walked the dogs around the loop trail while "the grownups" stayed at the table in the grass. We all walked up to the overlook where Mom and I spent Memorial Day, and sat and watched a couple of windsurfers and a blue heron. Amanda brought bubble-blowing stuff and some other toys, incredibly thoughtful and fun of her, and I took some sweet photos of John blowing bubbles to delight his little sister.

The day before they left we took them to The Riverside, a fabulous restaurant along the parkway overlooking the river just a few miles past Mount Vernon. I had reserved a table by the window for the six of us, and they tried to seat us farther inside. I was furious and stood my ground until they reset a table for us by the window. Really, I'll be damned if I'm going to take my mother to one of her last meals at a restaurant by the river and not get her a riverside seat! John said he was impressed with my determination and wouldn't want to cross me. I've finally impressed the General!

It was a joyous meal with great food, including an over-the-top lobster bisque. Despite an argument with the Colonel in the morning about his not going. I put my foot down about that, too, and he caught a handicap cab and joined us out there with his scooter. He was complaining that it was too much trouble and he didn't really need to go, and I said, "Your wife needs you to be there!" And, I insisted, it would be fun, and better food than in the dining room. The last argument was probably the most persuasive.

You'd never have known he resisted coming, the way he played the gracious host of the party.

I think we were all sad when they left, for knowing it might be the last time Ali sees her big brother and he sees her.

Monday, June 28

We had a rough night getting Mom to bed. Did some exercises right before bedtime—she insisted—and I think it wired her. She couldn't remember what she needed, or needed to do (which was nothing), and wouldn't settle down. I finally gave her another half of an anti-psychotic that Hospice prescribed for her last week to eliminate nighttime confusion—Seroquel. She really resisted taking it, I felt awful insisting, but she just wouldn't settle down. Then I rubbed her neck a little bit and it was so tense it was arched back—I gave her an Advil then, too, and sat with her awhile with the light off, before finally leaving. She had such a good day, too. I'm not surprised, just grateful it hasn't happened sooner. No more exercise before bedtime! The nurse is coming tomorrow, she may be able to help.

Tuesday, June 29

Executive Director

The Home

Dear Meg,

Parking space #237 has been vacant for nearly two months, with the exception of two weekends when it was occupied by apparent visitors. I have asked Kathleen several times about the possibility of switching spaces with the one my daughter is currently assigned, and she has said the space is assigned to a resident who "may be away."

My daughter is assigned parking space #227 in the island, and this space is too narrow to permit me access to her car door with my walker. The pie-shaped spaces along the curve are wider and allow me to walk directly to her car door. Soon I will be in a wheelchair, and will need that extra width even more. I have a handicapped parking permit from the DMV. It is ironic and disappointing that I can park in an accessible space in any parking lot in the state of Virginia except the one right outside my residence.

Because of this access problem, when my daughter takes me to doctors' appointments and therapies several times a week, she parks out front to pick me up and drop me off, which can take up to an hour each way. When there is a space out front, she takes up parking that other residents and visitors might use. Often, there is not a space, and then we must deal with trying to get me into the car out back safely.

When I gave up my car I gave up my parking space. Now I have a need for a parking place again and there is one empty that allows me safe access to the vehicle I use almost daily. At one time that space was a designated handicapped space. I would like for my daughter's vehicle to be assigned space #237 and for the person assigned that space who is not using it to have space #227. I am asking for you to facilitate this.

Incidentally, there was a space available at the curb when my daughter arrived three months ago to take care of me but she was denied it because she is "not a resident." It was given to another Adams resident whose car leaves the space only once every few weeks with that resident's *daughter* at the wheel. Surely I have as much right as any other resident for an accessible parking space for the vehicle I use.

I know you are very busy, but I am asking you in the name of fairness to help me with this request.

Thank you,

Alice C. Clagett

Tuesday, June 29

Gunshot just went off in the neighborhood, or nearby. I keep waiting to hear sirens—there are hundreds of other people closer to wherever it was, surely one of them will call the cops. Nothing yet, more than five minutes. Feels kinda weird.

That Hospice nurse came again today, Cheryl. I just can't believe how sincerely nice she is. Are they allowed to stay for tea with their clients, I wonder?

Mom had another very tough evening, this time with her bowels leaking steadily, several messes to clean up, a shower in between—poor thing. But she did discuss the feeding tube again with Cheryl, and tonight I read her a Q and A Hospice brochure on it, and she said, "I'm convinced."

"Convinced of what?" I asked. "Not to get it," she said.

She's stopped subtracting time since starting the Seroquel, but today she told the nurse that she'd only pretended to take the second dose I gave her last night. That it was on the bedside table. Well, it wasn't, and she kept insisting, and I said let's drop it. She promised us all to take a whole one tonight, and she did, and it was a pretty fast acting dope. Fifteen minutes, for sure. Maybe less. And she was out. Wow. I've never really seen that in real life. Only in the movies, which don't quite do it justice. At least she joked about being drugged, once she was in bed for good—assured me she'd be okay, that she'd "had this before" with the bowels.

Meanwhile, I'd called the Hospice night number to inquire if there was anything they knew of to do, and they offered to send a nurse as if it were perfectly okay anytime of night, and so sincerely that I was really reassured. And, when Cheryl was here she suggested replacing the Seroquel with natural melatonin to help her sleep for a few nights—experimenting, though she hated to call it that. Also raised the question of whether a scheduled swallow test is really necessary. I'm beginning to really understand the Hospice premise. Really minimal intervention, comfort only intervention. I wonder if I did get Hospice in too early, but I really don't think so.

I don't see what intervention with this disease at this time is going to accomplish. Cheryl said to Mom (and the question made Dad uncomfortable) "What are your goals with Hospice? You have to decide what you'd do if they say you are aspirating and you can no longer eat." (Could they really say that?) And she went on, "Would you do anything different than you're doing now?" What a concept.

I then gathered that she was asking us to think about whether any of these expert doctors were really something we wanted to keep on with. And Mom has been saying for awhile, "I think these doctor visits are going to slack off now." I wonder how she meant that.

She's made the tube decision. Now she has to make the shift from the medical paradigm to the hospice paradigm. There really is nothing the medical world can do to change the course of her disease. She and I, Hospice and the PSP Society, can now do for her all there is left to do. That is another inevitable step in coming to terms with terminal, isn't it?

Wednesday, June 30

She was always trying to control my life. It just manifests differently at this point. I remember resenting for years her being so overprotective. Tonight she says she wants to henna her hair because she wants to be like me. "Why?" I ask. "Why do you want to be like me?"

"So people won't think you're so strange." That was her answer. Later there was another reason, but still she wanted to be (look?) like me. She said her hair used to be this color, and she "put the shiny stuff on it." I don't recall her hair ever being this red—maybe when she was younger than I knew her. Maybe at a happy time in her life. In any case, she now wants red hair. Uh oh. What if I go along with the red hair and we henna or dye it, and it turns out in a week it was the dementia talking and she hates it?

I've resolved we shall make the anniversary party invitations. She has been wanting to do a project with blues. It would be fitting (irony) for her to weave her sorrow about her marriage into the blues of the anniversary invitation. I get frustrated when there is a problem to solve, and rejoice, return refreshed when I solve it creatively. Like the invitations. Clever, artful, should be a fulfilling project for her.

Yet—I really resent her! Just like that old doctor said I might. Who knew? But not when she is sad or weak or ailing. Only when she is demanding and possessive and snotty. A brat, really. Now, I just need to overcome resenting her even then, and life will go a lot easier. Today I had all kinds of plans, but was so emotionally strung out and just plain exhausted that all I managed to do was walk the dogs, read, nap, and start thinking about the long overdue zoo job. And sure 'nuff, she called twice and said, "I think you better come over."

I really should have discussed it with her more and been calm, claimed my time 'til five, but instead I capitulated and went over, bearing a grudge. She didn't need me. Is she capable of following the reasoning that if she lets me go and come freely she'll get a lot more out of me than when she is this demanding? She was mad because the Hospice social worker, Henry, didn't show up (at all, no call), and she was picking her nails because I wasn't there with the polish remover. When I got there she was fixing a snack. She ate, I made a sandwich. I didn't hate being there, I was just angry to be demanded of when I really did have other things to get to today. Like the fucking taxes. Bills. Stuff I put off all morning because I thought I had 'til five, with Henry coming. So it's all Henry's fault!

July

Friday, July 2

My friend Wayne has been pretty imperturbable through the years. We met when we were about sixteen. He walked through high school with one smart girl after another stuck to his hip, and introduced me to his best friend, who courted me with perfume and roses. It was effective but it never went anywhere. Wayne and I stayed friends forever, though, through all kinds of windy weather. We stopped speaking once for a few years out of both our stubbornness, but that's long since water over the dam. He's always taken care of me like a sister, picking me up at airports and delivering me back to them, unclogging the toilet and repairing the roof, answering when I call.

He laughs and his face compresses into an array of winks as he tells his favorite story about our family. It happened back in high school. "I come upstairs and here's Mrs. Clagett sitting in front of her TV knitting, and here's Grandma Clagett sitting beside Mrs. Clagett on the sofa with her needlepoint, and there's Col. Clagett sitting across the living room in front of *his* TV with the headphones on, asleep, and over in the other chair there's Bubba Clagett sitting with his feet crossed behind his head reading a book, and Rita's asleep on the floor in the middle of the room! Everybody looks up and says 'Hi Wayne' and I sit down and they all go back to what they were doing. So I sit there awhile, and then I say, 'Well, it was sure nice visiting with you all,' and they say 'Bye Wayne, thanks for coming by!' and then I go back downstairs and drive away!" His shoulders shake with mirth.

I was disappointed at first in how often Mom chooses to watch TV rather than do something else. When I arrived here I was bursting with things to talk about with her, while she could still talk. But I have not managed to steer the evening's activities away from TV. As I feared, she has trouble talking now, and we haven't gotten around to many of the conversations I want to have. But we watch a lot of television, and I've come to enjoy the time just sitting together, watching. Now that I am spending an evening a week at home, she's worried that I'll be lonely without a TV at my apartment. After living for more than fifteen years without one, I didn't object when she insisted on taking me out to buy one a few weeks ago. But she can't watch TV unsupervised anymore, not after last night. Another symptom of the disease made manifest.

Wayne brought me home from dinner and we found her on the couch watching TV, frozen to the screen with a terrified, dark expression. She looked up at us in utter confusion as we entered the room. I rushed to sit beside her, and Wayne took the blue chair on her other side. It took us a minute or two to figure out what was going on. I pulled her against my shoulder and said, "Hey, what are you watching?" It was some high school thriller movie, children were running through corridors, there was a mask, there was blood.

"I don't know! Something horrible is going to happen, I have to stop it!"

Oh my poor darling, I thought, and hushed her. "No, no, it's okay, you don't have to stop it. It's just a movie. You're right here at home, Wayne and I are here, it's all over. You don't have to do anything."

I had been forewarned that people with PSP can become overstimulated by television or movies, and that their viewing of either should be monitored. Mom hadn't had any problems so far, but I recognized this for what it was. She had lost the boundary between herself in her living room and the action on the TV. She thought she was involved in the drama, the fear, the blood and the chasing. She thought she could save these children from the masked man that was slaughtering them. She had let the story so deeply penetrate her fragmented mind that she thought she was responsible for the outcome.

"Are you sure?" she asked, trembling in my arms. "I have to help them!"

"No, no," I soothed. "It's okay now. You're not part of that story." By now I'd found the remote and turned off the TV.

"Oh, thank God."

"It's gone now," I said. "You don't have to see it anymore."

"Oh, I'm so relieved. You mean I don't have to do anything? I thought I had to do something."

I sat and held her. Wayne left and she barely noticed.

Sunday, July 4

I called Melinda last night after she left a message. So wonderful to have a cousin to talk with so freely about what's going on, and an experienced nurse at that. I'm really looking forward to going up to Syracuse for Gary and Lorraine's wedding in September. Have to figure out what to do about taking care of Mom in my absence. Mel says Lorraine is still suffering from having had to make the decision to remove her mother from life support. She said the doctors all encouraged her to make the decision, then after she checked with the whole family and everyone agreed, she told them to go ahead, and then they asked her again: Now? It was that final *Now?* that has left her with unshakeable guilt.

I am so relieved that Mom has made the decision not to get the feeding tube. Melinda had said pretty much the same thing as Dr. Sigmund, the neurologist, that it's a piece of cake with very little risk, and could extend her life or improve the quality. Then in our conversation last night, she said she'd just been reading a nurses' journal that had just come, with an article saying new studies reveal that not only may it not extend life or improve quality, but that in patients with dysphagia it can increase the risk of aspiration. Also that you take away the pleasure factor of eating with family, the feel and taste sensations.

Then she said that before she was teaching, when she was nursing and doctors had told her to feed patients with dysphagia, and as she'd fed them they'd begin choking and she knew they were aspirating, she had felt that with each mouthful she was killing them. She wondered if the doctors had spoken with the patients and their families and explained the risks to them of continued feeding. She had some of her own guilt left to deal with, and I think this article helped to wash away some of that, reassuring her that in fact she'd been doing better for them than if she'd been tube feeding them.

What else we have to do is write some letters, make some phone calls. To her friends Emelia, Robin, Carol, whoever else she comes up with. I need to get on the ball and keep her moving on these projects. We made the party invitations, and though I made ten and she made one, she enjoyed the process, and enjoyed delivering them to the invitees.

At one door, a classmate of Dad's, Dan and Barbara invited us in but we were on our way to Portia's for a visit and so couldn't stop. But Mom had started on and stopped in the corridor doorway when Barbara came running out from the back of her apartment to give her a hug, and say she was so delighted Ali had stopped by, and I leant against the door button to keep it open as they were hugging and chatting in the path of the heavy metal door. Barbara came back past me with tears in her eyes and said how happy she was we'd stopped and if there was anything she could do, be sure and call. She really seemed the most moved of anybody, and the most grateful for our quick knock on their door. I think the party will do Ali good. I hope.

On the other hand, as Melinda pointed out, the party might just make her reflect on her marriage and get weepy. She said when her mom and dad had their fiftieth party, that her mom just got all unhappy examining the fact that she is now married to a man she doesn't know; he isn't the same after his strokes. Mom has already said during the weeklong discussion about whether or not to have a party, "I have nothing to celebrate."

Wednesday, July 7

I had an earth-shattering dream last night. It was so vivid. I was on vacation on a large island. There were mountains all around, a road running through a valley, and I was staying at a place along the road but up a hill. My dogs were there, possibly my mother. I was sitting outside in the rain on a plastic lawn chair with my long-lost friend Dennis, who was old and chunky and didn't look at all like himself. There were lots of people around. A fire engine and ambulance had come, and we were all waiting to see who they were going to bring out. My dogs were still inside.

As we waited, I looked across the road and saw from the top of the mountain a great huge chunk of rock fall away. I yelled and people scurried, but I didn't fear it would have effects as far away as we were. It crashed down to the highway beyond a hillock, and I hoped there wasn't a car in its path. Then another chunk fell away, and more. People began screaming. Dennis and I ran around the back of the peak and he pulled me into a little alcove. "No, not there," I said, "We could get buried," and then a piece fell off that mountain.

"We need to get to higher ground," and I ran first toward the building hoping to get the dogs, but then the mountain across the road continued to shatter and boulders were bouncing closer and closer, so I ran up and up the slope away from the breaking mountain. Why I thought the mountain I was running toward wouldn't shatter I don't know.

Dennis was no longer with me. I kept running, wishing I had my hat and my shoes, for the sun was coming out. I climbed up onto smoother rocks with tundra-like growth among them. Behind me the rock was schist like in Ruby canyon, smooth, black, sculpted. I knew this rock wasn't going to shear off and I felt pretty safe. From there, on a ledge, I watched the mountain across the road break apart piece by piece, a boulder twice the size of a pickup crashed into a truck on the road. Clearly people were dying all over the place. I wished I had my dogs.

After awhile I heard voices. Where I sat was so steep that I couldn't see directly below me, but then I glimpsed through a hole in the rock a group of people coming up to where I was. Mixed feelings. I saw they were mostly older, a few younger women, a young girl, all of some early American religious sect. We all settled in together to watch the end of the world.

One of them gave me a handkerchief. Another a gift of a silk scarf. I realized I would be leaving them, they were preparing to settle in for the duration, and as the rock fall seemed to be diminishing I wanted to go back down and find my dogs and find a way out of there.

I realized that people down below were going crazy with fear and greed as they always do in such a disaster, so knew if I did go down I had to be extremely cautious. I slipped away from the religious folks, not sure whether to take their gifts or give them back. I got down, and met up with some other people who were all trying to find a way off the island. We knew it would be a long and dangerous journey with little food. I wanted to go back and try to find my dogs at the hotel. Somebody said there were two dogs who hadn't been shot, some were afraid they'd consume food people should have, others that they would attack us as food. I tried to reassure them, but don't remember the outcome.

Next thing, I was somehow off the island, looking back at the long bridge that connected it to the mainland, with a line of cars and trucks trudging across it. Mountains continued to crash down on the island. People in boats were trying to rescue people. Where were the helicopters? I could see something was going wrong on the bridge, and then it buckled and collapsed. That is about when I finally woke up for good, and reached for my warm sleeping dogs and hugged them tightly.

I felt very fragile for awhile. Everything, everything is so tenuous. I wondered if the world outside had ended while I slept this morning. I knew that it could at any moment. I feel so very unsafe here and want so deeply to be home on my mesa where the earth is safe, the people are safe.

My weakness is self-indulgence. Can't argue with that. Look at how I've lived my life 'til now. Even now. Here I remain self-indulgent, not giving my mother all I think I could of my time and energy. Not being there ten and more hours, but "pawning her off" as she says, on these hired caregivers.

I called Elizabeth last night and left her a message that I was thinking about her and wondering how they are doing there. I suspect her mother must be near death or have died by now.

Wednesday, July 7

Dear Elizabeth,

I'm so glad to hear from you this morning and know that you are OK. My continued sympathy and support for your challenges. Thank you for the food info, what great ideas! Using applesauce or jellied cranberry to thin meats when you blend them, adding chicken broth to pizza to make a cream soup! Mom insisted on having a club sandwich and french fries for dinner the other night, and I just made her chew everything 'til it was mush before she swallowed. I hadn't thought I could blend it, and I think she really needed to chew something for her peace of mind. Naturally she didn't eat more than a few bites. The sandwich she ate one piece of, (soggy) toast with lots of mayo and a thin slice of processed turkey, all pretty mushy anyway, and three or four fries, a couple of bites of bacon. It did her more mental good than nutritional. Otherwise all her food is pureed now.

She is being backed off her Sinemet gradually now, and that seems to help with the confusion, but it resurfaces occasionally. She rarely sleeps through the night, waking at three or four or five, sometimes calling me, sometimes waking my father. We tried various pills for that but she now refuses them because they make her feel drugged the next day. We'll probably have to go back to them but for now we're coping. Anyway, the last time we saw the neurologist she said she didn't think the Sinemet was doing her that much good and not to worry about the timing with food. About face from what she said five weeks before, and Mom had just gotten the routine down. So we pretty much stick to it except I don't feel I have to be strict about it, which is a help. Thanks again!

Thursday, July 8

The dream about the earth shattering and the dogs—it gave me a chance to really miss my dogs while they are still here for me to love. Tonight Mochi got a real massage, almost an hour. When I released them from the back of the car tonight she tripped over Brick's leash, which I had failed to unlock in time, and landed on her side on the asphalt. Poor baby! But she got up unhurt and happily trotted on up to the apartment. Once inside I realized how little attention I've paid to them recently, almost since getting here—certainly in the last few weeks. So Mochi got a real massage, and Brick got to learn to wait his turn, lying in splendor on the foot of the day bed, watching. He didn't want much, but when I finally got up to pee, and Mochi left the pillow, he came in to tell me, then went and sat on the dog bed and waited for me to come massage him! After a few strokes he stood on his head a bit and then curled up into that tiny little ball he manages to make of his bulk.

I thought about the dream: my foundation was crumbling and I didn't even have my dogs. Then I realized no, the ground beneath my feet remained firm throughout, what fell apart was the entire world around me. The edifice, or structure, the mountains surrounding. What could that mean? Globally? Personally? Psychically? But there is some comfort in that the ground beneath my feet was always solid. Though if I'd had my dogs I'd have felt better. And now I do. We all do. They are very calmly sleeping on their beds, and not right behind my desk chair as they so often have since we've been here.

Here. Here. Here. Not *there*. Not home. But here is home, here is always home, and what a lovely job I've done of creating a comfort zone. So comfortable that it's a mess of piles of papers, as usual.

I don't want to impose death on my mother, but I seem to be the only one who sees how close she could be, and certainly I'm one of few who see she has work to do before she goes. She can barely see, her speech is getting worse and worse, more slurry, less loud. Her muscles in her arms are getting stiffer, her balance more shaky, she's crashing into things with her walker all the time. Today she choked a number of times on nectar-thickness liquids: we are using a product called Simply Thick, and it comes in two thicknesses, nectar, and even thicker, honey. You add it to water or any liquid, supposedly it doesn't change the flavor, it just thickens the liquid. Kerry, the speech therapist, taught us that thin liquids are more easily aspirated, so as this problem intensifies for Mom we will be thickening all her liquids. Except her oh-so-occasional sips of vodka tonic. I tried the thickened water. I'd rather die.

She had a hard time talking after eating her dinner. I had to get her to cough repeatedly to clear her throat, as Kerry taught us yesterday, before she went on conversing. She dragged at getting to bed, the excitement of having her sister there, perhaps, or the anticipation, maybe even dread, of the anniversary party. She was like a reluctant child seeking diversion along the way, in the linen closet, in the guest room, with her fingernail polish. That one I gave in to and removed her polish while Rita rearranged knick-knacks on the dresser top where the new TV displaced them.

I need to find a way to tell her, again, to convince her, that she has enough time. I guess just focusing on doing the things she needs to do—art, letters, phone calls, whatever—not leaving her so much with aides. But I continue to need time to myself. Gaytha's right, there is no such thing as a normal day. I've managed to relax and renew a little bit more the past week than for a long while previously. Time out.

Bob and Ali in their first home, clearly in love.

The truth is I don't know how it was between them. Don't know if there was ever tenderness, ever absolute sweetness and harmony, if there was ever a sense of oneness, as I have sometimes felt, fleetingly, with some men I've made love with. A tenderness all-absorbing, a yearning toward essence, each for the other. Did she ever lose her self in his caresses? Did he ever hold her as though she were the most precious, fragile vessel in his history? Did he ever roll her on top of him while both of them laughed with the joy of their union? I don't know how it was with them. I can only hope she felt some of these things.

When I returned home from my junior year of college and announced that I was dating a man seventeen years older, Mom wept and wailed. "Don't marry a man that much older than you! You'll be young still, and want to go out dancing, and he'll be sitting like a lump in front of the TV!" The voice of experience. She was ten years younger than the Colonel. She said that as soon as they were married he quit listening to classical music and read only magazines instead of books. She was disappointed.

When I was young I used to catch them snuggling sometimes, in the kitchen while she was cooking, or passing in the hallway. My young eyes took in the implications as he wrapped his arm around her from behind and cupped her shirted breast in one hand, his mouth close to her ear. I never saw that again after they noticed me noticing them. Even at the age of eight I appreciated the gesture.

Perhaps they tired of each other. She thought of leaving several times, and told me only when I was in my thirties that, "It was something you said that kept me from leaving." What a load to drop on a daughter. "What did I say?" I asked. "You said 'Don't think if you leave him I'll necessarily go with you.'" I was fourteen at the time. I don't remember.

I asked her one day, as we sat on the patio, when it was that the two of them had stopped having sex. She could not remember. Maybe twenty years ago. Maybe more. Before his back surgery. "Why?" I asked. "He just couldn't anymore," she said. "One time I was stimulating him and he said 'Just stop. Just don't anymore.' And that was that."

I wanted to weep. That moment must have been the beginning of the end for her body. I know the humiliating sting of sexual rejection. I could not live with a man who would not touch me. But they were of a different generation, and she did not know she had options, and she could not speak of it. I can imagine how daily frustrations built up into resentments, which, without the catharsis of passion, became walls.

The Colonel also told me why they quit having sex, when I asked him later. He, too, could not remember when. "A few years ago," he said. "After we moved in here." A slightly different time frame. A different reason. "It got so it hurt her," he said. There was no real blame, just sadness, in both versions.

I believe years of bitterness and ill health hung on that one misunderstanding that a good psychologist could have helped them unravel. Or sex therapist. In my observation, people who are still having sex into their seventies and eighties are happier and healthier than those who aren't. I've noticed older couples who are especially vibrant and I've either asked or they've told me, they still make love on a regular basis. It makes sense. No wonder Mom pays so much attention to her ablutions—the only time she gets touched is by herself, or by the Colonel giving her a kiss on the cheek. I'm not saying either she or he could have avoided the physical ailments that came to them, but if they'd managed to overcome the misunderstanding, the shame and silence that ended their love life, maybe she would have something to celebrate at the end of fifty years.

We persuaded Mom to go through with the anniversary party. The Colonel made arrangements with the Dining Room to cater and bake a cake. Mom and I made invitations by tearing up bits of all her handmade blue papers and gluing them on cards. The making and delivering of invitations alone lifted her spirits. The night before the party I gathered up photos from stacks and albums and glued them in collage to a sheet of foam core board. We stood this photo-record of the marriage on an easel in the party room, and now it stands on the cabinet in the living room for her and the Colonel and everyone else to see.

Jock and Caron flew up from Florida, Auntie drove from White Stone and her daughter came from Arlington. I helped Mom dress in a rich purple skirt and blouse, and divvy up her jewelry to give to her friends.

"I want to give them something," she said, so she sat on the bench at her vanity, and I sat at the foot of the Colonel's bed holding envelopes with the names of the twenty women who'd be there. Mom pored through her jewelry drawer. "I want Luli to have the ivory necklace," she said, "and

Althea to have this jade. But which of these pins shall I give to Mary, and what earrings for Portia?" We spent an hour choosing the perfect piece for each friend, weighing aesthetics and value, personality and intimacy. This chance evaluation of her friendships warmed her grim determination to enjoy the party, and the giving of the gifts brought her great joy.

She carried the envelopes down to the Private Dining Room in the basket of her walker, and once she was comfortably seated and holding court in an armchair, she had me bring her friends to her one or two at a time. Party favors, she said. No one was expecting this. Most of them grew dewy eyed as they opened their gifts, some wept outright.

They celebrated their fiftieth wedding anniversary from opposite sides of the room. He sat on his electric scooter and drank whiskey with his daughter-in-law. She sat on a chair and handed out gifts of her own jewelry to her women friends. What makes a marriage have worked when one looks back? What makes it work when one is living it? And what is the definition of "work"?

When Mom visited me during the decade after the Colonel quit traveling, she spoke to him nearly every night before bedtime. She began to worry about his welfare the minute she arrived at my home. Would he fall? Would he make it through a day without her? He worried about her too, and if we didn't call he'd be sure to check in.

After having just listened to her tell me how awful he'd been to her in some situation or another, I'd overhear her asking for the most mundane details of his day. Who did he eat lunch with? What did Dr. Wise say about the rash on his hand? Had Frances gone to Tai Chi? And he'd tell her all the little bits of gossip from his day: what he'd eaten for lunch, what the waiter had brought Nell and how she'd railed at him for his error, who had gone to the Kennedy Center concert and who to the Great Beyond.

"I miss you too," she'd say as she hung up. Did they miss each other, or did they miss the idea of each other? She claimed one reason she came to visit me was because when she returned, he had missed her so much that he actually paid attention to her for a few days.

They move through their one apartment in two separate orbits, greeting each other in passing. He lives in his den, she in her studio or in the living room. Each morning they breakfast together while he reads the newspaper and she reads a book or a magazine, or tries to. Each night he says, "Good night, sweetie, I love you," and she sometimes says, "I love you too," or tries to. Who's to say it didn't work?

Tuesday, July 13

Got home tonight exhausted after taking Beth back to the airport in Baltimore. Her visit was perfect timing. She arrived the night after the wedding anniversary party, but came in late, so didn't get to meet Mom until the next day. We went over in the early afternoon, and as I knew she would, Mom loved Beth immediately. Before I knew it they were alone in the living room and Beth was giving Mom a foot rub. I overheard her say as she rubbed the ball of her foot, "You've got a little congestion in there," and heard Mom struggle to figure out what that meant. After that she did not want a deep foot rub from me, either it hurt her poor bony little feet or she didn't want to think about the "congestion."

Anyway, we took some great walks in the park and the wildlife refuge, a very long walk through the refuge on a foggy day. It must have felt almost like being home in Oregon for her.

In the parking lot, I pointed out to Beth the little culvert kitty I've been feeding with Mom's leftovers. Just a tiny thing that hangs out with his momma along the wall between buildings.

About a week ago, I was walking the dogs along the little strip of woods between Woodside Apartments and the Lorton sewage treatment plant. Only rarely when the wind comes from the southeast does the smell intrude. This little strip of woods is bordered by a chain link fence on each side, on the sewage side adjacent to more woods, on the apartment side atop a two-story tall retaining wall that holds the hill back from the building beyond. Brick strained at the leash toward the fence at the top of the wall and I let him have his nose, but followed at the taut end. He stuck his head under a vine and I saw between the fence and the wall, with just enough space to fit, a white cat with one tiny orange kitten. Just as quick as I'd seen them, the tiny orange kitten with deep blue eyes half-open shot halfway through the chain link and went nose to nose with Mr. Brick. Both boys sniffed at each other without fear or rancor, ninety pounds of dog and a few ounces of cat. There's my kitten, I said to myself.

The mama cat, blue eyes narrowed to slits and ears back, flattened herself to the ground against the wall with her tail puffed out behind her. I pulled Brick back and considered my options. I feared if I grabbed the baby now, I might injure him pulling him through the fence. Also, I knew there was an excellent chance his mother would shred my hand if I didn't move fast enough. In an instant I made up my mind. I pulled the dogs away, and came back alone with a plate of leftover chicken, which I set down nearby. I've been feeding them ever since, carrying rotisserie chicken carcasses and Mother's leftovers to a spot near the hole where I saw them disappear.

Beth and I spent a lot of time with Mom making collages. I found some colored folders, and we began pasting magazine pictures all over them, each of us working on our project at the dining table piled high with magazines, scraps, and glue sticks. Mom seems to really enjoy the tearing and piecing, and I see that she is more focused on creating an impression with the colors, rather than a story with the images as I am. I guess she can't see the images well enough, but can see the colors.

Beth keeps the conversation lively. So we worked on collages afternoons and evenings, and took one night off for ourselves. She talked with both Mom and the Colonel a lot about—well who knows? With Mom about death and getting herself—and her affairs—prepared to leave, and with the Colonel I imagine just giving him the sympathy I can't muster. Her decades of working for Hospice have certainly qualified her to help Mom through this ordeal. Some things I'm sure Beth or Mom will tell me later, but I don't really need to know, as long as Mom is finding some peace in their conversations.

It was a very healing visit for all of us. Dear sweet Beth. The Colonel proudly showed her all around the Home. She slept on the daybed in my apartment, and we talked late into each night, and had some good laughs watching TV a night or two. She dyed my hair red again, and I cut hers short. I was very sad driving home from Baltimore without her.

Friday, July 16

I come from a long line of women who have had other women clean their homes for them for generations. I remember my grandmother had Gracie. From my earliest memory, Gracie was a part of going to visit

Grammer. Gracie not only cleaned the bathrooms, vacuumed the rugs, and polished the silver, Gracie also cooked. And Gracie made applesauce.

Later, my mother hired Gracie's daughter, Gladiola, to clean our house on Masonville Drive. I grew up in this house, from age five to thirty, ceasing to return and removing the last of my belongings only when my parents moved to the Home. Gladiola died prematurely. Gracie explained that she had "roaches of the liver." Later, Gracie herself died of course, friends to the end with Grammer. Then Grammer died. And now my mother is on her way.

As long as I can keep my house reasonably tidy through constant vigilance, cleaning takes just a few hours a week, and cleaning itself becomes a pleasant meditation. This apartment, two rooms, a kitchen and a bathroom, is a breeze to clean. Perhaps when I get home I will finally have the rooms of my interior in sufficient order to cultivate the practice of housekeeping.

Every time I vacuum the rugs in my house, I hear my mother telling me, "Don't vacuum the fringe off!" She said this a few years ago after she'd sent me the oriental carpet that used to live in her dining room at the Home, and before that in the den in the old house. She was thrilled to have the parquet floor in her dining room showing at last, and I was delighted to have the rich burgundy carpet. I spread it out in my loft. She kept the larger carpet in the living room, and the smaller rugs.

When she said, "Don't vacuum the fringe off!" I bristled. Why, I wondered, would she think I'd be so stupid as to vacuum the fringe off? And how? Ridiculous. But I noticed as I vacuumed my new old rug how the fringe sucked into the vacuum if I drove over the edge, so I was very careful. And then I noticed that the fringe on my downstairs rug, the old flowered green rug I'd bought from Helen's Antiques, was frayed and tattered, and I wondered if I had been vacuuming the fringe off of rugs for years. Still, I mulled over, How did she know?

Now, living again with my mother's rugs in her home, I see. The small, worn prayer rug the Colonel bought off of a family's wall in a village in Turkey in 1951; the large living room rug; the small hall rug that has been in Ali's family for several generations. This little rug has only the vaguest remnant of a fringe. Somebody vacuumed its fringe off long ago. Was it my mother? Was this how she knew? Or had Gladiola or one of her other housekeepers vacuumed the fringe off the rug? I can imagine the scene if she'd caught a housekeeper ruining her family rug. I can imagine her dismay if she as a young wife had suddenly realized that she herself had been vacuuming the fringe off.

Tuesday, July 20

Today it's fine. I haven't left home. Yesterday was fine too, though Mom was a bit beat from being awake since four in the morning, by Dad's count (he's keeping a journal/record now, and he was exhausted all day too), and only since six or seven by hers.

Her judgment is getting worse. I was to pick her up at the beauty parlor two buildings over, and was just leaving the apartment to get her when she knocked at the door in a pitiful state, having walked the whole way by herself, dropped her water all over the place and picked up the cup. I'm afraid I scolded her, because the day before I had left her on the patio while I came in to make her a shake, and she got up and was struggling to open that heavy glass door—so I scolded her for both of those, and that didn't feel good. I guess I just have to be calm about the risks she takes— and let her out of sight less.

She continues to decline slowly and subtly. Hospice is providing a wheelchair sometime in the next week, and just in the nick of time. She's still getting around alright on her walker, but yesterday I noticed that she's veering off course far more drastically than she had been up to now. And she stubbed her toe pretty badly against the wheel by just not stopping her foot in time. It's just a matter of time before a severe fall if she doesn't get off her feet for the most part. Also she continues to sleep well some nights and then fret all night other nights, but is so averse to taking any sleeping medication that I will have to slip her something soon if I can't get her to agree.

There is a new National Museum of the American Indian opening this fall in D.C., and I drove past the building the other day. I was driving through all these square white marble boxes all over downtown, thinking, monuments to dead white men all, when I came upon this gorgeous yellow sandstone building, all curved serpentine walls of stacked sandstone block, and it really popped my eyes open. It was behind a big chain link fence, and

I thought what the hell is that? Then I got up to the billboard announcing OPENING SOON! And I thought, Perfect. I knew it couldn't be about dead white men.

Friday, July 23

Each night we deal with what comes up. Each day we deal with what comes up. After more or less of a plateau for a few weeks, with all the festivities included, things took a sudden turn today. Later Dad said she had been like this since afternoon, but I didn't really see it until after dinner. She was happily working on her collage, we were watching *Friends* and *Seinfeld*, and she was paying more attention to her art project than to the TV, which I thought was great, and I was cutting more photos out of the magazines.

Suddenly she said in a high voice, "I can't breathe." It was clearly real and serious. I got her Albuterol, and she did one puff—after only two minutes I let her do the second one because she was in such distress. Then a few minutes later she wanted to try the Flonase, which she said she hadn't done yet today—Dad disagreed, said she had done it this afternoon when she'd had trouble getting her breath. All because we had run out of Rhinocort? No, more than that, must be. Because she had talked with Henry about her frustrations, and maybe has been making some sort of peace with the finality of the disease?

Who knows. In any case, none of the puffs helped, so I called the Hospice night line, and the nurse told me to give her 2 ml of morphine from the dropper under the tongue and wait twenty minutes. She didn't feel much better after that, so I gave her another 2 ml. That seemed to stabilize her. In the meantime, between the two doses, we sat on the couch and I was going to read to her, but then I asked, "Would you like to talk to the recorder about what happened tonight?" and she nodded.

I have been thinking that I should record my conversations with her, and maybe when this is all over, produce a story about her journey with PSP. Here is a transcript of the recording:

"Were you scared when you couldn't breathe?"
Uh-huh.
"Did it come on all of a sudden?"

Uh-huh.

"Have you thought about what you want me to do if it comes on and nothing works? Do you want me to call 911 if that happens?"

Huh-uh.

A long silence.

"What are you thinking?"

I'm wondering if it's better this way... or not...

"You mean you don't know if you feel better now or not? You thought you felt better a minute ago. Do you feel bad again?"

No, I don't feel bad.

The timer goes off, that means she can have something to drink now. After morphine she has to wait at least twenty minutes before drinking. I go to shut it off. When I return she has composed her thoughts and geared up to articulate them.

"Are you feeling sleepy?"

Huh-uh.

"What are you feeling?"

I'm wondering if it's better to go on and go. Do you want me to? Go on and go?

"Do you want to go? Or you don't want to go? Are you asking me if I want you to go?"

Mm-hmm.

"I don't want you to go but I don't want you to suffer. I think when your suffering outweighs your enjoyment you need to listen to your heart. Remember your head doesn't always have the right answer, your head isn't always clear but your heart always knows. Are you feeling like it might be easier?"

Uh-huh. Only if you do.

"Do what?"

Want me to go. I want to go if you want me to go.

"I want you to go when you're ready to go. I'm not here to rush you."

I know it.

"I'm just here to be with you on the journey."

I know it.

Long silence. "Do you feel like you're dying now?"

Huh-uh. I don't feel good.

"Tell me where and how you don't feel good."

I feel tired. I feel like I don't wannoo… I don't wannoo do my collage anymore.

"That's alright. What else?"

I want you to go away.

"You want me to go away?"

Huh-uh.

"You don't want me to go away."

Uh-huh.

"I'm not going away, I'm right here."

I can't get my mouth closed…

I ask more questions about how she feels, what she wants.

I don't want to drool.

"It's OK if you drool. Want me to get you a napkin, something you can put over your shirt? Do you feel confused right now? No? That's good."

I dnn nnn what ih like oo be drooling.

We sit quietly, with my arm around her. "How's your breathing feel? Tell me." No answer for minutes. "Better? Not better?"

No better.

I turned off the recorder. At the same time that I was utterly present in the moment, heart to heart, responding to her concerns and questions, I had the microphone in my hand recording the conversation. What sort of blew me away was that she actually wanted to talk to the radio, and knowing she was being recorded she chose that moment to ask me, "Do you want me to die?"

Later when she was in bed, and her breathing had stabilized some, Dad came in and massaged her feet in his clumsy way, and I got her to giggle a little, and everyone relaxed together, and soon everyone was tucked in. I persuaded her to take half a Lorazepam as the nurse had suggested for relaxation, and I did so by agreeing to take the other half when she insisted. I took mine first, after letting her choose the small half, which she did meticulously by feel, and I showed her my empty fingertips after I took it, and made her do the same to me. As a result, I now feel a wee bit loopy, and think I will settle down with a cookie on the bed and watch some ridiculous TV.

I called Michael tonight because I had a powerful urge to connect with him as I was driving home. I miss him so much, which I just now realize. I miss all my friends so much. Anyway, I just once again heard him saying in the gallery that day in 2000, when he met Mom for the first time, and I told him she'd been diagnosed with COPD: "It looks like a degenerative neurological disorder to me." I reminded him of that tonight and he said, "It gives me no happiness that I was right." I said, "Well it gives me some—more, it reminds me how special you are to me."

For me this evening was a turning point. One of many, I'm sure. As she sat at the table and clearly could not breathe much, I realized there could come a time when in a crisis like this, unexpected, she could go—it could be *the* time. I had the barest inkling of what it might feel like to be there with her as she dies in a sudden unexpected way, different than the proposed scenario of a long drawn-out absence of sustenance while she lies in bed in the sunny room with loved ones gathered 'round.

Tuesday, July 27

Dearest Auntie,

She can move the wheelchair by herself now. I wouldn't let her use her feet for the first few days until Pat, the physical therapist, came by yesterday and showed her more about the chair, how to move it, how to transfer to the toilet, etc. So she can exercise both her arms and her legs, and do it more safely than with the walker. She had gotten really unsteady in the past week on the walker, and voiced a fear of falling several times. So it's a good thing. Pat says she's safer in the chair. And it actually will make it easier to take her other places, for the most part, because I really worried about her on the walker in stores, etc. You know she had a tendency to veer and crash into walls. So for outings I can push her.

She had an episode right before the wheelchair arrived of difficulty breathing, and since then has been noticeably weaker than she was up until then, and her speech has deteriorated an abrupt notch also. Pat suggested that we need to think about communication aids for when she may not be able to speak comprehensibly. I think she was surprised at Ali's decline since the last time she was there less than a week before. She seems to go down in steps.

Tuesday, July 27

This afternoon as I was driving past Seven Corners I had a startling recollection about the Bridge Dreams. In the Bridge Dreams I saw, at the tender age of nine or ten, the end of the civilized world through overdevelopment. Here I was today driving through congested traffic and thinking, I have known since I was nine years old how this world would become, how it would be now, how it will be. What a fucking hopeless feeling that is. There really is no hope for the world, for us as a species. And living in Our Nation's Capital proves it.

But here's the thing: That makes it easier in a way, to just go on living, loving, and doing the best, to live for and in the moment, to be kind. To let some idiot get in front of me who's waited too late to merge, because I have just gotten over waiting too late to merge and some kind person has let me in with a shrug and a smile.

To live in the moment and be kind, to deal with this awful deterioration of my mother, and the rape and pillage of the lovely forests here turned into semi-detached townhomes or strip malls, and creeks full of sludge and roadways ever widening, to see turtles smashed in the road. And to drive across the whole length of this huge county and arrive at my friend Jerry's house, where there are banana trees and tomatoes planted in the front yard, though he has to dig up the bananas and bring them in for the winter. To once there partake of fine red wines and broiled salmon with sweet potatoes and onions, to do all this in a small house crammed with music and instruments and books and a grand piano and a bunch of different colored shamrocks, and to discuss the Quaker meeting house which is all that is left of a large Quaker settlement that was confiscated earlier in the century in order to comprise one of the largest military bases on the East Coast. Fort Belvoir, right down the street from where I live. Sigh.

And the rain continues to pour down outside. It rains all the time here. Oh well, it's better than the thick cloying muggy air when it doesn't rain. And now here I am living in the thick of it. All your life you strive to escape a certain thing, and then just when you WAKE UP, you find yourself thrust into the thick of it.

Good thing I have a TV. I am now going to go vegetate in front of the Sundance Channel and forget about the threat of nuclear holocaust or some massive natural disaster. As Jerry pointed out this evening over chopsticks, if there was ever anything someone needed to run away from in Our Nation's Capital, there would be no way to evacuate anyway. I mean, you can't even move down the road in normal rush hour traffic. What the hell.

Thursday, July 29

Dear Elizabeth,

Yes, I think maybe my mom is moving downhill more rapidly than your mom. I don't think she has as strong a will to live as your mom, and that may be contributing to it. She's been in Hospice for about a month now, and they say they may have to discharge her because she's really not as bad off as most of their patients, and if they don't see decline in a couple of months... but her moving to the wheelchair, and needing suctioning, and they just today ordering oxygen, all suggests maybe they'll see decline when they evaluate her.

Sorry to hear about your mom's bedsore. That's interesting that it requires an intake of two thousand calories a day to heal a bedsore. I wonder if Mom is getting that much even now. And sorry to hear about Molly too. I wonder how your hives are? I hope next week to get to a store where I can pick up some things for you both that might help with the stress. I think about how stressed and frustrated I sometimes feel dealing with this half-time, and continue to marvel at how you manage full-time. Got to hurry up and pay some bills and head over there now, so I'll write more next week.

August

Sunday, August 1

New Church, Virginia, Delmarva Peninsula, near Chincoteague.

My clothes from the morning hang drying from the curtain rods in the Champagne Room upstairs in the Garden House. I breakfasted and dined last night in the Victorian House just across the lovely lawn and garden. The only place in the Chincoteague area that takes pets, and they're as blasé about my two big dogs as can be. High end places usually are.

Such a lovely, relaxing, unexpected spot. I called yesterday and said, "I have an unexpected weekend getaway," and Sarah said, "That's good, we have an unexpected vacant room!" I made believe to ponder it but in my deepest heart I knew that instant I'd be here instead of Uncle Cecil's basement this weekend. So sorry to miss camping with Chris and Dave down in southwest Virginia, but it couldn't have been as relaxing as this. Three hot baths already and one novel.

This morning we drove up to Assateague. I followed a slow stream of tourist traffic across the causeway into National Park land, followed cars stopping for ponies or those tiny eastern whitetail deer, down to the parking lot at the end of the road. After an earlier squall, many folks were heading back to the beach from the shelter of their cars, or to dry out in their cars after having been caught on the beach and drenched. A herd of ponies stalked across the dunes and through the parking lot. They came to me. They circled me and one of them nuzzled me. Then they passed, leaving a crowd of tourists staring, envious of me, and me feeling stunned and blessed.

After the ponies left I took the dogs out to the beach. We walked a mile up the island watching the storm raging out at sea. Then we turned around, and saw that a new squall had crept into shore behind us and was catching up. The dogs do not like rain, so we began to run straight for it, hoping to beat it back to the car. But I could not keep up the pace, and overtaken by the first drops of rain I surrendered to it, laughing and breathing in gasps. Then I half-walked, half-trotted through the downpour back to the landmark, past very few others still out on the beach, with two shivering, dripping hounds pulling at me.

A low mound of sand had a driftwood cross, behind it a rainbow beach umbrella shielded three young men—a black boy and a white boy surfed—clouds roiled and low waves were expected to swell to ten to eighteen feet later. I listened to my little weather radio when I returned to the car—halfway back to Virginia the skies were sunny and blue with puffy clouds, but now it's overcast and spitting. I splurged on nice flax clothes on Chincoteague and a handful of inexpensive used books.

I have thought about Mom some here, but not like back there. Not all the time. What a relief. I needed a break from her need. Though she needed me to call her and she needed to call me again today—said she "just didn't know where you were." No, and yes. She knew where I was. This mini-vacation reinforces and clarifies one thing—I have lived so far, and can no longer, in the shadows of her fears. Yet just when it is ever so clear to me, I cannot declare it to her but must just live it.

And it has reminded me—one can find peace anywhere. It is here on a seedy little lane beside a highway in this peaceful room and gardens. An exquisite, four-star dining room. Anything can be anywhere. I stumbled on a great public radio station last night that's kept me company since then.

Oh yes, and it's reassured me of life and pleasure after this mission. My capacity to indulge and enjoy is not diminished, no, it's just temporarily on hold—not even, it's just in general overrun with the need at the Home. Away from that for just a day I find again my light heart and good cheer.

Wednesday, August 4

A new symptom tonight, preceded by shallow breathing. I gave her a dose of morphine, then hooked her up to oxygen and shortly after that she became still and quiet. She didn't respond to my talking and couldn't get herself to swallow. Finally she said, "I'm very tense." I got her a Lorazepam and a second dose of morphine. Must have been about nine o'clock. Then I got her into bed, talked her into breathing and just being with, acknowledging, the sensation—got her a heat wrap for her neck, curled up behind her and held her as we listened to the music CD Beth sent.

Meanwhile, Dad was doing his ablutions and creeping into bed— feeling, I imagine, lost, lonely, left out.

But here's the thing to remember: the tensing up was preceded by this eerie stillness—a freezing up—I must watch for that in the future and anticipate the need for drugs. She had started drooling in the middle of speech exercises, froze up on the K-K-K's, couldn't swallow. I tried to talk her through it, brought her a drink, got the exercises finished. Then she called her sister and was very slurry and didn't say much—that's when I noticed her getting really sort of—catatonic.

After she relaxed with a few cuts on the CD, we got up and she did her ablutions, then meds, then back to bed. I sure hope she sleeps well. It's so—deepening—to have an event like this—takes me right into the moment and leaves everything else behind.

Thursday, August 5

As Mom's need for me intensifies I'm beginning to depend more on other people for distraction, diversion, and general cheering up. I'm beginning to feel some anger about her demands: When are you coming over? Why *not* right now? Why can't you be here all the time? Oh well. Not much to do but swallow (and thank god I *can* swallow) and try to call up more compassion.

Sunday, August 8

Last week Mom and I went to Amy's mother's for a nice lunch in her antique house in the country, and Wayne took us to see La Boheme in concert at Wolf Trap on Friday night. Maryann was playing triangle in the orchestra, I swear I didn't see her lift a finger. He picked up the binoculars at one point and I wonder if he knew when her part was coming.

With the handicap permit on the car we got great parking right by the back entrance to the theater. Mom and I sat by the wall between the amphitheater and the lawn while Wayne went to get us drinks. He brought Mom a glass of red wine, which we mixed in with her thickened water. I looked at Mom's guide to opera book which she had thought to bring along, and saw that she had made all kinds of notes in the margins of this one. Turns out it's her favorite opera!

Wayne and I had finished our drinks by time for us to sit, and of course she hadn't. At some point during the beginning of the show, an usher came up to Mom and told her she wasn't allowed to have a beverage in the theater. I about came unglued. We were in the next to the back row—I hissed at the woman that my dying mother was drinking medicine and she had to have it, and after a brief argument the usher went away. The program was lovely, it was just musical highlights of the opera.

She loved the music, but I noticed about halfway through that she was looking kind of still. Some time after that, I realized she'd not had her 5:00 p.m. Sinemet because we got all screwed up getting ready when her aide didn't show up. Then I'd forgotten to give her her 8:00 p.m. Sinemet too, being in the midst of an opera. So I could really see how the Sinemet is helping her, and how bad off she'd be if she weren't responding to it. I hated that I forgot not one, but two doses, and that she'd gone catatonic during the music, but I got a couple into her as soon as I realized, and she perked up by the time we were driving home, and said she'd loved it nonetheless. She didn't seem to have noticed any difference.

Sunday, August 8

Hello dearest Diane.

I have been thinking almost daily about writing to you, so your message last night was quite timely. I've been pondering something you wrote during our last flurry, and wanted to revisit it with you.

I was suffering a little nagging anxiety about what you must think of me. Remember you said, "Don't wish your mother a shorter life," or something to that effect, after I said I was worried she'd choose to have a feeding tube? I felt chastened when I first read it, and of course you were right, certainly I shouldn't wish that. But I swear, if you could see how she suffers, I think you'd wish for her to pass in her sleep this week. OK, that's an exaggeration. I don't wish for that either—I cherish the time I spend with her, feel good when I can make her laugh or bring some joy into her day, but I see her suffer every day and I do wish for mercy for her.

All these things we take for granted: she rinsed her mouth with a swish of plain water the other night, and for some reason swallowed it. She knows she's not supposed to drink plain water—she coughed for five minutes. Imagine if you couldn't tip back a glass of cold water and just guzzle it down on a hot day. All her liquids must be thickened with a gel consisting mostly of guar gum, and all her foods must be pureed to pudding consistency. She enjoys baby foods. Each swallow is an ordeal for her, and sometimes she freezes and can't swallow or speak or close her mouth.

She's now in a wheelchair, and sleeps with oxygen to keep her from waking up, and sometimes recently her muscles all seize up at once and she becomes as stiff as a little clay doll. She now weighs 108 pounds. She still enjoys things like going to sit by the bay and watch the boats and the birds, but her vision is getting worse—sometimes everything is just a blur.

Just in the past couple of weeks her speech is becoming unintelligible even to me. Often she says in the middle of brushing her teeth or getting dressed, "I don't know what to do." She is so tired all the time. I just feel such wrenching compassion for her. I am relieved for her sake that she made the decision not to have a feeding tube. As trying as it is to be with her sometimes (as her need for me is truly overwhelming), I am trying to be as sweet and loving as I can be every minute, to touch and hold her often and remember that one day I won't be able to.

I have now finally arranged the aide situation so that I have two nights off a week. This has me responsible for five days from about two o'clock 'til bedtime at eleven, and two or three hours the other two days, plus three or four chunks of time mid-day in any given week, either doctor appointments, or Hospice nurse, or something. I'm doing just fine with it in general, but really have zero energy leftover for anything else except reading novels or watching TV. Oh well. This is my main work now. My only work, so I'd like to give up the feeling that I should be trying to accomplish anything else.

I haven't meant all this to be a rebuttal to anything you said. I understand what you meant and I took it to heart. I've written this to help clarify for me (though it hasn't really) and for you exactly what Ali is dealing with, and why I was so anxious in the first place about the prospect of her prolonging her suffering.

As it turned out, Hospice provided plenty of information based on studies that suggest that a feeding tube in elderly terminal patients does not prolong life, runs a high risk of infections, increases hospital visits, and actually increases the risk of aspiration pneumonia more than in patients with swallowing difficulties who don't have the tubes. It turns out it's a completely different situation than with someone, say a stroke or accident victim, who cannot swallow temporarily but has a prognosis of full or partial recovery and regaining the ability to eat eventually. So many components.

So there you have the general picture of the situation here. Ali has really begun to make peace with the fact that she is going to die from this, and waffles between wanting to fight it, hold out for a cure (which is hopeless), and wanting to just surrender and ease on out. It's an awful struggle to witness. And is made worse for me by the fact that she makes clear several times a week that I am the only reason she has to stay alive.

You are very dear to think of me so often and to offer me love and encouragement. It is tremendously meaningful to me to have the support of my friends back home, and I could not be any luckier for that. My dogs are a great comfort to me, too, as is my certainty that I am doing the right thing being here with my parents. We all make the most of it and find some fun in every day.

Both my brothers are coming this month, and their visits will overlap by one full day, which will be the first time they've seen each other in thirty years. They never were close—one brother is a half-brother and wasn't around much anyway, but I've reconnected with him in recent years, and just adore his wife. So that will be fun. Then Michael is coming in early September, his niece is getting married in Pittsburgh (he's probably wishing it were Puerto Vallarta) so he's going to visit me for a few days too. Then I'm off to Syracuse for my cousin's wedding. So it's a very busy month coming up. After that I imagine fall will fall into a calm routine.

Wednesday, August 11

Melinda's husband mentioned he might be able to help out when Mom does go, with getting her brain to the right place for research. I'm getting a little anxious about that as I watch her decline—wanting to make sure I have everything lined up for a quick getaway—for the brain.

I had a falling out with a dear friend this week because I had counted on her for something, and she said, "It'd be better if you just think of me as a possibility." I finally wrote her back and said, "I have too many possibilities in my life right now—I need a few sure things!" That's what the brain thing's about, I think, wanting to get the plan laid for that. Mom is determined that her brain go to science.

Thursday, August 12

In just three weeks I'll be driving to Syracuse for Gary and Lorraine's wedding. Maybe I'll crash in the hotel room Friday night with a bottle of gin and several hot baths in a row. I know Saturday will be a big party afternoon and evening, and more than enough excitement for me. I'm just really looking forward to getting away for that long a stretch, and to seeing my long lost cousins all together, and my brand new ones as well.

Friday, August 13

Rob and Nancy came from California and spent a couple of days at the Comfort Inn in Lorton during their East Coast trip, between visiting his sister nearby and their vacation to the beach. One of my deepest gratifications is to see the Colonel on good terms with his eldest son, who spent so many years not speaking to him. Nancy promised me a girls' getaway to the mountains, but in the end Rob came along too. As long as he was going, I wanted to take Mom but just couldn't figure out the logistics with her erratic bowels, knowing we'd rarely be near a toilet should she need one.

We drove up the Skyline Drive, ate lunch at the café at Big Meadows, ran up the tenth of a mile trail to the overlook that always seemed so steep and faraway when I was little. The last time I was at that overlook was almost twenty years ago, when I took the black dog Sam's ashes up there to scatter. I remember climbing up the hill, standing on the edge of the rocks looking over the mountains in perfect calm (in me and in the weather), saying goodbye to her troubled soul, and casting the ashes (and grit) in a

A young mother, Ali on a park bench with her stepson Rob, and her two children, Rita and Jock.

great arc out over the abyss below. At that exact moment, a huge gust of wind blew up the slope and sprayed her ashes and grit back in my face, in my eyes, in my teeth. Some poetic justice there since I'd had her put down.

We returned before dark to the Home, then picked up dinner from Thai Herb's. Sat with Mom on the porch and the Colonel on his scooter in the doorway conversing for awhile, then moved inside. When Rob and Nancy left that night they hugged and kissed Ali and told her they loved her. Nancy and I were waiting out on the porch for Rob, who came outside in tears. "I told her I love her," he said. "I've never told her that." I could really feel his sense of loss for this sometime surrogate mother who treated him tenderly when he was young. His own mother, it turned out, was not so nice.

Anyway, it was great to see them, they actually arrived and had brunch the first day with Jock, who had come up from Florida a few days earlier. The first time my two brothers had seen each other in more than thirty years. Then Jock left, Rob and Nancy stayed a couple of more days, and the Home was bereft without them when they left. Though by this time, Ali is getting to another stage which I've read of on the Forum, and which Elizabeth's mother has been experiencing, where any disruption of routine, even a pleasant distraction, is upsetting. She's happy to see her visitors, but would just as soon see them go, it seems, and get back to her "new normal" routine.

Someone told us of the concept of "the new normal." Every step down begins a phase of a new normal. It's a helpful concept in terms of coping.

Saturday, August 14

Another nosedive today. I noticed in the past few days a lot of little burps, heavy breathing more than at bedtime, and an inability to load her own fork. For the past two weeks she's had real trouble seeing down, can't see her plate, her feet.

Rita A walked her a bit this morning, said she noticed her breathing changed so she got her home and on oxygen. She ate a good lunch, then her neck got very tense and her head hurt. Rita A gave her an Advil, then another around three and a Lorazepam.

I sat with her in bed from four 'til six, then we got up for Chinese food. She drooled a lot and needed me to feed her, couldn't get food on the spoon or spoon to mouth. And worst of all her speech, nearly completely slurred. She would not move her mouth to talk. Again, when pressed, she was able to articulate, but her best today was much worse than her worst yesterday.

Rita A said she was fine this morning 'til after the walk. 'Til after they talked to me. She was in bad shape then, around eleven thirty when I called in and said I'd be there at four. Was it my time off that exacerbated it? Did Dad even notice this dramatic decline? Can I be more kind, more present? Rita A said she wanted me a lot during the day. Can I possibly be there more? What life do I possibly need separate from her dying? What do I think I need?

Monday, August 16

My housesitter called and told me she doesn't want to be there for the winter. Said she would talk to Marla, Suzi, and others, and try to find me another housesitter, which is nice of her. Said her new boyfriend is afraid of snakes, so he won't come in my house. My snakes are in a cage. I think it's a bogus excuse because she just wants to move in with him.

My poor dear mother said about Sue wanting to leave, "Maybe we can accommodate her." I said, "What do you mean?"

She said, "I could just die and then you could go home." Jeez. I said, "Don't bother, she's not worth it." But I think that might be Mom's intention anyway. She's declining so fast just this past week. Still, I'll probably be gone several months after she dies, whenever that is, to settle things here, get the Colonel squared away. Then I think I'll do my Final East Coast Tour, visit everyone I could ever want to and then never return. Oh well. A bit premature to be thinking like that but I can't help it.

Or maybe not. Here is our conversation from this evening, after speech exercises:

"Tell me how you feel now compared to a month or a couple of months ago."

I'm looking forward to the day when I can put it all behind me.

"Tell me what you think about that day."

I'm looking forward more and more to zonking out at night.

She clears her throat. In the other room the Colonel coughs.

Trouble is it's too much work.

"Zonking out? Because you keep waking up?"

No. It just doesn't work.

"What do you mean it doesn't work? The drink doesn't work?"

No, it alway... I have to... it doesn't work...

"You mean—what doesn't work?"

It doesn't work because I have to clear my throat and then... there's always something... my throat clearing...

"Kerry was having you clear your throat a bunch of times, until it's really clear, and then swallow."

She clears her throat a bunch of times.

"And then swallow. Yes. Now say Ahhh. Good. Do you think that drink is too thin?"

No. I think it's below the threshold of where I can clear my throat.

"Okay. Try your chin tuck... and now your throat clear... now swallow... and say Ahh... good."

She clears her throat and clears her throat, then swallows.

I don't think that does it.

"You sound better. Is it just that drink?"

No.

"It's any drink?"

Um-hmm.

"What did you have for lunch today?"

I had a shit-on-a-shingle.

I laugh. "Which is what?"

SOS. And pasta primavera, and God only knows what it is, it had nuts in it. I pit 'em out. And gravy. And mashed potatoes. And okra, and tomatoes, jumbled up.

"Tell me how you feel today, you said some days you feel like fighting the PSP and other days you don't."

Other days I don't. Today is one of those days.

"Which one?"

I don't feel like fighting. I feel like giving up.

"Why do you feel like giving up?"

It hurts. I can't talk. Too much problem. That's about the size of it. Can't see. Just too many problems. And I don't know if anyone will help me or if I just have to not eat.

"I think there are a lot of people that would like to help you."

Well why... not then?

"What can we do, is the problem. How could anyone—How could I help you with these problems? How could I help with your vision?"

I don't know... I'm talking about helping me commit suicide.

"Oh! Is that something that you want to do?"

Um-hmm. Better than not eating.

"Well, there's the Hemlock Society to check with. I can get in touch with them. They know how, and we can have someone come out and talk to us about it. Not eating isn't a bad way to do it. Are you hungry?"

No. Just for sweets.

"Just for sweets. Sugar can sustain you for a long time. This is the first I've heard you talk about wanting to commit suicide. How long have you been thinking about it?"

Weeks.

Wednesday, August 18

I checked with Compassion and Choice, formerly known as The Hemlock Society. They asked to speak with "the patient," but I explained that she couldn't speak right then, but that I am her daughter and medical power of attorney. I asked what she could tell me about drugs and dosages, and if they could send someone out to help us discuss options. The woman told me, "We don't really use drugs anymore. There's a new method that came out of the AIDS movement. It's simple and painless and very effective. It involves putting a bag over your head and a canister of helium, that you can get at any party supply store—"

I didn't need to hear any more. There is no way that my mother would put a bag over her head or that I could do it for her. She was sitting in the chair next to me while I was on the phone with this woman, but fortunately she wasn't paying much attention, and she didn't ask me anything when I hung up.

Friday, August 20

How often and alluding to what diverse circumstances I've heard these words from Mom recently: "I don't know what to do." Every time it brings tears to my eyes. Except my tears are dry these days. Some time in the future I will be digging in the garden, or repotting a plant, and some broken bit of clay from her life will come to light, and then I will weep wet tears. Meanwhile another very stressful night at the Home, and I'm just starting to unwind. Maybe a glass of wine and some Olympics.

Monday, August 23

Hi Elizabeth.

I think of you so often also. I'm working late tonight trying to finish up a job I actually got paid for last December but haven't had time to sit down and focus on for the two weeks it's taking to finish it. I'm very nearly done! This will be my last work for the year, I just can't find the energy to do it anymore. I truly understand your eagerness to get away. I hope you have the best weather so you can walk and walk along the lake and see great sunsets. If nothing else the time with good friends will really rejuvenate you.

Killing Mother

Considering how quickly my mother is going downhill, it's really amazing to me that your mother continues to hang on! Mom's speech has finally become virtually unintelligible, but in a different way from your mother's. Hers comes out as just slurry, or open-mouthed moans, not the slow gravelly way your mom's did when I was there. Which after only a day with you two I was beginning to pick up on. Mom can still form words when she really focuses on it, but even in the past week that skill is going half the time.

She's beginning to suffer from acute and sudden stiffness in her neck, and bowel problems. But the language is really the worst, and it's just beginning to sink in to me that the time is actually coming when she won't be able to communicate by speaking anymore.

I too am looking at Hospice respite care so I can attend a wedding in Syracuse in a couple of weeks. But they can't guarantee her a room at the Hospice residence, and there's nothing available at the place where they live, so she may have to go to another nursing home and I don't know if I can tolerate that with her speech so far gone. I may have to give up my plans if she can't get into the Hospice residence. I understand your nervousness about that aspect of taking time away.

Speaking of Hospice, they are working wonderfully. They're so supportive, and though they might have thought they were here prematurely when they first started, I think they now agree that they're necessary.

I'm beginning to get my own stress symptoms which are largely centered in my gut. I tried an anti-depressant the doctor prescribed for about five days, and got an awful bellyache, so quit that. He swore it was unrelated, but I'm not so sure. If it gets real bad I just take one of Mom's Lorazepams.

Also I'm getting a little crabbier than I'd like to be towards the end of each day. Bedtime is becoming a trial, as Mom can't get comfortable, and has started having more trouble swallowing her saliva. She gets panicky every night about aspirating.

At the same time, oddly, she's been discussing the possibility of hastening her death. I've tried to persuade her that if she's ready to contemplate suicide she should quit worrying about aspirating. If she wants to die she can let herself get pneumonia—what challenges! On an intellectual level, I've been expecting them, but it's such a different picture when they actually arrive.

Other than that, I'm hanging in there. I consider myself very lucky that we can afford some help so I have some mornings to tend to my animals and have a little time to myself, though I don't do much with it except catch my breath and do the grocery shopping, or stop by the pharmacy.

OK, my hero. I'm off to bed or back to work, I haven't decided which. Have a splendid trip, and be of peaceful heart and mind while you're free.

Wednesday, August 25

She tells me that my father was mad at her last night. That she got up in the night and went to the bathroom, and she couldn't get back to sleep.

I was trying to get... un... whas the wor? Un... what is the word?
"I don't know."
Yes you do. Un... un... unasphyxiated.
"Oh, you were trying not to aspirate."
And I was trying to get my leg extended. Oh it was just a mess. And I thought, why am I here, when Rita A and you are God knows where, and here I am, no one cares about me, and your father's mad at me...
"Do you really feel like no one cares about you?"
I did.
"Even though it was the middle of the night and Rita A and I were sound asleep—
Um-hmm—
"—in our own beds?"
Um-hmm.
"What did you feel like we should be doing?"
I don't know. Doing something ahead of time, maybe.
A long silence.
I don't like the little frown I see on your face.
"It's not really a frown," I say, holding her hand. "I'm just sad that you feel that way in the night."
I know it, I don't like it.
"What?" She nods at me, indicating my expression. "Well, that's a worry crease because I do care about you."
I know you do.

"Well, we'll have to tell Cheryl about your leg pain and that you're having pain in your head. What does your pain in your head feel like?"

Just feels heavy. Heavy. Like it did yesterday, only I thought I could get rid of it.

"It's not from the champagne is it?"

Uh-unh.

"Feels like it did on Saturday when you felt so bad?"

Um-hmm.

"I'm afraid you might be in for more pain. I think that's something that comes with this disease. We'll just have to ask Cheryl to help us manage it."

Um-hmm.

"Did you talk to your sister last night?" She nods. "What did you talk about?"

Whether she can come see me.

"I know she's planning to come for your birthday, is that when she's going to come?"

Probably.

"Do you want her to come sooner?"

I guess, maybe.

"Well what do you think? Do you need her to come sooner?"

Hm-mmm.

"Are you sure?"

Um-hmm.

"Because she can come this week or next week. She can't come the week after that. She was planning to come on your birthday, but she can come sooner if you want her to."

I don't care.

"Are you sure you don't care?"

No, I just never say what I want to say.

"To her?"

To anyone. I just say, "When are you coming."

"That's not what you want to say? What do you mean to say?"

I don't know.

"What do you think you want to say?"

I don't wanna go... have a birthday.

"Why not?"

Cause I've blown it. I've said my last hurrah. Here.

"You mean you don't want to have a big party? How about a little family gathering, would that be ok?"

Um-hmmm. I'm so sleepy.

September

I've been glued to the TV for the past thirty-six hours, watching Hurricane Frances destroy the state where I used to live and still have lots of friends, and my brother. He's been incredibly lucky with both the hurricanes, they've missed his town except for a little wind and rain and power malfunctions.

I am thinking of all my friends: George with his many venomous snakes and very expensive fractionating equipment to work the venom into helpful components for medical research; Chris and Dave the Dog People in their little trailer in the holler by the creek with all those dogs in kennels; the zoos where people and animals I love are in danger. These are only some of the things I am thinking about.

Margo was here early in the week. She and Michael overlapped by one day, when they did some business meetings together in D.C. It was fun to have them both here. Margo and I spent Tuesday afternoon and evening with Mom and pulled out all her pastels. We painted paper with watercolor to get good background colors, and the three of us painted all day. Mom loved it, so did we. Mom worked on painting a peach, which continues to evolve, though it seems she's lost interest in finishing it. It may well be her last painting. Margo made a great African Gray parrot, a fabulous fish,

141

and a landscape I didn't like. I piddled. But it was a good afternoon and evening's activity. Even then Mom was hard to understand. Margo was able to get what she said mostly, but not all.

Then Michael arrived. He also stayed three nights. He brought elk steak and venison and the two of us prepared dinner on Friday night. We served Mom a very special meal of elk tenderloin tips, real mashed potatoes, and green beans. She ate about two tablespoons of it, and hasn't eaten much since. The venison was tough, and the Colonel said later that if he'd gotten that in the dining room he'd have sent it back. But Michael was good about the whole scene. He's such a dear friend to even have me as a friend. He's such an important person in the world, and to think, he's my friend, and he spent four days with me this fall when he could have been doing anything else.

Then there is the little kitty that lives in the storm drain. He and his mother have moved down from the wall and are living in the storm drain directly below my apartment. I keep feeding them. I set the food down just outside the opening, then walk off and watch as first the mother, and now the kitten, too, come up to eat. The mother has started to nudge the baby up to eat first, and follows only when he's had his fill. Often they bask together on the concrete top of the drain, the mostly white mother with Siamese points, calico markings and startling blue eyes, and her little orange kitten.

I keep thinking I will catch him and tame him, maybe trap the mother and get her spayed. I watch, and I wait, and I feed the kitten and his ferocious mother. Sometimes if I walk too close with the dogs, she rushes out and hisses at us. As my mother eats less and less, I bring home more and more of her leftovers for the mother cat and her kitten. The problem is, there are so many feral cats here in Woodside Lane. I saw what I think is my baby's father just this afternoon, a large orange Tom, living in another storm drain in the parking lot. There are at least half a dozen of them. A new one seems to turn up every week or so. So I don't know if it really makes a difference if I catch her and get her spayed, and I certainly have more things to think about than a little feral orange kitten and his fate. But somehow it seems to really matter. He is so spirited, so curious and bold, and I *want* him.

I'm still planning on going to the wedding, but if Mom really is stopping eating, it may not be such a good time to go away. She is so miserable. She is not in a lot of physical pain, but her mental anguish at seeing what has become of her is dreadful, and her discomfort with everyday things is awful. I certainly cannot argue with her if she chooses to stop eating altogether. Her birthday is coming up in a couple of weeks, she'll be seventy-six. I have this intuition that she may die on that day.

Michael, watching the hurricane on TV, said he wished someone would mention this outrageous hurricane season in conjunction with global warming. It's really an amazing phenomenon. It's kind of funny how all these meteorologists and residents of Florida, and people everywhere, think maybe they *get* the limits of a hurricane, and then something like this comes along and just blows their limits and their expectations out of the water, so to speak.

It's so huge, and moving so slowly, and not really inclined to diminish much in strength, that it's unique in recorded history. But this is what I keep thinking: it probably happens all the time in Florida, in the geologic time scale. This is nothing new. It's just nothing that masses of people in trailer homes and seaside mansions have ever experienced. It's Nature at her most wild, at her boldest, strongest, most unfettered. It's a beautiful storm. Even the weathermen have been saying that, though not recently; I think their voicing their admiration got squashed by management.

The scale and scope of the damage is astounding. And, amazingly, Ivan is right on the heels of Frances. It's really a stunning display of the natural world, and I cannot help but admire it, even as I worry and wonder about people in its path. I mean, just imagine, the entire state has been affected by this thing, and it's not even half over after forty-eight hours of wind and rain. The storm is as big as Texas.

Monday, September 6

My neighbors below smoke cigarettes, and it's annoying, because in this cool, gray, rainy evening I want to have my door and window open to let in the fresh air, and I'm smelling their fucking cigarettes. They also annoy me because they tried for several days to catch my orange kitty with a string noose, and now he is skittish. He wasn't before, and was taming down, and did not have that frightened look in his eyes. His eyes were curious and alert, and he reacted quickly, but he did not look wary. Now he is suspicious and it may be too late to tame him. What a loss. A trivial loss, but somehow one of the few things I've really cared about besides Mom since I arrived here.

The other was the dead hibiscus tree that I found behind the dumpster, which is now thriving and full of buds. I can hardly wait to see what color they turn out to be. Maybe two colors. There were four trunks braided together, and two of them died completely and I just cut them off the other day, but two are going strong. Any day now. It seemed to matter also to bring this plant back to life. Point counterpoint? Is it because the one life I love more than any other is dying that these little incidental lives matter so to me?

It is these small accomplishments, interests, and connections that keep me grounded here. I imagine my mother's other helpers think that I'm an ice bitch, as I am so calm about her condition and her choices, her thoughts of how to get out faster. Maybe I will scream with grief when she finally goes, but I think maybe I am at peace with death, at least hers. I certainly see a woman who has been unhappy much of her life, and is suffering awfully now, and why, WHY should she or anyone else want her to prolong that?

I speak calmly with her of her next life, and how she might want that to be. I asked her to consider what, of this life, she might wish *not* to take with her into that one—fears, limitations—and what she might wish to take. I told her that all the work she has left to do in this life she can do lying down. She doesn't have to cut firewood, she doesn't have to hoe a field, all she has to do is review and forgive and make peace, consider and let go and look forward. I hope this helps her. Probably half of each day her speech is barely intelligible, but she is in there thinking and feeling.

Tonight I'm going to work on a communication board with the alphabet so she can point and spell, and also some flash cards with words and phrases she needs or uses a lot. Or maybe I'll do it tomorrow morning. I have some serious denial, I don't deny that. I cannot quite believe she is losing her ability to speak, even as I see it going. It's amazing to watch the distance in me.

Distance from this process going on with her, distance from the hurricane, distance from the orange kitten. I am not agonizing. I care, and I act, but I am not miserable. I still laugh at Michael, at life, I still get engrossed in a good novel, I still enjoy, and care about, my orchids.

And the other night, Michael and I went to D.C. to see some friends of mine play and sing at a Spanish restaurant, and we danced and danced, and I laughed and had a wonderful time. I especially enjoyed dancing with Reuben, the Latin man at the bar that Deb introduced to me. He was the best dancer that I've ever danced with. Michael let go of me once as he spun me and I landed on the floor laughing, but Reuben, he never let go, and when he spun me somehow his hand was always at my back and I never felt out of control. He smelled good in a way that I could only enjoy when I've had too much to drink—in general I hate cologne. Anyway, how can I go on having that much fun, then come back and deal with this ending, and be calm through all of it? Is this the peace of mind I've been cultivating for years, or is this a serious psychological problem? Hard to tell. I cannot seem to weep. For anyone.

Wednesday, September 8

Hi Auntie.

I wonder if Mom called you last night? It was my night off, and I went to Amy's for dinner. I meant to call Mom and remind her to call you, but I forgot. She had said on Monday after you and I spoke that she would call you, but I'm guessing she forgot.

She had a rough weekend, and didn't eat much. I was getting worried, but then she had dinner Sunday and has been eating really well since then, so I'm not worried anymore.

I'm planning to leave on Thursday, and Mom has been guaranteed a room at the Hospice center in Arlington for respite care for the time I'll be away. Cheryl just told us that this afternoon, and Mom is looking forward to it. It will be kind of like a luxury vacation for her, with lots of attention, and TLC. There is a doctor there full time, and things to do like art therapy, lovely grounds for them to take her out in. I'm hoping that not only will this give her a fresh perspective and a lot of good interaction with loving people, but that the staff there will be able to get a better fix on some of the problems she's having, like constipation, waking up at four or five and being restless and anxious, the stiffness in her neck and feet.

That's all for now. Everything is fine. I look forward to your visit. Much love.

Monday, September 13

Well the wedding trip was a lot of fun. I visited other cousins on the way, so it was kind of a whirlwind long-lost cousin reunion, which was reassuring and comforting. I'm pretty tired tonight so I'm off to bed early. I go tomorrow to pick up Mom from the Hospice residence.

At breakfast the day after the wedding, Bobby asked about Mom. At some point we were talking about death in a general sense, and Scott's wife entered into the discussion with an unexpectedly avid interest. Soon I had turned to talk with her, and she told me about losing her father last spring to ALS. Well son of a bitch. I asked her questions, she talked about her mother caring for him, then shortly after his death wanting to meet other people. She talked about how she misses him, and how hard it's been, and how disappointed she is in how she fell apart at his deathbed, how it was the most awful thing she's been through to be in that room as he died.

I asked if she'd ever thought about looking at it as a gift he gave her, as an opportunity to know what it's like and how she reacted so she can prepare and do better by her own standards in a future scene like that. Seemed to provide some comfort, a different perspective on the whole thing. She wept as she told me this story, and when she was done, I paused awhile, then said, "Well, it gives me something to look forward to."

She was puzzled. I had not realized that she did not know about Mom's condition. I said "My mother—" and she crumpled into an apology for having told the story. "No, it was good, please don't apologize," I insisted. She kept saying, "I'm so sorry!" for having poured out her grief on me, for having not known, and mostly just for the situation.

I wonder how it was for Mom at the Hospice place. She mostly complained and whined every day when I called to check in on her, and tonight, when I called to let her know I am home and will be there tomorrow, she sounded like she was desperate to get out *right now*, but I'm hoping and thinking this was just manipulation and/or anxiety. They probably don't talk to her like she's cognizant of everything. It's all awful. So I'm fixating on the feral orange kitten and pondering when and how to snag him and bring him inside to tame.

Killing Mother

Thursday, September 16

Mom's experience at the Hospice center was dreadful. Apparently they were frustrated by not being able to understand her, and they did not take the time or have the patience to try to help her communicate. My worst possible nightmare. Beyond the worst I thought could possibly have happened there. Symptom management my ass.

Mostly they drugged her with anti-psychotics rather than take the time to understand and help her with her agitation. They never got her a letter board to help her communicate, as they'd promised me they would; they did not get her art therapy as they'd promised they would; they had one volunteer take her out in the garden one time in five days; and they did not get her symptoms managed either—among other things—so her agitation on the phone turned out to be warranted. I'm so angry at the fiasco this turned out to be. I intend to file a formal complaint.

On Saturday when I spoke with her she said she was having fun and, "Don't worry about me." I knew then that she was putting on a brave face, and chose to accept it, but didn't realize it was an outright lie. Every other time I spoke with her on the phone she whined and complained and mostly I could not understand her, but I did understand the whinging tone. When I thought of her over the weekend I was annoyed with her for not making the most of the situation, taking advantage of the opportunities I thought for sure they were offering her, but instead wallowing in her negative space. Turns out it might have been a little bit her attitude, her fears and anxiety, agitation, but they basically drugged her into compliance so they didn't have to do much with her. Or so it seems.

When I picked her up Tuesday it was like bringing a dog home from the kennel. I knew something wasn't right, but she couldn't tell me what had happened. Only the next day, when the substitute Hospice home nurse was there, was I able to get the information that she hadn't had thick enough liquids, hadn't slept through the night, indeed had been waking up every hour, hadn't gotten her bowels functioning again regularly. Hadn't been given paint and the opportunity to work with it, had only been outside once; had been shown her oxygen and suction by her bed but had not been helped to do it, and on top of all of it had been given an injection of Haldol, specifically contraindicated for patients with PSP. Dangerous, even.

I feel so sick about her experience there that it's really tempered my enthusiasm about my trip, not to mention just added heaps to the guilt I feel already about not doing my utmost for her on a daily basis. Everyone thinks I'm so good to be doing for her, but I know I'm a horrible impostor.

I keep losing sight of the fact that *she* is the mission, she is the reason I'm here. Not to enjoy my little apartment, or to adopt a kitty or agonize over not adopting him, not to buy orchids or beads or eat out or see friends, but to take care of her. I am a lazy ass, and I am not doing my utmost. I come home and veg out in front of the TV, and I watch TV all morning if there's a hurricane in Florida, or a good movie, or I am too tired to get out of bed. I haven't given the dogs a proper walk in a week or more. And I have let her communication failure sneak up on me.

Until last week, before she went to Hospice, she was having bad talking days or bad talking hours. Truly it was going downhill fast since before the company came. Michael said he couldn't understand her for the most part at the end of the same week that Margo had little trouble. But I guess it just blindsided me, this complete inability to articulate that she's been suffering the past two days. And it's clear she's in there. Behind the dark worried little eyes, the pinched face, the slow unfocused gaze. She's in there. When she spells out something with the spelling board I made, it's coherent. Even funny.

Friday, September 17

Mom hasn't done her speech exercises much since she's had such difficulty forming words. Catch 22. The less she practices the worse her speech gets, but the worse her speech gets, the less inclined or willing she is to practice. For the past two days she's been unintelligible except for a few phrases. She can't close her mouth, and when she speaks I see her little pink tongue in there just barely moving as she makes sounds from still lips. Now she has entire days where she can barely move her mouth and each word sounds more like a moan. Once again she's discussing how to die, though she's reluctant to stop eating. Maybe she'll perk up again though. Sunday is her birthday, and Jock and Caron are coming, and Auntie.

I finally caught the little kitty yesterday. It was so easy. I just picked him up. I put the food down, he came up to eat right away, I reached down,

148

grabbed him by the scruff, and dropped him into a pillow case I'd brought. I took him upstairs, closed the dogs out of the bedroom and let him out on the bed. He fit in the palm of my hand. But he didn't stay there long. He jumped away from me and fled to the far corner beneath the bed. I left him there and drove to Springfield to the Pet Smart to buy food, litter, a litter box and a few toys. I lay on the floor and talked to him for hours but he would not come closer.

Last night I kept the bedroom door closed, but it was still warm, and the window was open. Down below, about midnight, his mother began to wail for him. Inside, under the bed, he commenced a pitiful crying. By five o'clock I couldn't stand it. I had barely slept, and then I saw the bedroom door had come ajar. I opened it a crack more to see if he'd gotten out, and suddenly he streaked between my feet, around the corner, and flew at the patio door. Fortunately, that too was open so he bounced off the screen instead of breaking his neck on the glass.

But in that instant he broke my resolve. I realized: I can't be around enough to give him the love he needs right now in his fragile, frightened state; he really is a distraction from my mission here and that I had better *do better* what I already have to do than add another project; that if he were trapped in my apartment ten hours a day without me I'd be over at Mom's fretting about the kitten instead of concentrating on her; that this whole story I've made up about who he is and would be in my life might not go according to my plan anyway; and what will I do when I leave here intending to travel for a couple of months on my way home? Have two dogs, a snake, a turtle, *and* a cat? I realized that occasionally circumstances conspire against a relationship no matter who it's between. And I let go.

I put him back in the pillow case and carried him downstairs to his mother. I dumped him out at the mouth of the drain, and he dove right into it. She was sitting on the bottom step of the wall, and as I left I saw her slinking across the dew damp grass to the drain where her frightened baby waited.

Naturally, I had told Mom on the phone that I'd caught the kitten. Today I had to tell her that I let him go again.

"Why?" she asked.

"I can't afford anymore sleepless nights," I said, "and I have my hands full."

She looked at me, then said with great effort through clenched teeth, "A few days of aggravation for a lifetime of pleasure."

My heart sank. Perhaps I should not have let him go.

I'm still feeding them, and another day things might be different. Maybe I'll trap her and get her spayed and keep him after all. But in the moment, it was a flash of clarity to let them be together. Now, of course, with this wicked weather I'm second guessing, but oh well. Sixty-five tornadoes raged through this part of Virginia and Maryland tonight, one coming within a few miles, and today it's cold and blowing hard all day. Remains of Ivan. Not much rain here though.

Sunday, September 19

Jock and Caron walked in yesterday, just as I was sitting Mom down with a list of the four phases of PSP I got off the website, trying to get her to understand that it's not the Haldol from a week ago, not the Seroquel from a week ago that's making her sleepy all the time, which she's been for months in general anyway, and making it hard for her to speak, but that it's the PSP, that these are symptoms of PSP. So they and Bob listened for a few lines then all disappeared into the kitchen to fix drinks and talk.

And there I was left with her reading out this glum litany of things she has—we ticked off all those she agrees she exhibits, which covered most of Phases One, Two, and half of Three, and a few in Four. There were a couple she didn't want to acknowledge, but I marked them because I see them in her. Maybe it was cruel to show her that, but I don't think I'm doing her any favors to let her think it's the drugs, something that can be changed, or something that Hospice did wrong that can't be undone. She decided that maybe it was the Baclofen, a serious muscle relaxant, that was making it hard for her to talk, so I eliminated that from her regime. By the time I left this evening, I actually managed to get a sentence I could understand—barely. But it was a heroic effort of clarity for her.

I guess I never thought it would really come to this, or maybe I just hoped she'd go before it came to this. How do all these people on the Forum do it? Sit with these patients for one and two and three years who cannot move and cannot speak—and love them and interact with them, and keep their own spirits up? I find it so difficult to be patient in this short time, and have no energy to be creative and fun and cheerful. I just cope. I hate myself for it. I'm not nice. I'm not kind. I'm short-fused and ill-tempered. But I try. Each day I try again to be cheerful and competent and attentive, and try to cater to her needs and wants. Her every sentence, mostly, begins with, "I want—" or, "I need—."

I cannot imagine how awful it is for her. Any sense of gratification she may have once had about being the center of attention as the invalid has got to be gone now in the face of the terrible frustration of not being able to communicate. Not to mention the physical weakness which is increasing dramatically. She did walk to the dining room today for brunch on her birthday, with the walker. She ate a few bites, and the Colonel said, "That's the most I've seen her eat for awhile." Well, you're not there at dinner or lunch, ever. All you see is her struggle to eat some breakfast.

Not to mention that he's being a colossal ass again towards me. Mr. Super-know-it-all. While I was traveling I called him from the Comfort Inn in New Columbia, Pennsylvania. Later I spoke with him again, and he said, "Where were you when you thought you were in New Columbia?" Said it didn't exist, it wasn't on his map. Argued with me about where I was on a fucking interstate highway with large signs everywhere, because on his tattered old map it didn't exist. Argued with me.

I am so angry at this disease. It comes out in being snappish to everyone, even my poor mother. Last night I tucked her in and went to wait for the nearly inevitable call from the bedroom. When it came she wanted to roll over, so I helped her roll over, then she wanted the remote control for the bed, so I gave her that. She raised her head a little, then her feet, then she kept messing with it 'til she hit the flat button, at which point I took it away, fixed the bed, and said, "You cannot play with this tonight. It is time for you to go to sleep. Now goodnight."

She clutched my hand in her little claw, and I hugged and kissed her, patted her head, and said goodnight again, gently. She did sleep after that. But I was short with her, taking the remote away. I am so very tired of the same thing night after night, and I have tried and tried to teach her how it works, and she just can't retain it, and she can't see the buttons, and she gets all mixed up and frustrated—flustrated as someone used to say, a great mix of flustered and frustrated—and can't sleep all night for messing with it, unable to find her way back to a comfortable position. So I took it away.

At her birthday brunch today her sister said aside to me, "I don't think she'll make it to Christmas, what do you think?" I had to agree, but said you never know. Some of her friends dropped by the table and visited with her, and with us. Mary brought Rita to tears with her sympathies. All this right next to Ali as though she can't hear or understand. Now in reality, there was enough chatter around her she probably couldn't hear, but if she had heard she certainly would have understood. It's amazing how someone who doesn't speak becomes unpresent to those who aren't tuned in.

So I guess I finally got around to writing to the core of the matter. It's the awful decline she's undergone just in the last three weeks. Just astounding. She spoke again of not wanting to live, of wanting to end it, and I suggested again that the best way would be for her to stop eating. She said she doesn't want to stop eating. But then she ate only a piece of birthday cake for dinner after Rita A had warmed her up a plate of baby food. And why not, I'd have made the same choice. Tomorrow Rita S is making crab imperial for her.

I said when we were talking last Friday night, "Let's just get through your birthday, hmmm, and enjoy your company, and then see?" And so now we are officially through her birthday, and Jock and Caron leave tomorrow, and Rita S leaves Tuesday or Wednesday, if she can even stand to do so—to stay or to go. It was so hard on Rita leaving the last time she was here, she cried for days.

And still I do not weep.

Tuesday, September 21

I am angry all the time. I am so angry at this disease. Today I broke down for the first time since moving here. She was trying to tell me something simple, she needed eyedrops, but she could not speak and kept spelling sentences that she couldn't complete and that did not make sense. I found my voice getting very tight and panicky as I kept asking her to try again. Once I finally got it, and gave her the drops, I went into the other room and just cried and cried. Finally.

But my anger is making me impatient, and I find myself getting short or stern with her. I've been reading the PSP Forum again as Mom has gotten worse. I did think back in the spring that some of the people's

152

adjectives about the disease were a little overblown: evil, wicked, etc. Now I understand, and I couldn't agree more.

I find in the discussions such courage and strength, good humor, hope and support for each other, and useful insights about medication, aids for daily living, etc., that I am very grateful.

But I do not find many people expressing the dark, angry feelings I am experiencing. Almost every day there is some conflict or frustration so great that I end up saying in my head, This is killing me. Am I a monster? I know at the same time how much worse it is for her, and that it really *is* killing her, in so many ways. And I try and try to remain calm and patient with her. By the time I leave after nine or ten hours I am seething. Then I read about so many of these people who live full time with their PWPSP (People with PSP, Forum shorthand), and manage to stay big-hearted—I am just stumped with admiration.

I feel lucky these days to find a handful of bright tiny moments in any one day to cherish—all the rest is either struggle or despair. I look at her rheumy, half-mast eyes that don't see me half the time; at her slack mouth and flaccid tongue when she tries to express a want or a need, which she does constantly. And then it's even worse when she cracks a joke or offers an encouraging word: to know she is in there thinking, feeling, reacting, coming up with a sharp reply, and it is such a struggle for her to get it out.

This situation is an incredible challenge to me to live up to my highest expectations of my best self, and to continually deepen my compassion for her and, indeed, for all who suffer.

I have been watching on TV the devastation of Hurricane Ivan, and feeling wrung out with stunned sympathy for all the people suffering so tremendously in the storm's wake. And I ache for the little feral kitten who lives in the storm drain below my apartment, feeling the pain of his frightened, wretched life. Not to mention I can't even watch the war news anymore—I never really could. I recently re-met an old friend whose nine-year-old daughter has Angelmann's Syndrome—she was born in a condition resembling that of the latter stages of PSP. What a world.

Here's to all of us for waking up every day anyway, and managing to smile and laugh sometimes, and keep on living. Maybe tomorrow will be an easier day.

Wednesday, September 22, morning

I just heard from Auntie last night a stunning story about Uncle Jack, her and Mom's uncle. He was married to someone, and Minnie was married to someone, and they all four were friends. When Uncle Jack's wife divorced him, Minnie divorced her husband so she could be with Uncle Jack. Then Uncle Jack went off to war and got blinded and lost a hand when he was sticking out the top of his tank and got blown up. After that he wouldn't marry Minnie, said it wasn't fair to her. She persisted but still he said no. So she remarried her first husband and went off to the Philippines. Then Uncle Jack realized what a martyr he'd been, and how much he missed Minnie, and what a terrible mistake he'd made, so he wrote and told her so. Then Minnie's husband bought her a bunch of Philippine furs and a trousseau, and sent her back to Jack with his good wishes. They were married for many years until Minnie died at a ripe old age.

Mom needs and wants constantly, and she cannot communicate without the greatest effort what she needs and wants. She is using an alphabet board to spell, but often takes so long to find the next letter that she tries to write instead, and sometimes that works okay. It takes her half an hour to find the right combination of words to say what she needs: for example, last night Dad, Auntie, and Pamela, Mom's new aide, were all there, and they had to call me to figure what she was trying to say. Instead of writing "morphine," or "medicine," she wrote, "Beth collage first time." Then she wrote, "R did something simple." Then she wrote, "R called H." Jesus. When I called Hospice. And this took fifteen minutes, after I'd been asking her yes/no questions on the phone. The very first question I asked was, "Are you having trouble breathing?" and she said, "No," so I figured she didn't need morphine. Forty-five minutes later, it turns out she needs morphine. It's fucking agonizing. Then I read about people on the Forum whose PWPSP haven't spoken in two years, communicate yes or no with a finger squeeze code and that's all they can do, have been bedridden for months or years, and they *handle* it.

What really happened was that Dad and Aunt Rita panicked, but Pam was pretty cool about the whole thing. She just hasn't been there long enough, I think, to feel confident in making decisions. I also don't think I've fallen into the trap that I'll feel like *anything* is my fault—I am just fucking pissed off about everything, and perhaps holding myself to a higher expectation than I ought.

Killing Mother

Wednesday, September 22, evening

My feet hurt. This afternoon while I was waiting for new tires and visiting with a woman in the waiting room, we got to talking about pets, death, pregnancy, that sort of thing. I told her about a neighbor's daughter who went into labor before anybody knew she was pregnant. She told me about an Italian woman she knew in New York, whose family thought she was dying of food poisoning at Christmas but she was in labor—she'd been told she couldn't get pregnant, so hadn't even suspected.

Then she said, "We never knew when my sister was pregnant. She was big anyway." Well, she was big herself. She went on to say that they'd driven to visit her mother one time, and the baby was crying, and her mother said, "That baby looks like his feets hurt," and sure enough, she said, "My sister didn't know that babies' feets grew." She'd had his feet balled up into infant shoes!

That's not why my feets hurt, but I think today I finally figured it out. It's the clutch. It's all this driving around with traffic lights. Stop, start, stop, start, slow, go, slow, go. If I were to stay here I'd get an automatic. I might anyway. Now I'm trying to clutch with my big toe.

Today was a good day after all. When I arrived at three Mom was up and happy and speaking relatively well. She wanted to go to Best Buy and look at laptops, so we went. We bought one for her, in hopes that she will be able to type on it better than on her typewriter, and thus communicate.

She spoke pretty well all evening, until just after she got into bed. Perhaps the sleep meds were working by then. And the day was happy and smooth all through. Then her eyes were closed, the story was done, and she started up again, "I think there's something else I have to do…" I put the kibosh on it real quickly, said, "No, there's nothing you have to do." She asked about her face cream, last drop, and I said, "Don't start this tonight. We'll deal with it tomorrow. You have to go to sleep now." And she did. But how quickly the aggravation and panic rose in me—also the boundary. Don't start this tonight!

Today was a good day for her, ergo it was a good day for me. As we drove to Woodbridge through long traffic, I played *Man of La Mancha*, which always makes me teary. This time more than usual. Mom loved it. A good day is almost harder to bear than a bad day. It is bittersweet.

No meows from the storm drain this night. Both mama and baby were there this morning, and baby pranced out to greet the dogs and me, then of course shied away. I returned shortly with a bowl of food, and he came a meter away from the drain to start eating it. Progress! One move of my hand and he flew back to mama. I tried to catch him again a few days ago. In the night I'd heard cats screaming, and in the morning I saw his mother on the wall with a tom. I figured the tom had driven him off or killed him, but then I saw him emerge from the drain. I took the food over, but he wouldn't come close.

Every single response is a choice, and true patience only begins when one becomes impatient.

Tonight, when all hell was breaking loose over at the Home, and I was waiting tensely for a phone call from Pam to tell me if Hospice was sending a nurse (they didn't), I heard cats yowling then mewing outside. After I got the call, I went out with a chicken leg to find the wildest scene. Mama cat was under a car, two toms were up on the wall, the baby came down towards me along the wall above the Toms, mama came out to the storm drain. I left the leg bone there, and walked away after shooing the toms and talking to the kitty a bit. Then I sat on the curb and watched. The kitty sat at the end of the wall, the mama watched him from the drain as though trying to encourage him to come get the food, then went up to the wall with him. The toms slunk out of hiding and lurked around, and three more cats came from the parking lot, skulking along under cars. One of them came out boldly walking towards the drain, carrying something in his mouth with his head high and making that particular proud meow when they've caught something.

I had to just leave, leave them all to sort it out. How ironic that just over a week ago I had that kitten in my bedroom. I cannot (but must) forgive myself for thrusting him back out into that world in a moment of weakness that passed for insight. Or vice versa? He'll never be caught now, and already the battle for who gets to breed his mama next has begun. *I should have kept him when I had the chance!*

It's just ripping me up inside to keep holding an interest in him. I told him he was safe with me, I said I'd love him. Then all at once in that moment at five in the morning, I took him back out, thinking he'd rather be with his mother. When I came in and saw the cat stuff I'd just bought I felt rotten immediately, but was just too exhausted to care. If I didn't have such other pressing concerns I'd feel truly rotten about it, and if I dwell on it any further I will for sure. I keep flip-flopping between being realistic and detached, feeling shitty that I didn't keep him, and thinking what an awful life I've consigned him to.

Wednesday, September 22

Dear Elizabeth,

I've been spending a lot of time on the Forum in the past week, and I really miss your voice on it. I haven't checked in there much since arriving out here, but as Mom has gotten so suddenly so much worse I've been spending more time there. I hate that someone's meanness turned you off to it so completely. I kept thinking when I checked in now and then that I might find you posting again, and as you and I were in touch I didn't really mind when I didn't see you. I can't help but think that it might do you some good to have that outlet again, and I know that you would be doing many other people a world of good with your kind and insightful messages.

Maybe you are simply too tired and burnt out to have the energy to post anymore. I could certainly understand that. I wonder if you still check in and read anything on there.

Some of the things you told me earlier about your mother remain so vivid—like how she thanks you each night for taking care of her, and how when you ask what you can do for her, all she asks is for more time. I remember how she spoke so carefully one word at a time, so that by the time I left after less than twenty-four hours I could understand her last words to me.

Now I have watched my mother go in the past month from being articulate to unintelligible most of the time. Odd how different her speech loss is from your mother's. She is slurry, whiny, gets higher pitched with anxiety, and now speaks often in barely more than a whisper, whereas your mom's voice was growly and it seems she drew out every word, as though she had more intention behind it than my mom. I think she had (and may still have) more of her wits about her than my mother. Also Mom has times when she opens her mouth repeatedly to say a word and barely gets out the first phoneme, time after time. As though she can't get her breath to push out the rest of the word. Her words are often just moans, her lips and tongue barely move. And though I tell her a hundred times a day that she needs to focus on one word at a time, she just won't. Or can't.

Well, I didn't mean to go off on that, mostly, I just spent two hours on the Forum and came away realizing that I miss your voice there. Hope you're doing okay, and that you're finding some relief from the stress.

Thursday, September 23

What's going on here defies rational comprehension. It's so big. I begin to fear I will be here until the Apocalypse, but I continue to prepare by cultivating peace of mind. Mostly, what is hard to wrap my mind around is the insidious nature of the disease that is taking my mother. Inexorable as Hurricane Ivan, stealthy and coy as Coyote.

A most mind-boggling event took place at the Home this afternoon. Pat, the physical therapist, arrived to take Ali out for a long walk around the lake, and the Colonel called me in to his den, in a bit of a tizzy about Henry, the Hospice social worker. He came to visit Mom, and invited Bob to join the discussion. Then he asked Ali what she wanted to say to Bob, and she said, "He doesn't help me."

Bob said, "He probably came in here and just asked her, 'What's bothering you?' That's the way all those bullshit psychologists and sociologists talk, that's how they wor—" and he stopped because I was making a face.

"Do you agree with that? That I don't help her?" he demanded.

I had a choice here. I chose to dissemble a little, give a spoonful of sugar with the distasteful medicine.

"Well, not necessarily that. But sometimes the first thing out in a session like that isn't really the core issue, and precedes some much more important issues. I do have to say that Ali's got thirty years of resentment built up around you, and I certainly understand the ways you are that trouble her. She's been telling me and Henry about them since we arrived, and I do think, you know, she's *dying*, and it's important for her to resolve these things and find some peace before she goes. It's unfortunate that she didn't have the nerve to brave your reaction until *you* can't hear and *she* can't speak. That's really unfortunate," I emphasized.

And I told him that I knew of two times in my life when she had considered divorcing him. I spoke candidly about everything I knew,

158

perceived, and experienced, without venom, and he listened, more and more aghast. Cracked him open, I think.

I went on, and he was oddly receptive because I intercepted his first huff of defense with, "Now I know you think all this is bullshit and you're going to get mad, but I'm going to tell you anyway if you'll let me." I handled it well! I kept my cool! Most of all I kept my sense of humor, and *most of all*, I kept my detachment from outcome.

At one point he said, "But what can I do?" and I suggested he just try to be more attentive to and more patient with her, show her more physical affection. And I said, "If I hadn't had that kind of touch in all those years I'd have left you long before," which really popped his eyes. He was truly astonished at what I told him about emotional abuse, belittling, judging.

I said, "The way you talk about women's weight, often in earshot of them, I find deeply offensive as a woman."

"But don't you think Rita A just looks obscene?"

"That word would never have occurred to me. Many African women of different tribal origins have large butts anyway, whether they're overweight or not."

He argued, "How will they know they're overweight if I don't tell them?" I hope he was kidding. I said, "It's not your business to tell any woman she's overweight."

"You tell us we're ignorant," I went on. "You look at us with disgust when we disagree with you, or when you think we've said something stupid. You yell at us over the silliest things. You're a bully."

He said, "How can a person change a life of eighty-five years?"

I said I believed it was possible for a person to undergo a sea-change with a softening of the heart, instantaneously, though challenging to implement the implications as they unfold. "I know it's difficult to believe," I said, and he interrupted—

"How can I believe something I don't understand?"

"Do you understand god?" I asked.

"What?"

"Do you understand god?"

I received the most surprising answer. "I believe in a higher power that I don't understand, and I don't believe it gets involved in our everyday lives."

"Well that's exactly how I feel about it, but then why do you go to church?" I asked.

"Church has a lot of good things about it," he said, and went on from there. "When I read the Apostles' prayer, 'I believe in God the father Almighty,' it's really only the first line I believe in."

Well, this softened up everything inside me, not just my heart. Just about then, Mom and Pat came back in, and we clustered in the foyer, and he drove around through the kitchen to "join the party."

By the end of what could have been a disastrous conflict we came out laughing and mutually grateful. And he behaved so sweetly, considerately, presently all night. He joined the party again when I was taping Mom's discussion on stem-cell research and on being frustrated at not being able to talk. Later, as he passed me in the kitchen on his way back to bed, he patted my arm and said, "Thank you." Let's see how long this lasts!

Mom was speaking fairly well most of the evening, and wanted to talk to the microphone.

It feels so stupid not to be able to swallow.

"Here, take a sip of your milkshake. No, that's not your milkshake, that's the microphone."

We laugh.

Ink the micopho, she says. She laughs again.

"Drink the microphone. Here take a little swallow. A little more than that. Good. Let's try G-G-G again."

G-G-G.

"Good! Now say good."

Oooo.

"No. Gooood. With a good hard G back there."

Good.

"That's better. Now say stupid shit."

Ooo-la-la! Stupid shit.

"Good. Let's do the ooo-la-la's."

She loves the ooo-la-la's. She does them over and over.

"Let's try son-of-a-bitch."

Hun of a bish.

The Colonel interjects from the other room "You're stealing my stuff!"

"Whatever works," I tell him, laughing. He has come up with this little bit of spice to make her speech therapy phrases more interesting for her.

160

"Sssss," I emphasize.

Ssss. Sssson of a Bitch!

"Stupid shit."

Sssstupid shit!

I laugh.

Fuck Fuck Fuck.

We both laugh.

I call into the other room, "What were some of those other ones you had last night, Dad? Some other kind of a bitch—"

Son of a Bitch! she offers.

"Wicked bitch, or something like that," he says.

"Say wicked bitch," I tell her.

Wicked bitch.

"Say stem cell research."

Stem cell research. I think it's great that Bush has stopped it. Bush can drop dead.

"Did you say it's great that Bush has stopped it?"

No. He never should have stopped it.

"Why?"

It could help so many people. And he had no business stepping into it when he didn't know doodly-squat. He thought he could stop cloning human beings and it has nothing to do with it. They're apples and oranges, two different things.

"Why do you support stem-cell research?"

The only chance I have of getting well is stem cell research, and I don't care if they clone a tadpole.

"You don't care if they clone a tadpole, as long as you get well, long as you stand a chance. Where have you learned about stem cell research?"

Through my reading. It has nothing to do with cloning people. Or animals. It is a good thing.

"And Bush is a what?"

A fink.

"He's a fink, and a what? Ssss—"

Shit!

"Yes, and a son-of-a-what?"

Son of a Bitch!

The Colonel drives his scooter into the living room. He can't stand to be left out. He has news from the dining room. Their friend Paul has had surgery on his jaw, and won't be eating lunch with him for awhile. He asks me if I would make him some of the special boiled custard I've been making occasionally for Mom. I'm delighted to do something to help Paul and Luli, his sweet wife, one of Mom's dearest friends. This is one of the rare times that we have all sat around and talked, easily, about mundane subjects. One of them remembers a commercial jingle, and soon we're all singing, "plop-plop, fizz-fizz, oh what a relief it is!"

Eventually we get back to the subject of stem-cell research. Mom begins:

He wants to keep cloning down but all he's doing is stopping stem cell research.

The Colonel says, all stern and know-it-all again, "It's going to go on somewhere. Bush doesn't let it or not let it, all he can do is deny federal funds to the people who do it. If somebody else wants to do it, it's alright—"

I think it stinks, she interrupts him.

"Say it louder," I encourage her.

It stinks!

"I don't agree with him on that subject," says the Colonel. "I think he should let stem cell research go on. But you can't find a perfect man anywhere, he does something wrong for everybody."

"I'll say you can't find a perfect man anywhere," I throw in. He laughs.

I'll say it too!

The Colonel talks more about cutting federal funding, defending Bush's other policies.

I can't listen to any more of this. In a pause, I say to Mom, "But still, he—?"

Stinks! He still stinks!

The Colonel laughs. "You know what that tells us," he concedes, "a difference of opinion makes horse races."

No. It tells us that he stinks.

She says it with great conviction and clarity.

"What were some of the other things we had her saying last night?"

"You dirty bastard," suggests the Colonel.

You diry bastar!

"Now swallow and take a deep breath and say it again."

You dirt-ty bastard!

"That's the ultimate condemnation," he says.

I say, "I want to talk to you about one more thing while you're able to talk. What does it feel like to be losing your speech?"

It feels terrible. Unbelievable. It's terrible not to be able to be understood.

"It probably feels as bad as losing your hearing," says the Colonel.

I think not. I ask her, "Do you think it's comparable to lose your hearing?"

Maybe. I took a lip reading class to try to inspire him—

"I pretty much do all the hearing I do with lip reading" he interjects. "If I take a hearing aid out all I can hear is that she's making noise."

"Did it inspire him to take one too?"

No.

"No. Do you think losing your speech is comparable to losing your sight?"

"No," says the Colonel.

Maybe.

"Do you think it's comparable to anything, or is it all its own thing?"

It's its own thing.

The Colonel says, "I can see where losing your speech could be one of the most condemning things that can happen to you, because you get constipation of the brain. If you can't write and can't speak, nothing can come out of you and it's a terrible situation."

"How do you feel about what he just said?"

Very true.

"Tell me in your own words what it feels like to you."

Tis shit-ty. She chuckles. The Colonel laughs.

"What's the worst thing about it?"

The worst thing is just not having anyone understand. Aehh.

The Colonel whispers to me "You shouldn't be on this subject for long."

You go on and on, you rlyy and tmm, and no one understands any worrr… I want to type so badly. I can't make anyone understand me…

Here her speech deteriorates so badly that, in fact, no one can understand her. I encourage her to take a sip of her drink and clear her throat. While she struggles to drink he tells us, "When I came in here awhile ago my game was to go to the bathroom," so he takes off on his scooter. She regains her voice for a few more minutes.

I feel I should be able to say whatever I want and I can't. I can't even type it. That's very frustrating. I'm used to being able to express myself, and if I go completely raishy it's because I can't stop myself from talking. I can't say what I want, and I'm not saying that very well.

"Well, you are, I just didn't understand the one word, you said if I go completely—?"

Crazy. And I mean it. I just want to be able to express myself in the way I'm used to.

"You're speaking pretty clearly tonight."

Good.

"Do you know that with PSP most people lose the ability to speak altogether?"

I know. That's what worries me. But... I hope that I can overcome it.

"Overcome the PSP?"

The speech. By trying to say things in a way that I can not do... maybe I can't. Maybe I can. I don't know.

"Is there anything that you feel is really important that you don't want to leave unsaid?"

That I love people. That I love you, and Rita, and Jock. I love people. And Rita was so scared that I'll die. I know she was scared of me but she needn't of been.

"She was scared *for* you, not scared of you."

Well, she needn't of been.

"But you couldn't tell her that could you? You couldn't talk at all that night she was here. You were trying to write, but you couldn't write the words you wanted."

If I was a nurse I could have talked to her but I'm not a nurse. I couldn't say it.

"Well, if you were a nurse with PSP you couldn't have talked to her. You could have reassured her if your speech had been better."

Maybe.

"Sure you could have. It was because you couldn't speak that you couldn't tell her. What was going on that night?"

I don't know.

"You needed morphine but when I asked if you were having trouble breathing you said no."

Oh. That night. I wasn't having trouble breathing. I am now.

"I'll get you some more morphine. Can you tell me why you said no when I asked you if you were having trouble breathing?"

No. Except it was like the first night when I couldn't talk... and that is why... what you did that first night, and what I want done always.

"All I did that first night was I called Hospice and I gave you morphine, then I gave you more morphine. Then we went over and sat on the couch and you talked about it. Do you want more morphine now?"

Uh-huh.

"You have to put your shake aside for another twenty minutes. What do you call this?" I bring the morphine dropper to her mouth.

164

Marijuana.

"Morphine," I laugh. I give her the drops. I say, "I have to go pee, I'll be back in a few minutes."

Alright. I won't go anywhere.

Thursday, September 23

Dearest Auntie,

We had another easy night for some reason.

She took a long walk around the whole lake with Pat from physical therapy, who has been visiting her once or twice a week for a couple of months, for exercises and walks. She's done a lot for her, and is a dear person. But Hospice spontaneously laid off their seven PT's in a budget slashing measure. So today was the last time, and they took an especially long and lovely walk together. She came back jolly. While she didn't sound too good, and was short of breath, she was happy. Pat had forgotten Mom's shades and her drink, so it pushed her a little out of her comfort zone—which may have been a good thing mentally.

She enjoyed a shake and cake for dinner, took several doses of morphine between six thirty and ten, and talked at length to me about stem cell research, which she sssss'd all the way through, and then about the frustration of not being able to be understood. Somewhere in there, Bob came in and added his two cents on some unrelated things (such as drinking ammonia cokes at his uncle's drugstore when he was an early teen) and managed to do it in such a way that I rather applauded his softness, enjoyed his story, and tolerated his difference of political opinion. For it came down to Ali saying "Bush stinks," over and over, which was great for her articulation, and he had to take it, and agree that Bush should not prohibit federal funding for stem-cell research. It was a place they could more or less meet politically, and he didn't strut his stuff doing so.

Ali was in bed by just after ten, asleep. It was one of the most peaceful nights in recent memory. The most. I think your visit did her a world of good. Even though she didn't want you gone, now that you are, she seems very at ease. It pleased and sorrowed her at the same time that she scared you so the other night. Pam told me she said yesterday morning, "I think I scared her," and tonight she said with a regretful though impish hint of a smile, "She was afraid of me."

I am so glad that I got those two questions discussed while she was having a good speech night. I strongly suspect that with the expletives that carried some emotion, and with the tape recorder running to immortalize her, that she had a bit of core energy to invest in speaking articulately. Expressing herself.

I'm thinking as I write that I should incorporate the recorder every night. You said I should write something, and I have, actually, this kind of thing mostly. But I bet it would be good "expression therapy" for her to talk to the recorder every night, to turn it on after speech exercises to record some over-articulated conversation. She has no incentive to say the words and phrases that came with the exercises. She has no inspiration to say, "I cannot get up," "I need the toilet," phrases Rita A has been using with her, very useful I'm sure, but not the most uplifting phrases to practice. But get her talking about Bush and stem-cell research, or get her hurling expletives, you can have some fun with her!

This is one reason your visit is good for us. You bring into the equation that immensely special ability to make light of everything. Not to make fun of, but to leaven with your humor and your acceptance. "We'll know more later," comes to mind as one of my favorite of your unproclaimed (but oft-repeated) mottoes. And I thought you were just great during this last visit. I know how unfathomably painful it is for you to see her like this. So painful for me that all I can do is cope. You bring your light-hearted (open-hearted, soft-hearted) patience to bear on my less extensive experience in suffering and you lighten my heart, nourish my sense of humor, and inspire my patience. You're my hero.

I should have been recording her as part of speech therapy all along. I tried to start doing that months ago, but she was uncomfortable with the microphone, though eager to talk. I've brought it into the scene usually just after a time of crisis or achievement, and asked her to talk about it. Now that she can't see so well, she can't see the microphone; also, she is accepting the prognosis another notch deeper, and knows that whatever she wants to say, she had better say. She wants, she said tonight, to "express herself." The deepest need of the Twentieth Century woman. I had such respect for her tonight, and enjoyed her so much. She was present and grownup. And funny. I think now I could interject the recorder into her speech therapy and get inspired results from her soul, so that's my next objective. The time is ripe. And running out.

It's like all the unnecessary edges are knocked off and appreciation becomes very sharp. The good days are more emotionally complex than the bad days. They hurt a little more.

166

Again, I think your visit did her nothing but good. Please believe me. I know it was hard on you, but it opens your eyes a little more too, doesn't it, and makes your appreciation of all you love a little sharper. And you can't argue with that!

As for me, I imagine your visit had something to do with my having the courage and clarity to tell Bob all that I did tonight. He was devastated. It was all news to him. He has never seen into her world. (Where is the intimacy in that?) I was flabbergasted at how easily that unfolded, how I kept my cool and my sense of humor. I can only credit that to having you as a primary role model all through my becoming a woman, and to the exemplary softness of heart you showed this weekend. You know what I'm talking about. It's the endless consideration of every aspect, with kindness and humor, that you do all day every day. Correct me if I'm wrong. I know the rum helps. Gin is my medicine. And tonight I polished the dregs off the empty morphine bottle and palmed a Lorazepam on the way out the door. So I'm relaxed.

I hope it reassures you that all is not disastrous here—not far from it, but not always dancing on the brink. I could go on about how everybody loves you. My friend Peter was so disappointed to learn he won't get to meet you. They arrived from Florida this afternoon to spend a few days down at the Comfort Inn, to avoid the hurricanes and to play with me during my times off. I arrived in their hotel room on my way to Mom's this afternoon, and hadn't been there fifteen minutes when Peter asked if we were going to visit my Aunt Rita. He was crushed that you'd left town and he doesn't get to meet you. See how y'are?

Oddly enough, there are some similarities between the two of you: that laissez-faire joie de vivre that says "whatever" (a refrain I remember from you from many years ago) and in him that blows off a social or intellectual gaffe with a laugh and, "Oh well!" Something about the laugh, completely tossing off any consequence with a light heart.

Enough! Would you keep me up all night?! Love to Ford and you.

Monday, September 27

Today Mom required assistance with every transfer, not just with spotting. Over the past couple of weeks it's been gradually coming on, gradually noticeable, that she's getting weaker, and I've helped hold her back when she sits, more and more, and helped her stand with just a little pulling—but today I needed to use the gait belt for every up and down, she just couldn't get any lift from her arms, and once on her feet couldn't come to upright balanced. She could get upright, but was leaning back and without my support would have gone over. She looked and felt so very weak. Her poor little eyes were all squinty and bloodshot, tearing a lot. She seems to be choking more, coughing more during food and drink, needing thicker water. She had a great day yesterday though.

Or at least a good evening, with the art show opening, seeing lots of her painter friends and her neighbors. Drinking champagne. I could fairly easily interpret for her. Her paintings looked lovely in the frames I picked up last week. She stayed up late a few nights ago finishing the peach, a painful masterpiece she titled *Fractured World*. Not for Sale, at any price. The Colonel and I both covet it.

Tuesday, September 28

Dearest Auntie,

Well, it was the mother of all bad nights tonight. I got home at two thirty tomorrow. Poor Ali, she said about six that she had to poop and it hurt, but she pointed to her tummy and said "crampy." She'd had a suppository and a large bm two days ago, so it never occurred to me she'd have an impaction tonight! But at nine forty-five she was finally able to communicate what was going on, and we tried several remedies you don't want to know about that helped a little, and at eleven thirty I called Hospice. The nurse was on another call, but showed up about one, and did an oil retention enema, which helped a little more, enough for Ali to finally go to sleep by two fifteen. I got home feeling a little crampy myself, and guess what, had got my period a week or two early. Oh well. So it goes. She was very brave through it all, and we even managed a few laughs. Go figure. I told her my favorite line of Shakespeare is from Macbeth, "Who would've thought the old man had sooooo much blood in him?" and I rewrote it for this evening.

It's finally raining a little here. Did you get any?

Wednesday, September 29

I arrived this afternoon, just twelve hours ago, to find Mom talking beautifully with Cheryl. Her speech was better than it's been in weeks! She was restless, though, and started down the hall just after Cheryl left. I noticed a note in good handwriting that said, "Get rid of extra stuff," and asked her about it. She said she was going to her studio to do that, so we started in on the first corner of her work table. After a long time, an hour or so, I went to the kitchen to get her a new drink, and hadn't gotten it poured before I heard the crash and her cry for me. She hit the table on the way down, and the rest of the evening complained of "terrible pain." I said if she was going to use that phrase I'd have to call the clinic or take her to the hospital. I had a hard time gauging just how badly she was hurt. There was no outward manifestation, which was a little alarming for the way she complained.

I used arnica gel, gave her Tylenols, some morphine, ice pack, she ate dinner pretty well, then complained more. I got her in bed and read to her, and left her pretty well doped up with Terazepam, morphine, Tylenol. I hope she sleeps through the night and doesn't wake Dad with "terrible pain" in the wee hours. I don't think she was badly hurt, but do wonder about any internal injury. She kept insisting she wasn't wounded, but then kept complaining how she hurt.

Not a moment is easy. And I had so many things I thought to write while I was there today and cannot come up with a one of them now. I was so angry at her for trying to get up! She said she was coming to get her drink, tried to get from the desk chair she had insisted on getting into, to the wheelchair, while I was gone. WHY WHY WHY??? But I kept my temper pretty well, called on the principle of patience, and simmered down. Was calm outwardly long before I was no longer angry. So that was good.

Really, it could have been such a good day. It was a great day for a walk outside, and I almost suggested that instead of getting rid of extra stuff, but went with her inclination. What did she think? That she had to follow me to get her drink? Did I forget to say, "I'll be right back"? I don't think so. Did I forget to say, "Don't get up"? Yes. Damn! I have to say that every time I walk away from her!

I'm so glad for Pam and Rita A. Especially, these days, Pam, who is so good for her frame of mind. And so good with her physically, too. I wish we could have her as a live-in!

Thursday, September 30, morning

Balmy fall day, misty sun. Brick's sleeping on the balcony, Desmond is scrabbling to get out of the tub, Mochi lies behind my chair. Three orchids remain in bloom.

What's hard is the fluctuation. One day, or for one week, she seems on the verge of dying. The next day, she is talking beautifully and feels strong, and eats well. This is the "good days and bad days" noted in every description of PSP.

I'm thrilled when she's doing well. But there's a convoluted internal reaction to it, after a week or three of her seeming like she's winding down. Something in me prepares for the end, and there is a measure of relief in that. The tension shoots back up again on the good days, the "How much longer?" rears up again. This is a perfect practice for living in the moment and not anticipating the future. Just accept every moment with whatever it brings. And do not prepare, or rehearse. But it is like a roller coaster, and I'm getting a little nauseous on it.

I really didn't know what to do when she fell yesterday, with her complaints of pain. Take her to the hospital? That seemed extreme. I think I did okay. But what about next time? What is next time? What crisis comes next? Every day there is some crisis. Every minute there is a need to be met. Thank god I don't have to be there all the time.

Thursday, September 30, evening

Within two weeks of my returning him to her, the mother cat appears to have abandoned her kitten completely. The irony makes me laugh, the way god laughs when you tell him *your* plans. I have consigned him to a feral apartment life, with traffic threats and management control threats and bulldozer threats and the threats of ignorant but possibly well-meaning neighbors with their string nooses. I knew his mother wouldn't keep him long, that she, in her wild way, would run off with the best tom present when her hormones told her to.

This kitten, from the moment I laid eyes on him, has personified pure life. His bold curiosity in greeting my dog, his blue baby eyes just barely opened already so eager to take in whatever his world offers, his fearlessness. This kitten has a heart and soul that were an open book to me.

170

I knew him in that first instant, I knew that I knew him. But I doubted my knowledge and allowed myself to return him to an uncertain future fraught with threats. I doubted my knowledge and myself.

I have wanted him so much all along, that when I try to practice non-attachment to outcome, try not to care whether I catch him or if he lives, it is a huge effort. I continue to feed him, to be involved in his living but detached from his destiny, but I struggle with it every night. I drive into the parking lot after leaving Mom's, and I look for him. I come out with some sort of food and leave it at one of the usual places. I listen to the various yowls and screeches in the night and roll over, fatalistic, and a little sad.

I keep pondering, what is my attachment to this kitten I might never have known existed? Caught up as I am in the struggle between my mother's desire to die and her grueling will to live, this kitten has become an anchor for me. For months, he has personified new life striving against the odds to come to fruition. As my mother's life concurrently diminishes, their two lives intertwine. Two courageous souls contending with circumstance, the little orange kitten seems to take on the life that Mom is losing. And somehow, she knows this. Perhaps they both do. As he grows in strength and coordination, her balance, her muscles, her organs fail. The cruelty of her particular disease leaves her completely aware of her own deterioration.

What is a life? Who determines the value of any given life? Is a human life inherently worth any more than the life of a frog, or a kitten? Or a dog? What is the nature of life, that we swim through it, occasionally surfacing for a gasp of true air, and otherwise thinking we know the ocean around us, and our relative place within it? I believe in the divinity, the sanctity of all life, and draw very little distinction between kinds of lives. I do not see the discrepancy applied by most people to the deaths of different species. It is *Life* that I revere: we are each of us simply one shoot, one spark, of the great living force of Life that flows from the divine consciousness that permeates the universe.

Even science, now, insists that we are all one, that the driving power of the universe is consciousness, and that consciousness is Life unfolding in all its infinite individual manifestations. Crow or virus, tree or human baby, kitten or mother, life is *Life*.

October

Dearest Auntie,

Hi! I'm home, puttering and enjoying the lovely first of October evening in my light, bright apartment with plants, animals, colors and now after dark, candles and good music.

When were you supposed to go to the Islands? I'm wondering if it's soon, maybe you should go ahead. She's been doing so well the past two days, strong and speaking pretty well. I think you should consider taking advantage of the opportunity and have a nice getaway, especially if the airline is uncooperative about refunding your tickets. If she gets in dire straits and you need to come back we can afford a quick ticket for you. Really, just go whenever it is, given that we can get you back fast.

The neighbor dog downstairs gets put out at the oddest hours, and just barks and barks. The other neighbor, whenever he enjoys a cigarette on his patio, I also get to enjoy it in my bedroom or living room while my windows are open.

Saturday, October 2

Dearest Auntie,

What a nightmare of a day. Not really. But it started off bad, when Rita A called at ten this morning to report that Mom hadn't been able to swallow yet, and was in pain from the fall, and couldn't take Tylenol. I checked with Hospice and they said to give her .5 ml morphine, and later she was able to swallow Tylenol. In between, Rita A called back and said Mom wanted me to come, then put her on, and she kept saying, "I need you."

I asked, "Are you scared?"

"No."

"Are you dying?"

"No."

"Why do you need me?"

Finally she said, "It isn't fair that Rita A is having to do things you should be doing." This really pissed me off, and I started in again—I should know better than to bite! It's been months, though, since I did.

But she handled me! She just passed the phone to Rita A, and I was still explaining when Rita A came on and asked, "Are you finished with her?"

"No," I said, "I was still talking, but I guess she's through with me!"

Later, after our massages, I sat with her awhile on her bed, and she was talking well. She complained about some things, and then I said, "What else is on your mind?"

She said, "So much…. So much… I don't know where to begin." After a short philosophical discussion, we ended up agreeing that there is no beginning and no ending.

"There is only the moment," I said.

"The moment stinks," she said. I laughed. Then I asked again, "What else is on your mind?"

She said, "Why are you so cold?"

"Do you mean why am I a cold-hearted bitch, or why is my skin temperature not warm?"

She meant cold-hearted bitch. I asked, "Are you talking about why I wouldn't come over this morning?"

"Yes."

I tried again to explain that it is hard for me to do this; I don't begrudge it, but I need time that is just my time. That I have so little energy for anything except taking care of her, and that I need to keep my boundaries. How if it were an emergency of course I would come over, but that she can't cry wolf, I can't come every time she just wants me. "Do you understand?"

"NO." She doesn't understand why my life isn't her life.

I said, "You need to have a life of your own. You can't have mine." She said she has no life, and she still doesn't understand why I can't be there all the time. Fuck. Again. Then she brought up when Rob and Nancy were here, and had some screwy interpretation of that, and said she had wanted to go with us that day, and why had I taken Nancy to "our place" in the mountains? That was six weeks ago. I said, "Let it go. Are you trying to bargain that day off for me coming in here on some morning when you don't need me?"

"But I did need you."

"For what? There was nothing I could do for you that Rita A couldn't."

"She's too big to get in the bed with me."

"You just want me because I'm your daughter, and she can't be your daughter, right?"

"Right."

Well, break my heart.

Later we set up the plant stand, and then set up the laptop, and she did really well typing on it, and I am fucking exhausted by now, but had to get that down, that aggravating, heartbreaking conversation. But she's right. I really am cold. I just can't be brought to tears with that kind of demanding.

Then later, she was cheerful, speaking well, and relatively pain-free. Ate dinner pretty well, walked down to the dining room with me to get it, and afterwards was eager to meet Betty to set up her cat collection in the display case in the foyer, with some drawings and her framed Christmas cards. It looks marvelous, and when Dad came in after going to look at it, he commented on her stupendous talent. Later, after voice exercises, I was recording her thoughts, and she just went on and on about how awful he is, how mean he's been, and how she doesn't care if she ever sees him again in this life or the next. Sad, sad, sad.

We talked a good long time, though, and she talked happily about her siblings, and her art. Then we got her to bed, and I was home by eleven thirty. I fed leftover fish to the cats out back. They were hiding on the patio at the end of the building behind me, which is a good wholesome place, or looks to be. I hope whoever lives there gives them some attention. That would be ideal.

Thursday, October 7

Dearest Auntie,

Yesterday afternoon we had a fun little party in the dining room where Bob and Ali voted their absentee ballots. I was witness to both, and filled out Ali's little ovals with the number two pencil. Bob went first, and after about one second yelled "Oh SHIT!" He had accidentally voted for Kerry! I erased it for him because I had a better eraser, but I bet they'll throw out his ballot. Afterwards, after everything was sealed, I looked at the directions, which he had read already, which said if you mess up you can request a new ballot, but I figured if he hadn't read it before he started that was really his problem, you know? Not mine.

Then while we were all in the same room for a few minutes, I called a family meeting, and asked him about his legs. Dr. Wise gave him something new and his legs were fine that morning. I mentioned the possibility of them getting on the waiting list for the Health Center, and he got all terse and said, "I'm not going, end of discussion." But I pressed gently, and after some back and forth, he said he wouldn't get on the waiting list because that meant giving up, and he wasn't going to give up, and he still had some other options to look into. I said, "Well, see that you do that soon."

"For example," he said, "I've thought of paying an athletic trainer to come in and help get me back up to a better place."

I said, "You better do that soon, 'cause they can't bring you back up from nothing."

Then I said, "I have another subject to discuss at this meeting before you rush off. As you know, I'm here for the long-haul, and I'm beginning to suffer from burnout."

The Colonel said, "Yes, I know that."

I explained that I've arranged to have two full days off, that I realize that I'm not living up to their expectations but that's too bad, I have to do what I have to do. I turned to Ali and said, "I cannot be your life, you need

176

your own life too," and to both of them I said, "You've both guilt-tripped me in the past week, and I can't handle that."

Bob actually apologized for "whatever" he'd said. He said all he was trying to say was that he really appreciates my being here. I said, "That's a far more effective way to say it." He stammered a bit but the point was taken. And Ali wrote a note that said, "It's okay."

Of course, she called this morning, but I fielded that well, and she didn't ask me to come, anyway. I've spent a lovely day repotting some houseplants, rearranging furniture for winter after bringing houseplants inside, tending geraniums for fall, and tidying up the apartment. I'm having company this evening, that old friend from the early summer party, who it turns out is in the midst of an amicable divorce. We're going to take the dogs to the park for a walk, then eat in. He's picking up something for dinner on the way down here from Alexandria. Should be relaxing and fun.

Many of my orchids and some of the plants from Mom's patio are on a lovely new wire plant stand in front of the glass doors, in full afternoon sun. The rescued hibiscus has a huge yellow blossom open, and your grand-tortoise is basking under the plant stand midst all the greenery. He's enjoyed having all of us at home today, and the dogs, too, have enjoyed lazing about on beds and carpets, in sun and shadow, on the balcony, all day with music and me. So that's my update. Except right now Desmond is trying to navigate over one of the rungs of the plant stand, and his front feet are waving in the air, his back feet on tiptoe trying to kick him over —Oh, he's given up and is going around. OK, I'm off to lie down for a few and gear myself up for a social event.

You said you'd noticed that it's getting to me: I'm curious what you've noticed. Tell me sometime. Hope you and Ford are enjoying this exquisite day. Much love, YR

Friday, October 8

I record her singing *Smoke Gets in Your Eyes*. This is a woman who has never sung in her life. When I tried to sing as a child she would laugh and tell me no one in our family has a musical bone in our bodies.

One day I come in to find her sitting in her studio in the corner, hunched in front of the closet door where her boombox sits, playing the

CD over and over, struggling with the buttons to find the song each time, listening to the song over and over.

"I'm trying to learn the words to the song," she explains.

I buy her a CD walkman and burn a CD of the just the one song, so she can sit in comfort and simply hit repeat. She plays it for hours at a time.

One night, sitting together on the couch, I say, "Sing it for me." She drags the words from her soul, drones a flat dirge of melody. A few times I coach her with the words. I record her endeavor. She makes it through the entire song, though it doesn't sound like this:

They asked me how I knew
my true love was true
I of course replied
something here inside cannot be denied
They said someday you'll find
all who love are blind
When your heart's on fire
you must realize
smoke gets in your eyes
So I chaffed them and I gaily laughed
to think they could doubt my love
Yet today my love has flown away
I am without my love
Now, laughing friends deride
tears I cannot hide,
so I smile and say
when a lovely flame dies
smoke gets in your eyes...

"Why do you like that song so much?"
I yee o weshu...
"It leaves no questions? What do you mean?"
I mean it's positive.
Long pause. "It's positive? The song itself is a positive song?"
You can't question it.

178

Saturday, October 9

Mornings are fleeting, evenings interminable. This time, when I return to Colorado, will have been short. Even today the past six months have flown. Yet the next six months or however many stretch like an endless desert before me.

An inappropriate analogy since I love the desert, but, say I have to walk across it alone with little or no water—that kind of stretch. For it certainly feels as though I'm doing this alone. Yet even as I write those words, I feel the support of all my friends welling up from below my surface, I feel the strength of my certainty in my mission, and the power that motivates me. So I know I am not alone, yet I do succumb sometimes to loneliness.

If I ever write a novel about this experience, I will include all the awful aspects of myself that I cannot bear to admit to in writing now. (But I'll try.) I'll describe how at the same time, as I watch my mother drag herself through a meal, I am wracked with compassion for her difficulties and repulsed by the sight and sound of her efforts. I'll describe how her face, lovely and radiant in repose (everyone comments on her beauty still) pinches into a pointy rodent's mask when she struggles to swallow, or cough; how she grimaces when she sips, or chokes, or does her voice exercises, how her lips stretch wide and show her mouthful of uneven teeth; how her tongue lies like a fat berry in her mouth when she cannot articulate through motionless lips.

Then there are the times when she has tried thrice to say a sentence with patience, and the panic comes into her rheumy gray eyes. Sometimes, too, there is still humor in them, and her lips occasionally curl in the hint of a smile; but at wrong times, when she is smug that she frightened her sister who thought she was dying one night. Oh, to be fair, she does smile at little things she ought, like:

Yesterday, when she was finally settling down for a nap after an hour and a half of fussing, with the toilet, the suction, and telling me how mean and cold I am, she asked, "Will you please put some tuna fish on my feet?"

I smiled and said gently, "No, I won't put tuna fish on your feet, but I will put arnica on them." When she realized what she'd said, she said again, "But I want tuna fish on my feet," with a sly little edge of a smile.

Earlier, though, she said I was being mean. She referenced a couple of times. Once she'd asked me for the flashlight and I wouldn't get it; but

I explained, then and now, that she was asking for a white flashlight I'd never seen or heard of, and did she want the black one by the bed, which she didn't. She mentioned another time which I can't remember, and I explained my side of whatever it was. Then I said, "Ali, I'm treating you like an adult, and if that feels mean to you I'm sorry. But I'm not going to coddle you and treat you like a child."

"And besides," I added, "I'm burning out. That's why I arranged to have some days off each week, in hopes that it will improve my attitude while I'm here." And as long as she had opened the topic of being mean, I said, "Also, you've been mean and resentful to me for weeks. I understand that you're angry. Who's to know who started it, but we've got to both stop." How, she wanted to know, and when had she been mean to me. "I haven't been keeping score," I said, "I can't remember specifics, but your general demeanor has been dark with me, and you're very demanding."

At some point, before this when she was complaining that Rita A was mean to her that day, wouldn't give her coke when she wanted it and something else, she said, "It's very hard, when you're completely dependent on someone and they're mean." She has also mentioned in the past couple of weeks a few times, "I really am completely dependent on you." Perhaps the more she takes advantage of that dependence the more she realizes she doesn't really like it after all.

I had an interesting chat with her sister the other day, in which she said that Ali has always been spoiled. She said, "I was spoiled too, and I'm kind of proud of that, not ashamed of it, but she was really spoiled. The perfect little golden child from the beginning, and then after she got that awful burn Grandmother and Grandfather felt so responsible for her, and he in particular just doted on her. I think Grandmother felt a little differently but she always followed his lead in everything. So she was really spoiled—and now, she has someone with her every waking moment. She's the center of attention again."

We had touched before on the subject delicately, how she does like to be the center of attention, and while the two of us might not have any quality of life or reason to live were we in situations like hers, that for her simply being the center of all this attention may suffice to make it bearable, even enjoyable at times. And this is what bothers me the most right now, during this phase: that she seems to actually enjoy having me or Rita A or

Pam at her beck and call at all times. She certainly takes advantage of it. I cannot sit still for more than seven minutes at a time (I've watched the clock) before she rings the bell for something, however nonessential. How she struggles to get settled for a nap! Yes, it's sorry and sad, and I cannot possibly understand her discomfort—but sometimes she seems to relish getting helped to the point that she doesn't take initiative to solve things herself. What do I mean specifically? I can't bring something to mind right away.

And finally, her very childishness I find repellent. She is seventy-six years old. She has been childlike all her life. She has never grasped the most simple technological concept, and this is exacerbated now. She cannot find the return key on her typewriter after a two-hour lesson the day before. Yes, maybe the brain disease makes her not remember things, but I swear to god she just doesn't try. She has had hours of lessons and practice on the remote control for her bed, and still she struggles to make the buttons do the right thing. This isn't all the PSP! It can't be! Can it?

Specifics of her childishness? Maybe these accusations of people being mean. Her refusal all these years to deal with her resentment of her husband in an adult way. Just to harbor it and complain about it to me, her daughter, ever since I was a teenager, as though I'm supposed to fix it. And I guess I've tried, and thought I could help with that when I came out here, but now I see so clearly that I can't really do anything because she really won't do anything.

And of course, with his bad hearing and her bad speech, she cannot possibly address it with him without an interpreter, and I guess this is one way I could help, by being the middle person in that conversation, but what a delicate walk that would be! What a strain! Perhaps if I meditate to prepare for being intermediary I might be able to pull it off. It's possible I could be the only one with whom he would speak freely. I just am not certain I could stay fair between them, though I may be close to having had just enough of her to manage it.

That was the other way Rita A was mean to her: Mom said, "She wouldn't translate for me with Bob." I said, "But I heard you all in there talking away for a long time."

"But she left," she said, "after awhile. She hates Bob so much she won't talk to him. She wouldn't stay."

It's not really in her job description, I'm thinking to myself, especially if it's personal stuff. Certainly she has reason enough to not like him. He bullies her also. But I have seen her be very pleasant to him when she doesn't have to.

How to solve this one. Wait for deathbed enlightenment for the both of them? Try to be a bridge?

Sunday, October 10

Something is very wrong in me. This is not the way I thought I would be. I am so awful. By the time I left there this evening I hated them both. When she fussed about the blinds, when all else was set for her to go to sleep, I tried to fix the slats yet again, and I said, "You are killing me. You're killing me. This has to be okay. It's done. It *has* to be okay." And she said, "OK," and I left.

I *am* cold. I am so cold. Sometimes, I cannot bear the wispy touch of her little bird claw fingers on my hand when I hold the Advair discus for her to inhale, her weightless grasp; when she reaches to hold my arms as I help her transfer in or out I cringe. I can't stand the sight of her grimacing face when she is choking and she looks at me with those eyes asking for help, for understanding, at the very least compassion—she looks at me with anger and fear, she looks at me demanding something beyond what I can give her.

My throat screams in constriction as I sob here, and my eyes, my eyes and my throat ache with unspent grief. Pain from my throat presses out my ears. I want her to die. I cannot stand for her to be alive in this awful state. She chokes more and more with food, with any food, with pills, with drink. Her hands are permanently bruised between the thumb and fingers, her feet, her toes underneath the bases are bruised. More than half the time I cannot understand a word she says.

This is when I took a nosedive, after I came back from the wedding and found her unintelligible. I freaked out deep down then, and it's just now coming to the surface, in my increasing impatience and manifested frustration.

I hate them both for their smallness. She could have been a bigger person if she'd been with someone other than him. She could have done the work to get past her stuff and blossom as the creative person she could have been. He stifled her for fifty years. I hate him for that, and for the insidious way he continues to be abusive and yet comes across as softening. The way he yells at Rita A, now, instead of at Ali and me. He cannot change. He's retreating, but only out of fear; he's not facing the issues and addressing change.

And she let him stifle her for all these years. I hate her for that, for not standing up for herself. I hate in myself the same lifelong surrender to his bullshit.

They've both been generous with material things, and very stingy of spirit, all my life. I think she could have had a chance to grow and flower if not for sticking with him. What a pathetic waste of a life. It's no wonder she feels so worthless now at the end of it. And no wonder I want her to just give up and move on, relieve her suffering and sever my ties.

Is there any hope for her to redeem her life? Any hope for him? Is there anything I can say or do to ease the way for either of them?

They simply provide a screaming example of all that I do not want to be, in what is left of my life. For all that I have been like them in the past, please let me overcome such tendencies in the future. Let me be strong and clear and pure of heart, let me be giving of spirit and mindful of material things. Oh let me be mindful! And I am being so *unmindful* these days when I am there with them. I am filled with hate and rage and disgust and so very little else! The darkness in her eyes condemns me to distance. She looks out at me from a dark place, warily. Gone is the loving and light gaze she gave me often when I first arrived. What have I done to bring this on myself?

Been the bearer of bad news—brought her inevitable end to the forefront rather than simply made each day light and pleasant, filled with flowers and music and color and delight. I've told her how it's going to be, told her of others and their symptoms, worked her on her swallowing and speaking drills, scolded every time she tries to walk with her pants down, every time she gets up unaided, every time she takes too big a sip—actually, I dropped that particular battle months ago, but pick it up again every now and then, if she's drinking something thin and bubbly, or just goes on and on sucking from the straw.

I gave up for awhile reminding her not to turn her head while she's drinking—tried it out again a couple of times today, reminded her how

Kerry had spent months teaching her not to turn to put her cup down while she was swallowing, and you know what she said? This is the kind of idiocy that drives me fucking crazy. She said, "I thought that was only when I was doing the double swallow." Oh for fuck's sake. It's any time you swallow! It's all about swallowing! All I said was, "It's all about keeping you safe."

Yet she never ceases to amaze me the things she comes up with to say. Last night I was talking on the phone with Dottie about oil and the war and Dottie said, "Don't you think we could find a way to go over there and just tell those savages there's a better way than cutting off heads?" Startled at her use of the word "savages," I offered that we don't need the oil, that the technology exists to change the entire transportation industry to solar and other renewable powers, etc. Mom was listening this whole time, supposed to be eating her dinner, well into the second hour of one tiny plateful, and she leaned over and wrote on her pad, "What about Prius?" She is *in* there. She is aware, alert, educated, and involved. She is not an idiot. How can she be so simple minded about the simplest things, like not grasping the relevance of the swallowing technique? It's maddening.

I need an outside source to get me to a deeper level of compassion. I need to go into the city. I need help of a far more substantial kind than any I've ever gotten from pure counseling. Would meditating and yoga do this for me? I guess it's finally time to try. The drugs are all spent—the pot, the TV, the booze, the scrips, none of it is working anymore.

I need also to plan one fun outing a week for us, build it into one of my regular work days, to the bay, or to the mountains. Tomorrow I hope it will be to the orchid show at the Arboretum. To that end, I had better get to bed.

Tuesday, October 12

Today I took the dogs to the park for a walk, found a recently opened new trail, and actually ran a little bit of it with them. Last Sunday I took Mom and Rita A to the orchid show at the National Arboretum, which was lovely, and we saw some of the bonsai pavilions, too, before it was too much for her. She began to have trouble breathing in the bonsai pavilion. We needed morphine and we had forgotten to bring it. I asked a guard where the first aid station was, and explained briefly what we needed. She said the only thing they could do for us would be to call an ambulance. Mom and I conferred and concluded that would be overkill, so we just parked and worked on a little deep, slow breathing to restore her. When she regained her equilibrium, I stopped at the sales tent and bought my orchid for the month, a *Dendrochilum* blooming with sprays of tiny, pungent yellow blooms. Then we came home.

I've got to spend some of my work time with her doing more fun stuff like that. She's on a plateau where that's possible. Her nurse seems to think that she could go on like this for a very long time.

Wednesday, October 13

Dearest Auntie,

I think it's a splendid idea for you to ride up here for a couple of nights before Halloween. I'll double check with Ali, of course, but I'm sure she'll want you to come. Certainly part of the problem with the anniversary and the birthday visits was all the concomitant festivity. Let's try just a short, laidback visit from you alone. Whether you stay in their apartment or not is your choice—just the other day when we were discussing whether the dogs can come in when it gets really cold, and we'd agreed they could stay in the guest room, Ali said, "But what if Rita comes to spend the night?" I said you didn't mind dogs, and in any case they wouldn't be there while you were sleeping.

You know, she may have gotten riled up, and it may have had something to do with acting out while you were here, but remember that she began sleeping like the proverbial baby (the good baby) after you left. I think ultimately it calmed her and was very good for her to see you. If you don't want to stay there, or she doesn't want you to, of course you will stay here—as long as you'd prefer that to a guest room at the Home. I could drive you over in the mornings as early as you want, and then come back myself at my due time. All this is workable.

And as for getting here, or course I will come to Fredericksburg to get you. We'll just have to pick a place, probably on the south side of town to make it easier for Ford, as that is the long leg anyway, that we can both be sure to find each other. You just figure out the time and place.

I appreciate your concern over not causing more stress, but I think that it's good for you to come when you can, even if it does cause some stress. Better that she should get to spend time with you now while she can still communicate, however poorly. There may come a time when she cannot speak at all, cannot move, etc. I've been reading on the Forum more and more—it's just awful what these people go through, and how long they go through it. Let's take advantage of this time while she is still pretty mobile and has good talking days. With luck, she'll have two of them while you're here.

Plus, and the importance of this cannot be overstated: I love it when you come, for my own selfish enjoyment of you. I bet I can find key lime juice up here at Trader Joe's in two shakes. Keep me posted. And after all, you forfeited a trip to the islands during this time, you might as well make that worth it.

Thursday, October 14

Dear Pa,

Probably most everything I say to you in this letter falls under the heading of "psychobabble" in your world-view. This is really the crux of the problem: that different people can have completely different world-views. To some, everything is cut and dried, exactly as they see it and there is no other world-view possible. To others, the world contains much more seen and unseen than we will ever comprehend, and an awareness that everybody has a unique perspective.

Also, there is ample research and even more ample personal observation available to confirm that men and women see and interact with the world in some fundamentally different ways. Not all men, not all women, but most men and most women really do function in the world differently from each other.

We spoke the other day about some things I see as problematic in your and Ali's relationship. You are rational, linear, military, male, and inclined to yell when you are provoked. And, as you said this morning, you don't understand what people mean when they talk about "feelings." Ali is artistic, non-linear, nature-oriented, female, and the youngest child of an abusive, alcoholic father. She is emotionally complex (has a lot of different

186

"feelings"), and is easily beaten down. This, as I see it, is an unfortunate combination of people.

It isn't your fault. But the truth is, that Ali is looking death in the eye now, and her marriage to you has been the biggest part of her life. She doesn't find a great deal of satisfaction looking back. It's not pertinent here for me to try to enumerate her issues. I suspect all she ever wanted, like many women, was to be adored. It's true you loved her. But what does "love" mean in your vocabulary? I mean, really. What does it encompass, signify?

All I really want to get across here is that, like it or not, she has a lot of unresolved unhappiness about her life, her marriage is a big part of that, *and* she bears the ultimate responsibility for the fact that she is now looking back and grieving her life.

It is not just the way she drinks out of a cup that is childlike, as you mentioned. Again, research shows that most adult children of alcoholics don't really mature emotionally to the point that they take responsibility for their own lives, actions, etc., unless they do some deep emotional work. They can get on, succeed, make quite a splash in the world, but their personal relationships are usually fraught with complications and unhappiness. Ali is not especially emotionally mature. All you have to look at to confirm this is her current jealous fixation over you sometimes having lunch with Nell. But I'm sure you can find countless examples in your lives together that will support my contention.

She mulls over ancient events in your marriage that tore her apart at the time. She failed to confront you with them at the time, or did so unsuccessfully—meaning that she may have tried to talk with you about them, but didn't stand her ground and hold out for resolution; instead, she buckled under your habitually defensive angry reaction. Therefore, these memories now rear their ugly heads as she reviews her life. Furthermore, she held on to them all these years and nurtured her resentment. This is not emotionally mature behavior.

I know from my own life, and from the confidences of other women, that after a point in a relationship where there is a pattern of conflict, it seems easier to give up trying to resolve anything and instead to just get by. I think this happened a long time ago in her life. It doesn't necessarily make you wrong—but you are inescapably a part of it.

Today as you were preparing to leave for lunch, when she said she was worried about Nell, and you did a great job of offering her reassurance, and she reached for the pen to write something else, you muttered under your breath in that disgusted tone you have, "Oh gawd." Do you think that all the times you've done that over the years, she hasn't heard you? I certainly have. Can you imagine what that might do to someone's sense of self-worth, to have her supposed love-mate react that way when she has something to say? Can you imagine what it might do to her desire to even try to talk to you anymore, after years?

Now in this case, she did go on about Nell. What she wrote, and why I told you to go on to lunch, was, "Well he says that about Nell." Meaning, and I know this from previous conversations with her, that she is not reassured by what you say, for her jealousy is too deep to be assuaged. This is *not about you*, this jealousy and neurosis about Nell. She has said numerous times, "I've seen how Nell operates."

But the whole Nell issue does reflect, I think, rather sadly on the marriage. She is possessive of you, but resentful and unhappy. She wants you to have been someone you were not. But you are still her husband, by god, and nobody else will have you either. I think you did an eloquent job of reassuring her this afternoon, but I think she is so deep in her own story of dissatisfaction that she wasn't able to hear it.

Education specialists will tell you that it takes between twelve and twenty times of hearing a fact before a person remembers it. So maybe you have to tell her twelve or twenty times that there is no other woman in the world you want to be your wife, or have more than a casual conversation with. And still, given that she can't change who she has been for seventy-six years any more than you can change who you've been for eighty-five, and given that she has a brain disease, it still might not be enough to make the problem disappear. I can understand your impatience with this. I told her after you left that she has precious little time and energy left, and she needs to choose whether she wants to spend it worrying about Nell or doing something more worthwhile. This may have been a waste of breath, but it's all I have to offer her when she sinks her teeth into a petty worry like this.

Please remember that Ali is really confronting the ultimate fear right now. Many people do not ever have to face the knowledge of death because it snatches them without warning. Many people, like you, do not even think once about it until they are old and their friends begin to die. But I have thought about it all my life, and feared it, and it has informed my choices since I was a child. And now Ali is looking at THE END, and is trying to make peace with whether she did the living right after all.

My advice on what you can do now is simple, but unappealing. It is simply, to find an opportunity when you can sit down, hold her hands, look her in the eyes, and apologize for every time you've ever hurt her, intentionally or unintentionally. Tell her (whether you agree with it or not— you said you'd fake it) that you know you've been mean, unfair, awful, to her at times, and you're sorry. That you never meant to belittle or denigrate her, and if you failed in your time together to fully appreciate her and give her the respect she deserved, you are terribly sorry. Etc. Then, re-commit yourself to her for the remaining time the two of you have together. Commit to not yelling at her, not belittling her or her beliefs, and not taking her for granted. Then do it.

And maybe you have to tell her these things more than once. And maybe you don't bring yourself to tell her these things until she is on her deathbed. And maybe that will be soon enough. But I do think that this kind of full confession and full apology from you is the only thing that will give her peace.

She needs to forgive. She needs to forgive you for all the wounds she has added up and attributed to you. And she needs to forgive herself for all kinds of things too—for being less than she hoped to be, for all the failures of confidence, creativity, character, that she and most of us berate ourselves for. If you can "soften your heart" sufficiently to beg her forgiveness for things you don't even know that you did to hurt her, she may be able to forgive you, and then to forgive herself.

OK, that's the best I can do on short notice. Please know that while I am often frustrated with you, I am also frustrated with her. I am hurting and angry at this disease also, just as you are. I hate your politics and it really pisses me off when you use certain tones of voice with me. But I do love you, and you have been a supportive and loving father to me, and I am very grateful to you. I feel deep compassion for you in this terrible time, and in this terrible message I bring that your marriage was not all that you thought it was.

I also know that for all her resentment and anger with you, Ali also loves you deeply and has relied on you for strength, support, and love for the past fifty years. She has told me this even since I have been here this year, and many times in the past when she was visiting me. One reason she loved visiting me was that you were always so happy to see her when she came home, and she felt you appreciated her a little more for awhile after she had been away. And she missed you while she was visiting me, every time.

What I have put down here is only the dark side of a multi-faceted relationship between you two. But it is a side, in light of her imminent death, and your ultimate one, that really shouldn't be ignored any longer.

So, sleep on it. I love you, dear father.

Thursday, October 14

Dear Uncle John,

I want to give you an update on your little sister. It seems that her most recent plateau of the past few weeks may be starting to drop again. If you are considering trying to get up here and see her again, you might think about coming within the next month. She is very tired of living this way. Who can blame her? She's spoken a couple of times before about just stopping eating, and is talking that way again in the past two days. She may rally, as she has before, and she may not. It is impossible to know. But if she chooses to stop eating she may go within a week. If she rallies and continues to eat she could go on for months this way. I'm sorry to lay this on you but did think I should give you a heads up.

She is still mentally competent, and though her speech is awful the past few days, she can understand everything that's said to her, so you might just call and tell her things, news about the kids, whatever. It was nice to get Clara's note, and she enjoyed hearing it several times. I know it's terribly frustrating to be on your end of a conversation when she is trying to talk back, but when you're done you can just say that you love her and you know she loves you, and that will help her from trying to say it and not knowing if you understand. Take care.

Friday, October 15

I saw Mom in the hallway today, and for a second I didn't recognize her. The tag sale finally rolled around. The sale where the toaster was supposed to be. I went early because I wanted to pick up some plates to put under all the houseplants that I just brought in from the patios. Then I walked down through the glass corridor toward Mom's apartment. I came around a corner in the hall and saw a black aide pushing a very old person in a wheelchair. The person I recognized first was Rita A. A split second later I saw it was my mother, but she looked so unlike herself. It was shocking not to recognize her immediately. She looked like she was at death's door. She was tiny and frail, white-haired and drawn, her face open-mouthed, dark-eyed and pale.

It took my breath away. Seeing her out of context and not knowing her instantly, as I might have even a couple of weeks ago, shattered me. It happened so fast. I was glad she couldn't see my face. They were on their way down to the tag sale. I said hello and told them what I had bought, and Ali struggled to say, "What did you leave for us?" which I finally understood. I gave a hug and a kiss to my mother whom I had not recognized, a smile to Rita A, and off we went our separate ways, they to the tag sale to shop for bargains, and I to the park, to walk off the shock.

Friday, October 15

Dear Uncle John,

Me again. I just got a call from Ali, and she sounded much better today.

This disease is so grueling for this reason, among many others. It involves something called the "unresolved cycle of grief," when a patient approaches the end, and then improves, over and over. Caregivers and loved ones prepare emotionally for the end, and then have to get back in a different mindset. Anyway, I'm glad to report that she is in better spirits, and talking much better. Just like that.

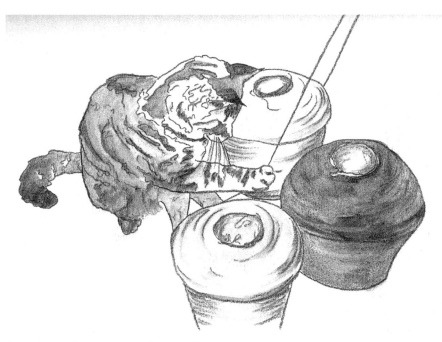

One of countless drawings Ali made of Olive, her cat for a dozen years through the 1990's.

Saturday, October 16

At last! Just about a month after I let him go, I caught the kitten again! I hadn't seen him for days, but this morning I took food down when I walked the dogs, and he popped up from the drain across the parking lot. Seeing him across the road for the first time, I felt a terrible certainty that he would get run over. I tied the dogs to a tree and walked to him. He approached hesitantly, ducked back, then came out again and ate as though he hadn't seen food for days.

I reached down, grabbed him by the scruff of the neck, pulled him into my shirt, and picked up the food. One-handed, I shut the dogs in the car, then carried the kitten upstairs. This time he is mine for good, and we both know it. He began to purr as soon as I wrapped him in my shirt, he purred through the whole can of food which he ate sitting on my lap in the bathroom, and he kept on purring. He is old enough now to be grateful. I named him Brat Farrar, after an orphan who makes good in Mom's favorite novel.

She is relieved to hear that I have captured him again. When I told her tonight, she wrote, "There's a toy in the top drawer of the hall dresser."

"A *cat* toy?" I asked, unbelieving she would have a cat toy in the house, years after Olive had died.

Olive was a little tabby stray that showed up on the porch of the quonset hut where I lived twenty years ago. She was three when I moved and couldn't keep her. I asked Mom if she wanted her. No, absolutely not, she swore she'd never have another pet after Mittens died. So I gave Olive to my neighbors, who kept her for a week then said she wasn't working out. I was crying to Mom about what to do, when suddenly she said, "I'll take her."

After that there was no stopping her. She wanted that cat as passionately as she ever wanted anything. I argued that she had allergies, she said she would get shots. I reminded her about her vow, how she'd said she couldn't bear to lose another pet. She insisted she could. I assured her that I could find another option. She assured me I had better not. The olive-eyed cat went to live with my mother.

Mom painted and drew Olive over the dozen years she had her, hundreds of renditions, from quick pencil sketches to intricate pastel portraits. That cat gave her more pleasure than any other single element of her life. She had painted a number of pet portraits before Olive arrived, for friends and for paying customers, but in Olive she had a permanent inspiration. Hundreds of people received her Christmas cards for nearly a decade in which Olive posed with presents, poinsettias, ornaments, stars. Hanging around my parents' apartment in frames are drawings of Olive reaching for the knitting yarn, Olive sleeping on a cushion, Olive looking out the window at a chickadee. Olive became the most drawn cat on the planet, and Mom developed a finesse with her lines that made her pen strokes unmistakable.

Because of her allergies, Mom could not love Olive the way she would have liked to. She had a special towel that she'd lay on her lap and then Olive could lie there. She covered her needlepoint footstool with a pillow case so that Olive could sit there. When Olive sat on her lap on the towel and Mom had to get up, she lifted both cat and towel from her lap, then turned and placed them on the sofa with such considered tenderness that Olive barely cracked an eyelid. Olive was fifteen years old when she died, but she left a legacy both tangible and intangible.

Indeed there *was* a cat toy in the top drawer of the hall dresser, a brand new Styrofoam bob dangling on string from a Lucite wand. I didn't think to ask Mom why it was there.

Sunday, October 17

As soon as I arrived in spring we began walking the dogs together. At first, I took the dogs on leashes, and she walked her walker. She couldn't hold a leash then, for if a dog had run, at best she wouldn't have been able to stop it and at worst, it would have pulled her off her feet. Now, though, she holds Mochi by the leash and I hold Brick and push her wheelchair.

There is a guy who lives in the Jefferson building who has a little black poodle, and occasionally we cross paths with him at the small pond. Sometimes at the big pond. Usually we're coming back home in the evening and he's heading out, and sometimes he only walks the little pond. So do we, sometimes, though while we still can, we go for the big one too.

My dogs go nuts when they see that poodle. Mom loves it. It's excitement, fun, she is surely laughing inside, for sometimes she laughs out loud, which sounds a little like a bark. I rein in the dogs, and the old guy keeps on walking, and we avoid any close encounter. The path around the lake is less than three feet wide, asphalt, and engineered incorrectly all the way around. In some places the grade tips you into the lake instead of away from it, which might have made sense if your first priority was drainage, but it should have been the safety of the old people who use the path.

We take walks in the evening, sometimes after dark if it's warm enough. The other night we strolled through the cottages, then back along the road until we came to the Adams parking lot. It was well after dark, but we hadn't had enough. We decided to keep going, and went along the south side of the lake in the balmy, humid night, listening to the frogs and enjoying fireflies, then we came in through the breezeway doors.

Ali loves walking the dogs like this. "Here's your dog," I say, handing her the leash as soon as we're out of the hallway onto the path. She grasped the mechanics of the retractable leash quickly, and was so well able to maneuver Mochi that I only rarely have to intervene and grab both leashes to handle a crisis, such as the black poodle. These last warm evenings of autumn, she is like a stick figure in her chair. I pass the leash into her bony hand, and off we go, her jaw set.

Monday, October 18, morning

What kind of sewer cat could come into a house at four months old and use the litter box the very first time? I'll tell you what kind. My little orange Brat Farrar. He's very affectionate and poury, pouring himself all over me like mercury, and purry too. We are both so happy. The dogs, of course, are not, but they will adjust. I'm in love! He's brilliant, gorgeous, precious. He loves the bob toy that Mom sent him. He flies through the air chasing that bob and catches it. He snapped the wand from my hand the first few times, but I quickly learned to keep a better grip. It is his best playmate and his tamer too: I flip the bob first near to the dogs, then over them as they nap. First he pounced beside them and now he leaps over them. I told Mom how much he loves that toy, and she articulated with difficulty, "I'm going to play with that cat with that toy." I promised to bring him over once he gets less spooky.

Michael asked if I might get home for the holidays. The only way that might happen would be if Mom dies before then. I guess I could drive a load of stuff home to storage if that happened, and spend a couple weeks before coming back here to take care of Dad and finalize everything, then do my Final East Coast Tour before returning for good. Feels weird to contemplate the future, but I do find myself making fanciful little plans. Most likely scenario is that I'm here for the duration and would make it home only when my work here is done.

It's also strange to find myself tacitly trying to persuade my mother to stop eating. She has days now pretty frequently where she simply cannot swallow for hours at a time. No juice, no pills, no food. Yesterday was one such. I finally coached her to the point that she got going on a shake, and got down maybe a couple of ounces before losing the ability again. I cooked her favorite eggs for dinner and don't think she took more than one or two bites. She did manage a vodka tonic, about two ounces total with a thimbleful of vodka in it, but that took her two hours.

She asked me again the other day, when she was only able to write and not speak, which is also more the status quo, "Do you want me to die?" Well, this destroys me. I don't know how to answer that. I said, "I don't want you to die, and I don't want you to stay alive for me. I don't want you to suffer this way. This is all about you, and about your choices. The question is, what do *you* want? This isn't about me." I mean, I can't tell her, "Oh please, yes, would you?" and I can't tell her, "No, I absolutely don't want you to die." Neither of these would be true. But I did say, "If you are asking if it's OK with me if you die, I give you permission. You can go anytime you want to, and that's OK. Nobody will force you to eat if you don't want to eat."

She says she doesn't want to stop eating because that will take too long. She wants somebody to bop her on the head and be done with it. In her place, I would get all my regrets redressed, all my material possessions disbursed where I wanted them to go, and all my last words down on paper, and then I would stop eating. I'd likely have done it months ago, but for sure at the point she is now. She can still walk for exercise, with someone holding a gait belt and a walker in front of her, but for everyday moving around she's in the chair. She can still enjoy flavors sometimes, but she can barely see. She can still enjoy going out to the lake and sitting by the water. But poop is a daily management issue, and most of the time she cannot make comprehensible words.

And I'm trying to keep her siblings informed but not alarmed, and wonder when to tell her son he should come—I'm sure, actually, that when she gets to the end she won't want some of them around—So I want to be sure I get them all up here before it's too late, while she can still appreciate their presence and they aren't too freaked about her condition.

Monday, October 18, evening

Had a good day with Mom, was there from two on. Pam and her daughter and grandson were there when I arrived. They had all been downstairs to the art show for a walk. Mom had trouble swallowing this morning and Pam called me at nine to tell me how bad off she was. I don't know if I helped her figure out what to do, but shortly after we hung up I guess she got Mom's pill down, and things started looking up, so they had a nice day.

First, I made her a shake, which she sat quietly and drank all of, while I knitted and talked a little bit about the kitty, and some other things. Then we went out to the lake around three and didn't get home until just before five. We sat and watched catfish on the deck by the water, and she walked a little on the back stretch. There were lots of people out, it was such a fine autumn day. Then she rode over here with me so I could feed the dogs, because I'd forgotten to bring food. I dashed in and gave the kitty a snack too, and he was all purry and rolly. Then we had a nice dinner that I'd bought at Whole Foods: lamb, asparagus with blue cheese and walnuts, and corn fritters. She ate all the asparagus, and a bit of the other two, all of which I had blended up for her separately.

Then she typed some notes, and I proofed and retyped them, and we addressed them to some friends, and then I read a bit of Kubler Ross, but we both found it too dry and rambling. Then it was bedtime. She did really well, right up until it was time to sleep. I was reading the story, and I read longer than usual, a couple of extra pages, and she just lay there and stared at me the whole time. When I tried to stop she said she wasn't ready to sleep, so I offered to read some more. I finished the chapter, and then tried to leave, and that's when it started.

In the first place, she can't talk by that time, with the sleep meds and everything else. Then she tries to tell me she needs to know where things are. No things in particular. We go on and on with a note and finally I just tell her I cannot do this, it is time for sleep, and she must let it go and go to sleep. I explain that everything is in its proper place, and it's time for sleep, and I'm not going to stay around for this. Bob tells her to go to sleep. I cry out something about every night being an ordeal and that I just can't take it. I say I'm sorry to get upset with her, I kiss her and leave the room. I hear her continue to moan on and on and Bob try to talk her down, and then he finally stops talking and she keeps moaning. I go in, flip on the light, give her a card and pencil and say, "Write down what you need, leave out extraneous words, and write big." She writes, "Close door to bath." So I say I'll do that, and will that make it OK, and she says yes. Well, she nods.

Every night is an ordeal. After a just fine day, when it wasn't so bad, I end up riled at bed time. After bedtime. When I should be leaving. I end up so angry, after such a nice day. So angry I could shout, or spit. Or kick something. Every night. I wonder if she pulls this shit with Pam or Rita A when they put her to bed?

Then I get home and have some cuddles with the kitty in the bathroom, and leave the door ajar so Mochi can see in and he can see her.

She leaves, and he follows her out, so I get up to follow him out, but he sees me rise and it spooks him, and he vanishes in a flash. It's two hours later and I haven't seen him. I know where he is because I heard a rack in the kitchen cabinet fall over. He managed to find the one hole in the framework, and now is in a narrow slot behind the kitchen cabinets. I just pray the drywall is whole and secure, and he hasn't ended up next door or between the walls. I cajoled, I cried, I tossed a chicken wing back there attached to a cord, and nothing. Finally I darkened the house, locked the dogs in the bedroom, and took a shower. Then sat down to write my sob story. I can't bear to not have him secure and happy, but missing and terrified instead. Or maybe I'm projecting. Either way, not what I needed at the end of a hard night.

Tuesday, October 19

When you fill and empty a pill box each week the Tuesdays fly by. And the Mondays, and the Saturdays—Oh! Here it is Tuesday again, oh, here it is Wednesday. Time flies. "Tempus is fugiting," I heard in a movie.

And the gin goes so much faster than any other thing. Oh my, Beth will be here in just over a month, what joy! My lifelong friend, my precious angel of death, incredible girl. She comes for Thanksgiving and her fiftieth birthday. Oh to be fifty! I know life will be so different then. This will all be a memory, and perhaps I'll have a big shebang on Fruitland Mesa where I hope to grow old with Suzi and Geoff, Marla and Charlie, Linda and Richard, so many more… The rest of my life—today is the first day—but it all seems so far away. Surely in five years this will all be over.

She ate, tonight, fully two bites of fried egg. I talked her through drinking, sucking through the straw and swallowing, perhaps one ounce of shake. No water. And a tiny vodka tonic.

Tomorrow I look forward to dinner out with Wayne. What a lucky girl!

Thursday, October 21

Speech therapy tonight, transcript:

"Try to do K-K-K."
Uh-uh-uh.

"K-K-K. Does your neck hurt? Try to drop your shoulders down. Try again, one good K. Do you need something?"

She writes.

"A massage? It's a good thing she's coming tomorrow. Let's try K-K-K again."

Huh-huh-huh.

She forces a swallow. We have been at these speech exercises for ten minutes. She managed the facial stretches, Oooo-Eeee-Oooo-Eeee. She accomplished the kissy noise and the fish face. But she cannot, this evening, get the back of her throat to make the K sound. These exercises we've been doing twice a day sometimes jump start her into being able to articulate.

Uh-uh-uh. She switches to the kissy noises.

"Nooo, now come on. That works a whole different set of muscles than the back of the throat. That's why you need to practice the one that's hardest for you right now. Do K-K-K."

Guh-huh-huh.

"That's better. Now take a deep breath and push it out. K!"

Kuh.

"Yeah, good."

Kuh.

"Yes!"

K-K-K.

"Yes! Very good!"

G-G-G.

"Very good. Keep going. Say good."

Gooo. Ooo-ya-ya.

"Let's stick with G. We'll get to ooo-la-la la-later."

G-G-G.

"Your eyes are tearing, do you need some eyedrops?" She nods. "I'll get them for you. Keep trying to do K-K-K, that's what's really important and will help you swallow."

I go into the kitchen to get her eyedrops and heat a pillow in the microwave for her neck. She struggles to swallow, to do the ooo-la-la's, the K-K-K's. She falls silent. I peek back out. "Can you do any of your practice words while I'm out? Try son-of-a-bitch. Remember to exhale when you say it! I've got to turn your pillow over."

Huh-uh-uh-ish.

"Let me put some arnica on your neck. Let's take your necklace off for the pillow. Can you say Bush stinks? Work on your Sssss sound."

Uuu-iiii. Uuu-hing.

"Good! Try to get your S sound. Can you go ssss?"

Uuu-hiiin. Hiinng. Sssss. Stinks! Muu-stinks! Buuh stinks!

"Here's the pillow, wrap it around, wrap it around high. There you go. Say it again?"

Buuh sting. Bush stinks!

I go back in the kitchen, leaving her repeating a phrase that gives her pleasure. Bush stinks because he won't allow stem-cell research. All summer she has hoped that he would pass a stem-cell research bill, because it might provide a cure and make her better. Election day is coming. She will tell anyone she sees that Bush stinks. If she can say it.

While I am mixing a gin and tonic, the Colonel hails me over from his den where he sits in front of the TV.

"I'm worried about how to get her her flu shot," he says. "She gets one every year and she's always after me to get one too. Dr. Wise has them at his office. I don't know if you can get one from him or not."

"Flu shot? What for?" I ask, incredulous.

"What if she gets the flu?" he asks. "She could die."

I wait a moment to see if what he has said will sink in. "She is dying," I finally say.

His eyes widen. He hasn't thought about it like this. "You go ahead and get yours," I tell him, "I'm not getting one."

"I'm not either," he says. "But she always insists. What do I do when she asks about it?"

"Let's just don't mention it," I reassure him. "If she asks we'll cross that bridge when we come to it."

I go back into the living room to bring her the vodka tonic she requested. She is able to speak! We discuss her sister's plans to come visit over Halloween.

"I think it's best if she sleeps at my apartment," I say. "She was so worried about you the last time she came that she didn't sleep very well. The last night she was here she didn't sleep at all. She was very upset with what happened. You seemed kind of gleeful the next day that you had scared her so badly."

A shadow of a smile plays on her tight lips. *No.*

"I know, but you seemed like it."

I nee the morphee, I know I noo.

"I know you needed the morphine. That's fine. But you weren't able to tell us that, and everyone was worried, and I wasn't here, and it just put her in a state."

I'm sorry.

"I'm sure you are. So Thursday night I'll come pick her up about nine thirty and take her home with me, and then Pam can put you to bed like usual."

Nu she wan tha?

"What?"

Does she want that?

"Yes. She's worried about not being able to sleep. She's old and frail, and she's very worried about you. She wants to come see you while she can, but it's hard for her to see her little sister so sick, so I want her to have a good night's sleep. If everything goes okay the first night maybe she can sleep here the next night."

Or na. Mayme she ca have two goo nighs.

"That's fine too. Would you rather she not stay here at all? Maybe it's agitating for you to have her here. Do you think it is?"

Anything out of the ordinary is agitating.

"That makes sense. And that's what I understand from reading about people on the Forum with PSP, and from my friend Elizabeth whose mother has it. Routine becomes very important and very comforting, and anything out of the ordinary is really hard. So let's have Rita come and stay at my place and I'll bring her over here in the morning. She doesn't have to be underfoot while you're getting your morning going."

Hello.

The Colonel drives his scooter through on his way to the bathroom. "You've been talking pretty serious in here, I just want to see what's going on, please."

"We're practicing our articulation. Give her some words." She doesn't wait for him. Or maybe she speaks to him.

Son of a Bitch!

He laughs. "There she goes! Bastard."

Bastard.

"You dirty rat."

You dirty rat.

"She's okay, she's talking great," he says.

Yes and no, I think. You don't know what it took to get here.

"We're talking about her sister's visit," I tell him. "Rita's coming up here on Thursday. Ford is driving her up to Fredericksburg and I'll go down and pick her up."

When will she come see me?

"As soon as she gets here. I'll pick her up and bring her straight here."

What time?

"We don't know for sure what time she's arriving. Thursday's the only day she can get her flu shot, so she has to do that first—" Oops. I know the minute the words are out of my mouth I've opened a can of worms. She interrupts.

When are you guys getting your flu shots?

I translate for the Colonel. We exchange a look. He takes a deep breath. He says "I'm not. It's a scarcity, I've done without for years and years and years, and I'm not going to fool with it."

I think you both need it.

"Well, I've never had one," I say, " and I don't intend to ever have one."

But times are different now.

"I don't think any of us need one," says the Colonel.

I do. You touch everything here that all the people touch.

"Aww, I don't even go out that much," he argues.

But she's right. He touches everything, door buttons, desk edges, the wall, handshakes. "How about if we all promise we'll extra wash our hands?" I ask. "Every time you go out you touch at least three door buttons that everybody else touches. I personally always wash my hands every time I come in. I don't like touching that button. I use my elbow."

"I'll wear rubber gloves," he says, hopefully, joking.

I turn back to Mom. "If you want a flu shot you can get one."

I need one. You don't think I need one?

"I don't think you need one for several reasons." I take a deep breath. "In the first place, in your weakened state, if you get a flu shot you run a much higher risk of getting sick from the shot than we do."

The Colonel interrupts, "Every time I've gotten a flu shot I've gotten a mild case of the flu." Whether this is true I don't know, but he feels it will bolster our position.

"Also," I go on, "in the second place you really don't go out very much—"

He interjects, "You never touch anything when you do go out, I don't think you're going to be exposed to it."

But you could get it and bring it back to me. She is looking at me.

"If you really want me to get a flu shot so I don't bring it back here to you, I'll get one for you, but only for that reason," I say. "But I feel that if I do get a flu shot, I'll get the flu. The only time I've had the flu in years was when I was here last fall—"

"How did you get the flu then?" asks the Colonel.

"From you! You had it first. I nursed you and then I got sick."

"I did not have the flu last fall!"

"You did! You puked and shat your guts out, and I cleaned up after you for two days before we sent you to the hospital dehydrated. Then I got sick, and then Mom did."

"That wasn't the flu, that was some sort of a food poisoning," he says, though without conviction, as though his memory of the event is a little fuzzy.

Mine is not. "Well whatever it was, you had it, then I had it, then she had it. It was a whole week of 'gastroenteritis of a bacterial or viral nature,'" I quote Dr. Wise. "That's not food poisoning."

I turn back to Mom. "And the final reason: there are about a third less flu shots available this year. You have a terminal illness, and you are begging to die every other day. The flu might help you with that. So I don't think you should be too worried about getting protection from the flu."

I'm not, she growls. *Bu yu nee wu.*

"She wants us to get one," he says.

"I know you do," I tell her. "But we don't want to get the shots and that's our choice. Your choice is whether you get one or not, not whether we get one. You can't be the boss of me! And you can't be the boss of him."

I made him get one one year.

"Well it's different this year. Eighty-five million people need the flu shot this year and there are only fifty million shots. That means there are thirty-five million people at high risk who need a flu shot who can't get one. He doesn't feel he needs one. He's giving up his shot to someone who does. I have never had a flu shot and I certainly don't intend to get one in a year when there's a shortage."

The Colonel digresses back to last fall, insisting again that he didn't have the flu.

"That's fine," I laugh. "I'm not attached to you having had the flu. But you got sick and then I got sick. I sat in the parking lot of the hospital and puked time after time while she was in the ER waiting for you."

"What hospital was this?" he asks.

"Alexandria hospital. And then I came home and shat for forty-eight hours. I was sick, that's all I know."

"Did you have any lung troubles then?" He asks.

"No," I answer, puzzled by his question. "I had headaches, though. Three days later I thought damn, I'm still sick; then I realized it was only because I hadn't had my morning coffee for five days!"

We all laugh.

Mom says something that sounds like, *I know what makes you sick all month, it's the flu.*

I explain about my special little homeopathic pills that I take when I get the first symptoms, and that I therefore never get the flu.

Wu di bu na anamo.

"You practice over-articulating," I say.

I'm just saying that one time they did, but flu shots don't make you sick anymore, and Dr. Wise has them... and you both need them.

The Colonel says he doesn't need it as much as thirty-five million other people, and I say I don't need it at all.

One time I had the flu and you were all playing Monopoly on my bed, and I couldn't stay up and play Monopoly.

"Well we don't play Monopoly anymore," I laugh, "so you don't have to worry about that! And Michael says this year is not going to be an especially virulent year for the flu, so there's no hope for the Coming Pandemic to rise up and eliminate 90 percent of the human population this year."

"It would be a good idea, though," says the Colonel.

"Michael and I are counting on it. But it's not going to happen this year. So your only choice in this matter, I'm afraid, is whether you get one or not, and I don't think it's a good idea for you."

"I don't either," he says, "I'm afraid for you to get it."

I don't need one, she over-articulates, *but you two do.*

I chuckle. "We're just going in a circle," the Colonel says. "She's pretty stubborn when she gets her mind set."

"I know she is. You're pretty stubborn yourself," I add. "I'm the only flexible one in the whole bunch."

He guffaws. "That's the funniest thing I ever heard! You've got two sets of stubborn genes in you."

"I understand that you want us to have flu shots," I turn back to Ali. "But we each have our own compelling reasons not to have flu shots, so I don't think we're going to get them. This is part of the point of what's coming down here in your life. You have choices about you. Those are your choices."

Well what if you two get the flu and bring it to me?

"That's the only good argument you have," I say. "But I want to ask you this: I'm very curious about how you go from one extreme to another. Just days ago you were begging for someone to kill you. Just minutes ago you were saying 'I'm so tired of this. I want someone to bop me on the head and end it fast.' So why are you afraid of getting the flu? If you got the flu, it might be your ticket out, and Hospice would make it painless."

I don't want you all to have the flu.

"Well, that's a different thing. Your argument has changed, and that one's not going to work on either of us. Why are you afraid of getting the flu?"

I'm not, she slurs. *I'm afraid of you getting the flu.*

"Well, we're not afraid of it, and your fears for me don't count. I've lived my whole life trying to escape your fears for me, and I'm not going to suck back into it now, just because I'm here. You're in charge of you. You're not in charge of me and you're not in charge of him."

If he gets sick, I get sick.

Round and round we go. "And that brings me back to my question. You've already agreed you're not worried about you getting sick."

What about if you get sick?

"Then I'll sleep it off for a few days. We'll ask Rita A and Pam to come in extra."

What if they get the flu?

"Mom," I laugh, "you can't stop everyone from getting the flu!"

"You can't stop *anyone* from getting the flu, as a matter of fact," says the Colonel.

"That's what I just said! You can't stop everyone from getting the flu, you can't stop anything from happening. All you can do is make your choices. I don't think it's wise for you to get a flu shot this year."

I won't.

"And now we're at the end, I think. It's bedtime. It's waaay past bedtime."

"We're done talking about it for tonight," says the Colonel. "If you want to talk more about this, we'll talk about it tomorrow."

I won't be able to talk tomorrow.

"We'll get you geared up again," he says.

Uh nee ma booies.

"You need your boobies?" I ask.

I need my booties, she articulates. I slip them on her bony little feet one at a time.

K-K-K, she says. *G-G-G. Oooo-la-la.*

Friday, October 22

Mmmmmm. I opened a bottle of very fine port when I got home tonight, just to celebrate a good, easy day, the new kitty, and not much else. I've left the bathroom door wide open for him for the first time, and if I sit here long enough he just might find me in the candlelight. The dogs are shut in the bedroom, and little Brat Farrar is feeling expansive. The port has made me warm-bellied already after only half a glass.

When we started our exercise conversation tonight, we talked about the other night at bedtime when Pam "slipped her a mickey" (gave her two sleeping pills when she wasn't expecting two, which was my fault because I'd accidentally put them in the pillbox). Then I asked her about bedtime in general, and asked her to help me understand what is going on when she calls for things after the lights are out and she isn't able to speak. She said, "The lights are too bright for me to close my eyes." I said I'd shut the bathroom doors and leave on whatever light in the front she wants. Some discussion ensued about light bulb wattage. Then I asked her why she needs to inventory her bedside table items each night. She said she needs to know where things are. We discussed which things she might actually need in the night, and narrowed it down to her lip balm, which I promised to put at hand.

I read a pamphlet last night that Wayne gave me. His mother died of cancer last winter, and his father is declining from Parkinson's now. It was a Hospice pamphlet called *Gone from My Sight*, which outlines the kinds of changes that take place in the last months, weeks, days before death. One of the first is withdrawal, first from worldly things like TV and newspapers, then from friends and relatives. This is the natural process of separating oneself from life, and turning inward to process one's unique history. I suspect that as more time passes, she'll begin to withdraw more, so it's good for her family to see her now. Of course, as Cheryl is quick to point out, she could go on like this for a very long time.

But with the amount she eats and drinks, and the increasingly long and more frequent spells she has of not being able to swallow, I still think it won't be more than some months—maybe six at the most?

So, for the moment, in the moment, I'm celebrating what I can: an easy night and a new kitty, with port and candles and music.

Saturday, October 23

Yesterday another fascinating conversation with Mom. She was napping when I arrived, and I lay down behind her, and held her for awhile. She felt down and too quiet. After awhile I asked if she'd had a nice visit with Henry, and she said no. I said, "Did it upset you?"

After a long pause she said, "Henry said I have to take responsibility for not leaving him sooner."

"Bob?"

"Yes."

"Did that upset you?"

"Wouldn't it you?"

"Yes."

"Why?"

"You tell me why it upset you first."

Silence.

"Because you think he's right?"

"Yes."

"It's hard to take responsibility for the things we've done and not done that we should or shouldn't have."

"I feel like I wasted the past twenty-five years."

We talked about regrets, and she said she doesn't really have any regrets—paradoxically. Said that Jock and I are her greatest accomplishments and she's known that for years. Later, when a cute note on black cat paper arrived from her friend Kay, thanking her for the wonderful cat drawings she'd given her over the years, she got weepy and very emotional. I pointed out that she's done other wonderful things during that time.

Back in the bed, though, I said, "You could still leave him, you know—by dying."

"I wish I could."

"What?"

"Die."

So that opened that up again, and we talked long about the not eating option.

I brought up the question she's asked me a number of times, "Do you want me to die?" and said how awful it made me feel. I tried to explain once and for all that I couldn't encourage her to quit eating, couldn't tell her I want her to die, and wouldn't, that I'd feel too awful when she was finally gone if I thought anything I'd said had hastened her departure; that I wanted her to understand that I did not want her to die, but I did not want her to stay alive for me—she said, "It wouldn't be fair"—I explained that I live with a low level of terror just being in this place, and that I came here to help her live her life to the fullest until she dies, but please not to live it for me. I can't remember many of the exact words and phrases, but it was a good and deep conversation, and we understood each other quite well.

I also said, "If you decide to do that, I will support you 100 percent; at the rate you're eating and drinking now I don't suppose you could go on more than four or five months, and stopping eating may seem like it takes a long time but it would take a few weeks at the most, and be quicker than the way you're going now."

I told her that I completely understand her many reasons for wanting to die, that I will miss her very much but know that she'll always be watching out for me. She said, "I'll miss you too," and I laughed and said, "No you won't, you'll be one with god, there's no room for missing mere mortals at that point; but you might think of me and watch out for me." She insisted she'd miss me forever.

So it was inconclusive, but was a good first step for her in beginning to separate from me, and in beginning to take responsibility for the fact that her life didn't turn out the way she'd always wanted it to, that she can have no more expectations of Bob. She said she could forgive him—what does that mean?

"I have no expectations of him," she said, "but I don't like him—I may love him but I don't like him."

"Yes," I said, "I understand that. He is trying, though."

She said, "I never finished reading *The Prayer of Jabez*, and I don't know the whole thing." This is a book that Gaytha gave her a couple of months ago. I told her I think the gist of it is, "Ask and ye shall receive," that god wants us to ask for what we want, and also maybe it's like, "Thy will, not mine, be done."

I said I believe in surrender, she said "So do I." Then I said maybe the Jabez prayer isn't really about surrender but about asking for, and that I'd always asked for, and I've lived a blessed life.

"Why do you think that?"

I said, "Look at my life. I have everything I could want, land, and friends, and security, and you've made all that possible."

"You are a blessed child."

"Yes, I know, I have been from birth, maybe even from my conception."

And here she said the second weirdest thing of the conversation:

"Your father got turned on when grandmother died."

"You mean he heard the news that she died and—"

"—and he fucked me," she finished.

Well. "Were you crying?" I asked. "Maybe he was trying to comfort you, and you were crying and he held and kissed you and one thing led to another. Many people seek and offer comfort in a physical way when someone is upset."

"Maybe. One time he woke me up."

"What?"

"One time in Germany he woke me up and wanted to fuck me."

"One time? In all your married years he only woke up you one time wanting to fuck?"

"I don't remember it."

"But you just told me it."

"I can't remember if it was in Heidelberg or Mannheim."

"Mom," I said, "I can't even count the number of times a guy has waked me up wanting to fuck."

"Well, I think it's rude."

Only astonishment kept me from laughing about this exchange.

Before I'd gone inside to lie beside her, I'd been walking the dogs outside, and thinking, There is a certain measure of attachment even to an uncomfortable routine. When she dies, this routine that I complain about will change. But the thought of the upheaval of her dying and the changes it will bring about made me settle in to the discomfort of this routine with more comfort. At least it's known. I know what time to come there every day, I know more or less the range of things to expect, more or less how the day will go. And she is still here. We can still talk and laugh and love. When she declines further, we will slip into a different routine, as we have been adapting all along. *A new normal.* Now the frustration of her poor speech has dissipated with familiarity and we have settled into the routine where she speaks clearly for some hours of every day, and those hours arise spontaneously and disappear.

Sunday, October 24

Little Brat has extended his territory into the back hall, moving freely in and out of the bathroom, with a water jug, a sheet, and some old clothes providing cover, and a quick dash through the doorway to safety. Ah, we are working it out. What a fine little being. As he stretches, makes a transition to a more trusting, interior environment, so must I. For several weeks I have been angry all the time, and I think not keeping that cat the first time I caught him I really let myself down, on the one hand, and took a leap of faith that tested me on the other. Now the kitten lives in my apartment, in my life. The dogs are having a tough time accepting him but are coming along. They just get a little too tense for my comfort when he gets close to them, but now they're both sleeping in different rooms and the kitten has the run of the place. Where he is now I don't know, but I hear thumps from the back now and then.

I stretched a bit on the hall floor, and the ache it drew out of muscles and bones, the massage has only disguised the depth of despair of my body. I am completely alienated from the shell. I have focused on the fire, the belly (the belly of the beast) and ignored the structure, the skeleton, even the skin. Certainly I need to stretch, in heart as well as limb.

The Prayer of Jabez. Gaytha, the irony, you will love to hear of it one day. How you gave the book to save my mother, and in fact it gave me strength in a most unexpected way.

Bless me indeed,
And expand my territory
Lend me your hand
That I may not do evil and cause pain.

Bless me indeed. God has blessed me indeed for all the intervening years since—since my conception. And I have asked god to bless me, asked a lot, as a matter of course.

Expand my territory. I have land, lots of land. I have asked for it all along. I have friends, buckets of friends, many people I can trust with my life, I can love. Children to dote on, to give to, to teach. Their minds really are like a sponge, as Kim said. As they grow, she said, "It strikes me how much their little minds really are a sponge."

I have animals, I have plants, I have the love of the natural world, I have a freedom from fear of the natural world, and that guarantees me endless territory—terrain.

Lend me your hand in my endeavors. Take me to the point where only you can help me. Overwhelm me that I may call on you to give me a miracle. Make me ask for help and clarity, again, as you did last winter, and give me the courage, strength, compassion to take this next leap you have in mind for me.

And do ye no evil. This is the Buddhist part of the prayer, the one I have been living, striving to live, for years. Let me not cause pain.

Needless pain? You sure caused your father pain yesterday. But look how he came through today! And I saved all the invective, saved myself the agony of writing all the invective last night, to enjoy the story today. Pam was wowed. "You musta lit into him somethin' fierce, girl." Yeah, I did. And

I felt a tiny bit icky afterward. I cut him no slack. I did not tolerate any of his excuses, his bullshit, and I hit with hard words.

"You are abusive! You can be an awful person. It's not right to talk to anybody the way you talk to people." Women, mostly, it occurs to me. Maybe his father was this way? That small, kindly looking, big-eared little newspaper man? I guess it could have been.

Anyway, he came in this morning and apologized to Pam, "from the heart, I could feel it," she said. Explained himself without trying to excuse his outburst. I hope he remembers by Tuesday to apologize to Rita A also. And it was her birthday! She showed tremendous strength of character not to walk out on him at that moment on her birthday. I'd surely have left. Of course, I wasn't there, so I don't really know, but they've never spoken so strongly about his behavior before, though they've hinted at it.

So maybe my outburst did a bit of good. It sounds like he thought about it. "It's wrong," he told Pam, "and I've got to stop doing it."

At this point, Mom is able to speak, on any given day, randomly, and the rest of the time she writes. We ask her to write big, remind her to move the pen. At least she can still write with coaching to make the letters clear. Without coaching she gets them tiny and all crammed together.

Friday, October 29

Well, I really agitated Mom tonight, and she fell to gagging and couldn't swallow saliva, and this went on for an hour. Now I see the direct result of upsetting her emotionally: While she was supposed to be brushing her teeth and wasn't, I said, "Come on now, let's make this an easy night, let's just do the normal stuff and move on to bed, not drag things out." Once she was upset and started gagging she couldn't relax. Shit.

Sunday, October 31, morning

Hey Auntie. I just wanted to let you know that Mom was better by evening. She was in bed when I arrived this afternoon, just a few minutes before you called to say you'd made it home. Pam had just left, and only told me on the phone this morning that Mom had banged on the table and said she was frustrated, and that you'd gotten a little teary, and then that you two had a long talk.

At the moment you called, Mom was trying to arrange herself and the bed so I could lie down with her, and was reaching and twisting and not waiting for me to hang up so I was pretty distracted. But I'm glad you made it home, and I gave her your message. Then we lay there for an hour and a half, both of us drifting in and out of sleep, and it was very peaceful. She couldn't talk, and I just held her hand and told her not to try to talk. When we got up, she could talk some for the rest of the evening, and just before bed she was enunciating brilliantly for a few minutes. But she'd had trouble breathing about nine, so by the time I left she'd had one ml of morphine, twice what she normally gets at night, and she zonked out pretty fast.

So I gather it was an awful morning, but you see this is the cyclical nature of this heinous disease. You saw the whole range in the forty-eight hours you were here. It's like a downward spiral. I think it was important that you came, and that you had that conversation—she is gradually assimilating all the pieces she needs to make a peaceful passage. Please tell me about your talk.

Sunday, October 31, evening, reply from Auntie

Sweetest child, thanks so much for your note. I really appreciated it—especially as I know you have so much to do and so little time to do it in. Our guests left about five and although I enjoyed them and we had a good time, I was glad to be alone again with Ford who has now gone to bed. Am so glad Ali called me awhile ago. She sounded great and I feel better about her tonight—although I realize it's only temporary, as I realize the bads are temporary for the present also.

Yesterday morning was *not* a bad scene. Ali was completely unable to talk. She wrote lots of things to me and did bang on the table in frustration, writing that she had no time to do what she wanted, that she had not done enough in her life, that she hated not to even be able to talk to me on my last morning with her, that the best two things she had ever done were her children, but they were half Bob. I told her they were, but every ounce of creativity which is what she was so proud of came from her and from our grandmother. She agreed with that and said they had never given her trouble

213

like other people's children and agreed that it might have been because she was such a good mother.

She told me she was sorry she had refused to let me use the phone, which she had previously clutched in hand so I couldn't call Nancy about my pick-up time. (I called from the studio.) She said she did it because she wanted me to stay another day and didn't want me to go. She wrote that she was furious inside, but that she loved me. I took both her hands, tears coming on and off down my face, and answered all of the above and more. She had such a strong grip on my hands I thought she was going to break my fingers. I had no idea she had such strength. I told her I hated, hated, hated what was happening to her and that I, too, was raging inside about it. That I wished it were me instead, but there was nothing either of us could do about it—as much as we both hated it. That we both must get over our rage as best we could and remember the love we have always had for each other. I smiled through my tears and said, "Well, almost always," and she actually chuckled.

Pam left the room when I started to cry and a few minutes later Bob came in to tell us he was off to lunch. Ali had just written saying, "But I am so ugly," and I told her she was not. I told her she was still beautiful (Bob agreed and went on to lunch a little after that) and I said she couldn't expect to look like she did at eighteen, and that if she wanted to see ugly to sit out in the hall and look around for awhile. She chuckled again and started to show me her wrinkled arms and I told her to forget that, as I had enough of my own to look at. I told her how much *everyone* loves her and how lucky she was to have all of us and to be able to dress, have her hair, nails, etc., all look so nice. I brought up an old joke between us and said that her "best feature," her eyes, were still as beautiful as ever, and she smiled. I told her that all she had to do was work on keeping her mouth closed as that did distract from the rest of her face.

Then we got on the subject of Nancy and face-lifts and the great wrenching emotional scene was over. So that was a lot (probably most) of it, but I don't regret any of it as it brought us *very* closely together, giving us closure if it comes to that and I don't see her again. We moved on to the etchings above the sofa where she wanted information from the backs read to her, etc., and then Nancy called and I had to go. And then she started to cry—so, of course, did I, and I had to leave her like that. I wouldn't let Pam help me with my baggage as I didn't want Ali left alone. I piled the Bean bag on the top of the suitcase and wheeled it out.

The styrofoam cooler was the problem so I put it over my head like a hat and blew her a laughing kiss. Just as I cleared the front door Bill was there, and Pam came running after me with an umbrella she said Ali wanted me to have. I told her to hurry back as Ali must have thought it was raining and that's why I put the cooler on my head. I felt good about that, also, as I thought she had stopped crying and was thinking of me instead of herself and not wanting me to get wet. THE END.

I love you. Aunt Rita

Ali on her last walk through the woods at Mason Neck National Wildlife Refuge.

November

Monday. My Friday. I am so tired. Weary to the bone. I read Eudora Welty's *The Optimist's Daughter* the past few days. What an exquisite book. Can't believe I never read her before. Gives me courage in a way.

Took Mom out both yesterday and today, and it was lovely. She was exhausted by bedtime both days, which was good, though Dad told me tonight that he got up about half an hour after I left last night and sat with her, and she was talking, she wanted Pam, and he finally gave her a few drops of morphine and she went right back to sleep. She was coughing a little tonight when I left, but seemed to be otherwise sound asleep.

The leaves have been just lovely this week, and the weather warm and sultry. Last night we got out to the bay about an hour before sunset, with the sun behind a deep cloud bank, so she didn't get to see the dappled drive in to the park. But when it came down below those clouds, we got a gorgeous sunset, and she enjoyed sitting on the water looking out at the muted trees, the clouds, the few boats—a couple of kayaks rode just below us, geese flew overhead, some gulls. We sat mostly in silence because she just couldn't talk much at all yesterday, until later that night when we did K-K-K and G-G-G, and got her jump-started. Then she talked pretty well

217

for a short time, during which I had her call Rita S, who said, "I will go to bed with a happy heart now."

This afternoon we got off an hour and half earlier and drove down to the Great Marsh Trail. She walked the first few feet pushing the chair, 'til I asked her to sit while I ran back to the car for the recorder. I had wanted to record the sound of our footsteps in the blanket of fallen leaves over the trail. When I got back to her, I discovered that the battery was dead, and that she wanted to ride from there on. It was a long lovely stroll through dappled trees to the marsh, and there the light was lovely, if a little bright. She put on her shades again which she'd had off in the trees, and we were looking right at the setting sun again. I said, "Hey, it's setting over here tonight. Last night it set over there," and pointed across the river. Of course, we were on a completely different bay, but it's funny how I get all turned around out here with no mountains for reference. The river has all these pieces sticking out of it so I can't keep directions straight.

She stood and walked around the deck there, and took some pictures, which if I weren't so damn weary I'd put on the computer right now. I took one of her. She has on her favorite earrings, silver and glass cubes that Jock gave her, and her black fleece hat, her black coat, and dark glasses that shadow her cheeks. Her nose is bright in the sun, her mouth and jaw, her earlobe. She has taken to pulling her lips tightly in over her teeth, curling them 'til they all but disappear into her mouth, as though she has no teeth at all. She does this to keep from drooling.

Trees yellow in the background, and between her and the marsh is the rail of the boardwalk. She is standing, walking for perhaps the last time in her life. I had parked her chair, and walked around the tiny space with the camera. I looked back to see her attempting to rise, and hastened to her side, ready to chastise. Quelling my first impulse to prevent her, I helped her up, and steadied her to the rail. She walked on her own, me ready at her side should she need me, but she held herself up with the physical manifestation of that iron will to live, and helped herself around the perimeter along the rail. I took the picture.

She said, "It feels so good to walk." Food for thought. She reached for the camera.

How she took two perfectly framed photos of me when she can barely see I can only imagine has to do with her innate artist's eye for composition.

She can still see shapes and colors, though she can no longer make out letters an inch high. The digital camera, of course, focused for her. Bright red leaves of sour gum below me and yellow sycamores above.

We talked little. We have become comfortable with silence as it has increased. What matters is that we were together. What matters too is where we were—in the wild marsh, amid geese and blackbirds and autumn-colored trees, in the wild moist air; what matters also was the time—nearing sunset, nearing the end. As we turned from the boardwalk in the descending dusk and started back along the trail, I took another picture. Mom in her chair holds both the leashes with yellow dogs streaming in front of her. All three of them are lit by a shaft of pure gold coming nearly horizontally at their backs. The pack on the back of her chair blazes yellow and red while the dogs glow. Ali, all in black save a streak of white hair between hat and coat, casts her shadow long into the arrow of light, deep into the trees.

It was dark by the time we got back to the car.

Tuesday, November 2, late night

I'm so tired of this. Tired of watching her suffer and being expected to read her mind, to help with every little thing, to be *able* to help. It's killing me a little bit every day. I'm losing my joie de vivre, if I haven't already lost it, and my sense of humor too. I'm not even angry anymore. I'm just plain tired. Living on coffee and gin, or scotch. Trying to hang on to compassion and peace of mind.

Trying to be the best person I can be. Every day, every moment. Seven months I've been here now. If it didn't look like it could go on another seven, or more, it would be maybe a little easier. I do want her to die. And I don't. She is already not my mother. She is already someone I miss, have been missing for years, really, watching this disease take her away ever so slowly, bit by bit.

These days, she has hours several times a day where she can't swallow, and shorter spells where she can talk. How does she keep on? What is she living for? Why doesn't she just bite the bullet and do what she keeps talking about doing? And that's part of my suffering, too, as I know it is hers. She keeps talking about wanting to die, wanting someone to help her die, and I'm getting to the point I've gotten to before with other people's suicide talk: Just go ahead and do it! I want to cry out. But fear of my future guilt restrains me. And that burden of knowing that what I say carries so much weight with her.

I think back to ten years ago when she told me it was something I said that kept her from leaving the Colonel. "Don't think I'll necessarily go with you!" I know she didn't tell me that to hurt or burden me back then, but it sure did both. It occurred to me tonight that that's probably one reason I'm here. On some level, I was responsible for her staying with him, and he turned out to be helpless in this time of need, so I've stepped in to fill his shoes.

I talked to Henry about this the other day. If the Colonel were any kind of a real husband I wouldn't have to be living here in terror. He could do all that I'm doing except the physical stuff, and if he'd been a better husband to her all these years he'd be someone who wanted to do this for his wife, and took an interest. I know he'd say he participates, but really it's like he's standing on the sidelines catching the ball if it goes out of bounds and throwing it back in, while I'm in the game as referee, quarterback, and wide receiver all in one. I'm fucking exhausted. I'm doing this job and have so little life outside of it. I'm alone in this. Nobody can really help me. Hospice helps some, but there's nobody to share the burden with. Not her husband surely. And he has the nerve, when I deliver him a glass of wine or a pill, to say, "Thank you, my love."

I'm not your love! I'm your fucking daughter. Don't call me "my love." It gives me the willies. It's fucking creepy. Call your wife "my love," not your daughter. It's inappropriate. If we'd had a different relationship over the years, and if I had a love for him that wasn't tempered, contaminated even, by disrespect and dislike, then I might not mind being called "my love." I recoil every time he says it.

And I want her to die. How she coughs and sputters, gurgles and mutters, gags and tears and holds the Kleenex to her open mouth to catch the drool. What is she holding on to? She could be gone in a week or two if she'd turn her mind to it. And she keeps saying she wants to die. What has she got left to live for?

Yes, it's true I arranged for her brother to come up again in a couple of weeks, and her son a couple of weeks after that, and Beth to come in between those family boys. Maybe when Beth comes she'll come to terms more with not eating.

Yes, I want it for my own sake, so I can relax again. I live in a constant state of fight or flight, alarm response, all the time I'm on edge. And OK, so meditating might help that, well I'm going to take a workshop this Saturday. But I really need to get home to my sanctuary, and it's months away from whenever she does go. That I know. I guess I also just want release from the constant worry, the task, the enormous need. I want release from this disease as badly as she does. But all this would not make me want her to go, if it weren't for the fact that she talks of it so often, she wants release for herself so dearly, she comes right up to it, then backs away.

Tuesday, November 2

Dear Elizabeth,

Thank you so much for writing, and for the wonderful photo to remember your mother by. I'm sorry for you that she is so close to going. I know you made the right decision because you did such a wonderful job taking care of her. You know she appreciated it, and that nobody else could have done it. I hope she continues peacefully until she is released from this torment. Please let me hear from you again when you can. I know you will be completely absorbed for some time now.

Please don't worry about sending back the straw holder. I'm just sorry I didn't mail it sooner. I got it, as you guessed, mostly to show you how someone else had done it, I know you wanted to invent it yourself. I'd had it a few weeks but didn't get time to package a bunch of boxes and get to the post office. Keep it or give it to someone in your Hospice who may be able to use it. Mom has special cups with lids that hold a straw so she doesn't need it.

The brushes are surgical scrub brushes sold by a garden supply company I favor. I use them for everything—nail brushes, in soap dishes by the sinks, mushroom/vegetable brush in the kitchen, and they're cheaper by the dozen, so when I run out I always buy a dozen and share them. Use them for whatever works!

I know this is going to be hard for you, but hold yourself gently through it and know that you have been an angel on earth for your mother—you've done all anyone could possibly have done, more than anyone, really. You will be sad and you may be lonely as this will make such a change in your life. But remember that she will finally be at peace, and keep taking deep breaths, and let yourself venture back one slow step at a time into a life that will be all your own. I'm sure it will take time to recover your equilibrium. Please don't berate yourself if you feel a sense of relief. Please stay in touch with me through whatever comes next! I treasure your friendship and your example, and want to be there for you as you wake up to a new and different world after PSP.

Wednesday, November 3

I am hot and tired. It's hot in here! I've got the door open as well as the window, and that is beginning to help some—but hot! In November!

Elections remained up in the air at two minutes to midnight on Tuesday. Preliminary results look grim for the planet.

A measure of just how tired I am is that when the roofers started on the roof over my bed this morning at seven forty, I slept for two more hours. Early on I moved into the living room, but with little respite. There must have been twenty Sauls up there: I dreamed, though I heard the banging the whole time, that I saw Marla and Charlie, and though I was home here, and they were home there, I saw them in the parking lot, and Charlie said, "Saul is up on the roof finishing it," and pointed to the top of an apartment building. I said, "There must be twenty Sauls on my roof," and pointed across the apartments to my building.

I heard the feet, and heard them rip up the old roofing and nail down the new plywood, and they'd gotten to putting the tarpaper on before I woke at nine twenty with a call from Dad. At that point I surrendered and got up, surprised it had been so long.

Then, amazingly, after leaving the house for most of the morning, I returned around one and rolled onto the guest bed again and slept for two more hours. I was simply too tired to go back out, and too distracted by the noise on the roof to do anything else. Until the sun came in strong and burned me up I slept. Then just as I managed to get some energy, after drinking a coke, and got up to take the dogs to the park, it was three thirty and they had finished for the day. So when I came home after five I had peace and quiet. To read a little, watch a little TV, listen to a little election coverage on Pacifica.

Had a brief conversation with Mom on the phone, in which I could not really understand much except her asking me if I could understand her. She began to try to tell me about some problem with Bob and Pam and Rita A. I said I couldn't understand her and it was frustrating to me to hear that they were having problems, and that if I didn't need to know about it today, I'd like to wait until tomorrow to hear about it, because I'd been having a really nice day and wanted to keep having a nice evening and not get upset about Bob and them. She said that was okay, and we parted amicably; still, I felt bad about blowing it off—though I did say, "I understand you're concerned about it, and if you need to tell me you can do it tomorrow, and I'm sorry if they're having problems. I just can't hear about it right now if I don't have to."

Oh so tired. One drink here puts me out. Two or three over there each night and I'm barely as exhausted as I am now.

Thursday, November 4

On Halloween night she said to me, in the few minutes that she could talk, that she wanted to die. I encouraged her to quit eating whenever she felt like it. She snapped at me and said petulantly, "How can I do that? You won't let me die when you keep planning fun things!"

"Like what?"

"You invited my brother to come up here in three weeks, and Rita this weekend."

I had to laugh. I said, "Sweet, dear Mother. I see that you want to die, but I also see that your will to live is stronger in you than your will to die. And as long as your will to live makes you eat every day, I'm going to keep planning fun things for you to enjoy while you're living. As soon as I see that your desire to die has overcome your will to live, then I will stop planning fun things. You can begin to die at any moment you choose."

"By stopping eating, I know, but I don't want to, it takes too long!"

"It can take from three to twenty-one days—there's not a faster way for you. I cannot help you with a bag over your head or even with pills. Since I've been here, and seen the power of your will to live, I have had to reevaluate my thoughts on some things. When I arrived, I was sure that I'd jump off a cliff if I ever got to the point that you were then! Now, I can't say I'd do that. Even now. I see the strength of your will to live, and I marvel at it. I no longer think I can help you kill that. That is what is in your power. That is what you have the choice to do, you alone. And the best way I can see for you to do that, the way where you have the most power, the most opportunity to say goodbye and set things right before you go, the best chance to talk to angels, the most dignity, is to stop eating. And only you can make that choice."

"It takes too long."

During her visit with Cheryl the next day, Ali asked again how she could die, and Cheryl again explained that Hospice could keep her comfortable should she choose to stop eating.

"How long?" Ali wrote.

Cheryl settled in for the conversation that had been waiting to happen for weeks. Near the end, Mom wrote, "This is going to be harder on Rita than she realizes." Cheryl said, "Of course it will be hard on her," and I said, "Of course it will be hard on me, but it's not about me. It's about you, your choice, this is where you get to be in charge of how you end your life."

Instead of, "I will miss you so much, Mother, you are the love of my life." If I force myself to now, I can think of all the things I told her that I should have, but that was earlier in the process. I've told her those things less as she gets closer to dying. Maybe now is when she needs to hear them most, but I feel that I should back away and give her all the space she needs to take her leave, not say things that would make her cling to living.

Later that day when I came back, I told her that I'd been thinking about it, and that what would be hard for me would be remembering that I hadn't done enough for her while I could. She picked up a little white pad and her pen, and she wrote in big, clear letters, "No guilt trips!"

She can only swallow very limited times during the day, and so is barely eating or drinking. She hasn't been able to speak except for a few minutes each of the past couple of days, and not at all yet today. It is very unsettling how these symptoms come and go—she won't speak for all day and then suddenly say something clearly and be able to speak for a short time, and then not anymore. Fortunately she can still write, but barely. She told Rita A this morning that her whole body was hurting. It may be a matter of only a few weeks, or even less.

Friday, November 5

Yesterday I began finally what I had intended—one of the things I had intended—to do weeks or months ago, which was to set up the brain donation. I finally got in touch with Mayo Clinic after several turns of phone tag, and spoke with Dr. Dickson's office. Apparently he is the leader in the field of motor disorder neurology in the country, perhaps the world. His lab will do the autopsy and send us a report, and even have the brain shipped from up here, all at no charge to us for donating it to research—but we must find the pathologist to do the "harvesting of tissue."

The receptionist gave me a name of a doctor at Fairfax hospital, who, as it turns out, is no longer there, and she also suggested some other places to start looking. So I spent on the phone from ten in the morning until five forty in the afternoon trying to track down a pathologist in the Northern Virginia area who could "harvest" my mother's brain. It became a little surreal repeating the story and the request to receptionist after pathologist. Most of these people were very kind when they heard the story. There was the initial "I'm sorry" when I began to explain that my mother has a terminal illness and may only live a few weeks. Then at the end of each conversation, there was some feeling not usually present in conversations with professionals—a slight hesitation and then a well-wish: uh, take care, bless you, god bless you and your family—kind phrases like that from nearly everyone. More than just the words, though, there was an honest sympathy in the voices of these people. Of course, in their field, I'm sure they're quite conversant with death.

Fairfax Hospital, when I finally got through to them, suggested one of the university hospitals in D.C., but both George Washington and Georgetown don't do autopsy on non-patients. They suggested Johns Hopkins. It had occurred to me to call them, but Mayo had told me to find one even closer than Fairfax, which is only half an hour away. The woman at GW said she knew Hopkins sometimes does outside autopsy.

And in minutes, after I reached pathology at Hopkins, I was assured that they could do the brain removal in a timely fashion and get it to Mayo, that they often do that for this PSP program, and that funeral homes frequently drive bodies four and five hours to get them to the facility there. Then I called the funeral home to find out about transporting the body—

and finally, after seven hours on the phone, I nearly cracked and said to the woman, "This is so intense." "Yes," she said, "I know."

More and more I see how experience with the death of a parent, or someone else close, can truly change your life. Change your attitude to certain situations, to people in certain situations. Walking in the other person's moccasins. Increase empathy. Why then is there still war? Killing of any sort?

And so, after an alarming report from Rita A this morning, and a day's work on the project, all the preliminary arrangements are made, and even should she die this weekend the valuable brain can be harvested quickly and sent to Mayo where it can do the most good for the many. Time is of the essence.

Mom can only take a few bites a day. She hasn't been able to speak at all for several days, except for a couple of minutes when she sporadically articulates a few sentences. Which are coherent, and relevant to the moment, but not significant in content. She can still write, which is good for she is fine tuning her funeral arrangements now. Her face is pale with dark sunken cheeks. She's having trouble hearing.

I despair that I did not do enough to encourage her to live while she still could, that I focused on her impending death rather than on her remaining life since I've been here, that my motivations for being here and for how I've been with her have not been pure. That I did not bring her as much delight as I could have in her last months, did not make every meal delicious while she could still eat and that I have been selfish with my time and energy, and have failed in my mission. Only I know how self-serving (or evil) I truly am. But my mother has forgiven me everything when I asked her to, and made me promise no guilt trips. So I will let this one little wail be my last about it, and try to do the best I can through her remaining time.

Sunday, November 7, morning

The meditation retreat yesterday with Sally Kempton. I felt a wee bit anxious about driving to the community college campus, the parking, finding the building, all the usual first day of school anxieties, and just as they welled up and I recognized them, I laughed and dismissed them. I had just spent the entire day before on the phone trying to find someone to "harvest" my mother's brain, and the thought that anxiety could arise about going to a meditation workshop made me laugh.

In the heart-space meditation when I was supposed to be visualizing a flower opening and closing in my heart space, I ended up with a little guy dangling from the ladder, letting go, floating in the heart space, then swimming back through sludge to get to the sunlit area in the back where he swung in a hammock until she spoke again about the flower, and then I got all confused. So I told this at Q-and-A when others were telling about their rose that expanded to fill the room, the scent of gardenia, etc., and everyone laughed. But Sally was helpful in telling me that, "If something else besides the instruction takes you deeper, you should follow what takes you the most compellingly into the space."

I can't believe I forgot. Yesterday was my grandmother's birthday, and I had fully intended to do a little ritual with Mom, light a candle, say a prayer, ask for her guidance for Mom in this process. I thought of it at some point early in my time here, then forgot. Scotch? TV?

Mom was eating when I arrived at four, and talking, then shortly after Rita A left she was able to do neither. Her neck was hurting terribly, so I gave her morphine, arnica, Advil, and beer, and sat with her awhile, told her about the meditation retreat, kept reheating her neck pad, and helped her to breathe "hamsa" as I had learned earlier that day. This mantra is supposed to align one with the cosmic Om. Then I made ravioli, spinach and artichoke, with organic pasta sauce. It was too spicy for her, so I gave her some plain ravioli with butter on it, and still she only ate about a tablespoon. Then said she wanted sherbet, and when I served it, she had to go potty, and from there she brushed her teeth and went to bed. She was asleep again by ten. When I open the Restaril and mix it with fruit it seems to hit her a lot faster than when she takes the caps. She was out.

Then Sophie, the new night nurse we hired yesterday, came about ten fifteen, and I went over with her the things I thought she needed to know for night duty. About ten thirty I took her into the bedroom, introduced her to Dad and showed her things on the night table, the suction, oxygen, etc. Then Mom woke up and must write some things, and she could barely hold the pen, much less move it across the page. She wrote "welcome" and Sophie anticipated it, and then something else we couldn't read, and when I said it wasn't important, that we got the message, Mom insisted and wrote again, more clearly, "welcome aboard." A sense of humor even then!

Another effort to write something, and again I tried to dissuade her, telling her it didn't matter right now, it was bedtime, and getting a little short with her, not too bad, and finally got that she was writing, "I thought we could plug it in in her room," referring to the electric chime. Well, it did matter at bedtime to her, but it was a moot point. Again, I was too short, too quick to dismiss. Sophie was wonderful. I think she'll have the kindness and patience to deal with nights. Just before I left, Mom rang the bell, so I took Sophie back there and showed her how the flashlight works, and then I walked out and left them together. Heard nothing after that so it must have been fine.

Sunday, November 7, evening

Wayne came over to visit this evening. I had asked him to come and talk with Mom. His father died Thursday morning. He had quit eating about a week and a half before that, and hadn't moved from bed for some days before that. Wayne and his wife went down to Florida, and Wayne's sister also showed up from Arizona, after not speaking to their dad for the past twenty years, since he left their mother.

Their brother showed up Wednesday night at ten, and the father died three hours later.

Wayne said his dad would look out into the room and ask, "Why did you come down if you don't have all the answers?" then wait a bit and ask again, "But why did you come if you don't have the answers?" then wait a bit, shake his head, and say, "Well, that doesn't seem like a very good way to run things." Wayne thinks he was talking to god, or Jesus, or an angel.

Wayne has talked before with Mom a couple of times about his father, who was also diagnosed with Parkinson's, and had been declining for the past year. It helps her to know of someone else going through a similar process. Wayne told her it took his father ten days to die after he had quit eating. She said, as usual, "That's too long."

Monday, November 8

Mom is religious about her ablutions. She has exquisite skin to show for it. Except for on her worst days, her skin is radiant. People comment all the time on the beautiful quality of her skin.

I'm not there most mornings when she starts every day the same particular way. I don't really know what she does every morning besides brush her teeth. But I am there almost every evening. When she's ready to head for bed she goes into the bathroom first to do her ablutions. First she "cleans her teeth." She brushes her teeth, and flosses them, then she rinses her mouth with water from her silver baby cup, rinses the cup, refills it, and sets it on the counter for the morning. She picks up a plastic cup and fills it with water to swallow her pills. The silver baby cup is only for rinsing.

After she has cleaned her teeth, she washes her face with Phisoderm on a special washcloth, and rinses. Then she washes each eyelid separately, with another special washcloth, a coarse thin cloth called VIC, and a prescription cream, because she has some kind of bugs in her eyelids. At least that's how it sounded to me when she first started this procedure twenty years ago, after some kind of eyelid encrustation and malfunction. I tease her about her eyelid bugs. "She's got bugs on her eyelids," I tell people, and she laughs. She long ago gave up trying to explain the condition to anyone, especially me.

After she has cleaned her eyelids and taken her pills, she "toilets." I'm not sure when "toilet" became a verb, but there you have it, in the healthcare profession, it is in fact a verb. Then she washes her hands, and moves into the bedroom to her vanity.

For most of the nights of her life she simply walked from the master bathroom into the bedroom and sat on her wooden vanity bench to begin her emolliation. In recent months she can no longer stand at the bathroom sink for her ablutions. At first, she sat on the seat of the walker to do them, then walked her walker into the bedroom and sat on the bench. After a few slides off the bench that could have broken bones, we removed the bench and she turned and sat on the seat of her walker. This phase only lasted a few weeks. The turning and sitting was simply too dangerous. Since we have persuaded her into the safety of a wheelchair, I wheel her in to the sink, wheel her to the toilet, wheel her back to the sink to wash her hands, then wheel her out to the vanity.

She sits at her vanity, and now, she opens the jars and bottles by feel. Each application of each emollient is done symmetrically, both hands moving at once in a mirror image. First she takes a finger-dab of Clinique Dramatically Different Moisturizing Lotion, and smoothes it over her face, cheeks first, then forehead, then chin. Then she opens the bottle of NuSkin eye cream, drops one small drop on one index finger, smoothes it between both, and applies it simultaneously to each eye. She follows the eye cream with a small dab of cortisone cream, again divided between two fingers, and this she spreads across her forehead, along her scalp line to her ears, for some skin condition there I know nothing about. Finally, she applies a Vitamin E stick to her lips as carefully as if she were using lipstick.

After her ablutions, she slips into her silk dragon pajamas and then between her raspberry red cotton sheets. I sit and talk with her while the Colonel finishes his ablutions, a whole 'nother story, and we wait for him to come to bed. Then I sit in her chair or on the side of his bed, and read a chapter from her childhood favorites, *The Peterkin Papers* first, then *When We Were Six*, *Alice in Wonderland*, and now, *Eight Cousins*. I give her a dropper of morphine, kiss them both goodnight, and turn out the light. As I walk down the hall every night, I hear the Colonel say, "Goodnight, sweetie. I love you." "I love you too," she said when she was able. And now that she can't anymore, he has started saying a little more. "I love you so much," he says. I wait five or ten minutes, and if she doesn't call for me, I slip out the door, lock it, and go home.

Wednesday, November 10

Dear Elizabeth,

Thank you for letting me know that your mother is free. She fought an incredible, brave fight. I'm so glad it was peaceful, and that you were with her. I'm so glad I got to meet her. She helped me tremendously. You are my hero. Love, Rita

Wednesday, November 10, morning

Had a nice relaxing evening last night at Amy's with bar food for dinner: wings, twice-baked potatoes, shrimp, and baked feta on a balsamic-olive oil bed with olives and thinly sliced red onions. Yum. Watched a little TV and came home early to my Anna Pigeon novel. I'm a little envious of Nevada Barr's writing ability, engrossed in her stories, and totally enjoying the new fancy.

Waiting for the nurse to summon me. Pam called this morning to report more idiocy from the Colonel last night. More pig-headed control-freak jealous interference in Mom's care. No doubt I'll hear about it today while I'm over there, but I've made up my mind that the best course for me is non-involvement. If he has a problem with Pam he can address it himself without involving me. It gave me a headache just hearing about it from her placid point of view.

Apparently Mom suffered neck pain again last night, complained of hurting all over again. I think this is probably because of dehydration and starvation, breakdown in tissue and joints, but she won't give up entirely and so prolongs the process. And she won't give up communication, or trying, even though her writing last night, Pam said, was doodles, just circles, like Elizabeth's mom's was when I was in St. Louis. And she could not speak at all today nor swallow. Oh please, dear, surrender!

Pam said, "What are we going to do when she can't communicate?" I told her the finger-squeeze code, and said we will just have to ask her yes/no questions to figure out what she wants. She is not going gently. Her brother comes in a week. I wonder if she is hanging on for that. Or for her son? I need to ask her. I need to breathe deeply and shake the image of my father's face contorted in suppressed rage, which Pam described so perfectly on the phone this morning.

I said, "I think he's jealous of you, for coming in, being an outsider, Ali loving you and having a rapport, being easy and happy with you the way she is not with him. He's jealous of the relationship you have, he's suspicious, he's a control-freak."

Good form would have it that I oughtn't say things like that to the hired help. I also said, "He doesn't see people as people, he sees them as positions—that's the military way."

Mom isn't able to swallow at all this morning, couldn't get her Sinemet down after half an hour so Rita A had her spit it out. I said to have her rinse with plain water after, and then do that periodically. I think she's so close, but who knows? Who knows? It's terrible.

Elizabeth wrote to say that her mother "lost her fight with PSP on Monday." She had stopped eating for one week exactly. That might offer Mother some comfort. I will tell her this afternoon.

Wednesday, November 10, evening

I have nothing new to say about death. There is nothing new under the sun. But I've been told by people who've seen many deaths that each person's death is unique. So each person's death is a new thing, an unforeseen experience for any witnesses.

Mom asked me from two thousand miles away to help her die when the time came, and I said, "Of course." Once I arrived at her apartment, once I spent hours with her every day, I still thought I could do it, for awhile.

Examining both sides of the feeding tube issue cracked open my first inkling of doubt. It became clear to me when discussing the option of a feeding tube with Mom, her doctor, her Hospice nurse, my friends, that simply quitting eating would be the ideal way for her to end her life. Not putting a bag over her head and inhaling helium.

Mom has been asking Cheryl repeatedly about quitting eating. How long will it take? Will there be pain? Will she be hungry? Cheryl has explained that as a person approaches death, the organs shut down one by one, they take only what they can as they slow down, and then quit functioning. She has told Mom that she will not feel hungry when the time comes because her body will be shutting down. Still, the moment of decision took me by surprise.

Just last night, driving to Amy's, I was composing my thoughts about Mom's refusal to give up. She knows that we can't understand her efforts to speak, most of the time. She knows we frequently can't decipher her less and less legible notes on paper. And yet she continues to speak, she continues to write. What amazes me is that for all the effort it costs her to communicate, she usually has nothing to say. She struggles to make the same kind of idle chatter, or worrying observations, or irrelevant questions, in her disintegrating voice or her agonized scribble, as she used to make in her old voice. In fact, it seems, with the urgency of knowing she has so little time left to communicate, she "speaks" more than ever her inconsequential thoughts. Just think, I consider her thoughts inconsequential, but to her they are all that she has left. All that she has left, and she is damn well going to let them out, every observation, thought, and question.

I arrived for our weekly meeting with Cheryl a few minutes late this afternoon. I came in the bedroom—Mom has always gotten up by afternoon on the few days she's slept in—a little after one o'clock. The Colonel was sitting in his scooter by the bed. Cheryl sat on the bed opposite Mom. Cheryl delivered the big news: "Ali said she forgave Bob."

He unfolded a small piece of white paper and showed it to me. "I Forgive You," written in large letters, clearly.

Then Mom asked Cheryl again for help to end it, and Cheryl offered again to make her comfortable if she chose to quit eating. She said, "OK."

Cheryl and I looked at one another in surprise, and at her. "OK?" I said. "Do you want to stop eating now?"

She nodded.

"OK," I said. "You brave girl. Do you want me to call your son?" She nodded. She indicated she wanted me to call her brother, who was due for a visit in exactly one week. She wanted me to tell him please don't come, it would tire her too much. So I called her brother, and I tried to lie to him but I couldn't. I covered the phone. "Mom, I have to tell him. Please." She nodded. I said, "John, the truth is, Ali may not make it until next Wednesday." He offered to come immediately but she shook her head. A few minutes after that she asked if anyone had called her son. So I picked up the phone and called him, asked him to come as soon as possible.

After her months of agonizing, knowing she had a choice and wanting to make it, her actual making of the choice came without fanfare. The energy in the room shifted. Cheryl made phone calls to order more morphine. I made phone calls to her son and siblings. The Colonel left to go to lunch in the Dining Room. OK, so maybe it wasn't different for him, but everything changed for me. One kind of waiting is over. She has set her mind to leaving.

She stayed in bed the rest of the day, until evening. She wanted to see her studio again. So I helped her into her chair and pushed her into the studio. She sat and looked around, looked at each side and corner of the room, at all her paintbrushes, her piles of papers and projects left undone, stacks of photos, drawings, boxes of beads, the sewing machine, her typewriter that had her flummoxed the last time she tried to use it; her art on the walls; she reviewed the tools, byproducts and fruits of her creative labors over the years. She looked in silence, slowly turning the chair around.

"OK," she said. I pushed her out of the room and asked if she would like to tour the rest of the apartment.

"No," she said.

"Are you sure?"

She nodded. I took her back to bed, and sat with her.

Then I brought the dogs over and moved into the spare bedroom. Sophie was taken ill last night, and can't come back. Life would have been easier if we'd gotten her here a few weeks ago, but now it's a moot point. I'll be here until Mom goes anyway.

Last night, the night before she decided to die, she did her ablutions just the same as always. I wonder if she knew then she was ready to quit. Tonight, I washed her face as she would have done, and smoothed on all her emollients.

Thursday, November 11

"I want to see the kitten," she scrawled on a notepad this morning. I jumped up and drove to my apartment, lured the kitten into the carrier using the bob toy, and drove him, trembling, to visit her. I set his bag on her bed, on her thighs, and zipped open the door, catching him as he tried to flee, holding him gently as she reached her wraithlike fingers out to touch him. They connected. I took her other hand and put the bob toy wand into it, carefully let my hand off the kitten.

I'd like to say she wiggled the bob, the kitten pounced, and Mom laughed. In fact, she was too weak to maneuver the wand, and I had to grab the kitten before he bolted. She did not get to play with the kitten with the toy she gave him. I waited too long to bring him over. But she does have the satisfaction of knowing it was her words that encouraged me to catch him again, and she does know from her own experience the deep and constant delight in store for me in the coming years.

Jock flew up today, and will stay in my apartment and take care of the kitty.

She slept most of the day. At one point she woke and asked to pee, and I told her she didn't have to get up.

"Just one last time," she said. Why did I try to deter her? She seemed so fragile. I feared dropping her, feared her weakness. But of course I gave her what she wanted, as I have done the whole time, no matter how resistant I was at first; I gave her what she wanted, helped her into the wheelchair, helped her onto the toilet.

After she had peed her pungent brown pee, thick from dehydration, I lifted her off the toilet, and held her in my arms. Her tiny, cold feet in her cotton slippers, her birdlike bones at the surface of her fragile flesh, her delicate soft skin—I stood, tall and strong, the mother, and held her as though she were the infant, small and naked. I wrapped my arms around her and held on as she became smaller, as she became the baby I had once been in her arms. We traded places in that naked embrace. I took into myself her motherness, and gave up to her my dependence. We breathed the new air between us. We shifted our feet and came closer. Time paused. There was at least one moment of true communion between us.

Then we moved. I turned her to place her in the wheelchair, and I wheeled her back to the bed.

Saturday, November 13, morning

Last night her friend Inma, a nurse, burst in like an avalanche of comfort. She responded to Inma only by squeezing her hand. Inma said, "Oooh, honey, you so strong!" and to me she said, "It won't be long." Later I called and asked should I turn her again—she came about an hour later and said, "No, don't bother, if you turn her now she will go." So I left her through the night lying on her right side. At some point she peed in the night, in the wee hours, so when Rita A came I said, "Let's turn her and change her pads," so we did as quickly as possible. Rita A put more force into her roll than I was expecting and I didn't catch Mom quite right, and her hand, or her arm, I didn't see, slammed onto the bedrail with a crack—I can't forget that awful moment—I grabbed her hand and leaned close and said, "I'm so sorry, did I hurt you?" But there was no answer, only the agonized eyes looking up at me darkly.

As soon as we turned her she shifted into a different gear and the breath came louder, more ragged, more urgent immediately. So we got her comfortable on her back, and returned all to vigil. That was just after eight.

Saturday, November 13, afternoon

Mother died, eleven twenty this morning.

What I perceived as one sort of struggle at the time I see quite differently now in retrospect.

She had been asking me a question—it started some time earlier, when she was gasping out, "wha—ah—the—" and I could not understand the last word. I was so frustrated that I could not understand the last word, and I wanted so to be able to help her. After I had a little cry with Beth on the phone, and then with Rita A in the hall, I pulled myself back together and was able to return to her calmly. I settled beside her, and stroked her and kissed her. She said, fairly clearly, "Flowers." Aha! John's flowers, that she'd not been able to really appreciate when they arrived last night. So Jock brought the flowers over and we set them on the bed. I took her hand and touched the flowers and told her what they were, I held the vase up in case she could see, I pulled a tulip from the vase and told her its colors, and stroked her cheeks with it, and laid it on her breast bone under which that tenacious heart would simply not give up.

Then she began another question. "Wha—ah—th—" Again I could not understand the word, again I felt despair! Finally I said, "Oh mama, if you are asking for something here, I cannot understand what you want. There is nothing left here that you need, you can let go—if you are talking to someone on the other side, ask away, and they will get you what you need." She continued to ask the same question—breath—word—breath—word—and by word I mean a barely intelligible sound, intelligible only because of the very slight change in her lip shape and tongue placement in an open mouth that could not shape the full syllables—breath—word—breath—word. Then I joked, "Hey, your last words shouldn't be asking me for something that I can't understand what you want, your last words are supposed to be 'Cut the crap!' "

Immediately her lips shifted—her words became "cut the crap"—though it sounded like so much less, but I could tell, it was very clear. And she stuck on those words for a long time. Dad said something about it being an involuntary reaction—maybe it was, something for her to hang on to to get the breath out, I don't know. Anyway, I knew even then it was the joke. Her daughter-in-law had told us over the summer that when her grandmother died, her last words had been "Cut the crap!" and we had all joked ever since that those would be Ali's last words. But the effort in her face—I thought it was an effort to hang on.

I see now it was her effort to let go—she was not struggling to cling, but struggling to leave, and despite all the morphine and the Ativans, she was very present up to and including her last breath. She was willing her soul to leave that body. She was cutting that disease down to size. She was shedding all from this world that she no longer needed, cutting the crap. And then she was gone.

The Hospice nurse that came laughed when I told her Mom's last words, and she said, "People are fully themselves at a time like this." She said how much you can tell about a personality by last words. Then she noted the raspberry bed sheets, and said that all this told her what a wonderful woman Mom had been and she'd have liked to have met her. She said, "She was taking herself out with that phrase, and what could be more better? Cut the crap! Get it over with. Leave it behind."

And so Rita A and I uncovered her, bathed her, and dressed her in her clean blue hospital gown and laid her out on her bed. And just then the men came from the funeral home. They wrapped her in a sheet and lifted her off the bed onto the gurney, leaving her face uncovered as they wheeled her out. Bob came from his desk for one last look, and broke down, said, "This is bad, I shouldn't have done this."

The Colonel spent his time since she died making phone calls, both to make it real to himself, I think, and as a way of dealing with his feelings. He went back to making arrangements. In the end, he gave her what she needed, and she forgave him. They crossed the chasm between them on a filamental bridge. He held her hand as she lay dying, and wept when she was gone.

He was in the room until a few minutes before she died, and so was Jock. They left, I think, burned out by her struggle to cut the crap, so Rita A and I were left there each holding one of her hands. She pulled her hands away from us, maybe just muscular contraction, but I think, more, that she was reaching for something else, and letting us go literally. I let hers slip from mine with the first pressure from her and looked over to Rita A who was hanging on. She asked, "Should I let go?" and I nodded; she did, and that hand too rose. Then the breaths—Jock came back in during her last gasping, rattling breaths, and Rita A said, "This is it." He sat on Dad's bed and watched. I never took my eyes from her and still I cannot say I saw the moment.

Rather, I did see the moment, but I can't describe what I saw. Her hands lowered, and I let her curled fingers rest in my hand for her last breaths. I said, "We're here, and we love you." I saw her flooded with rest, her body at least, relieved. Peace washed down her. I kept my eyes on her face as it went through its changes, as her lips paled. A few more sips of air, and she washed away. I waited. Then I checked her wrist pulse, and it wasn't there. Then I put my hand on her heart, that tenacious heart, and it was still. I looked over at Jock, who had tears in his eyes.

"Is she gone?" he asked.

"Yes," I said.

And he sobbed, and got up and left to cry outside. Rita A also began to cry, and she got up to leave, as though only my words had made it real, though they had seen it with their own eyes. They, I guess, had not felt the absent heart, so needed confirmation. I had some minutes alone with my mother to cry. I heard them offer comfort to each other in the hall and then they came back in the room.

"Did anyone tell the Colonel?" I asked. No. "Jock, please go tell the Colonel."

When Dad came in he went to her side and reached for her hand and kissed it, and then he too wept. Rita A was kneeling on the floor at the foot of the bed weeping, and the Colonel made an angry face and jerked his thumb toward her, and looked to Jock for support of his righteous indignation, but Jock was in the dark about Dad's dark feelings; I refused to participate in his selfish effort to keep the grief all his own. But in a moment I did get up and draw Rita A out, said let's leave them alone with her, and we went into the living room to weep some more. I went straight to the phone and called Hospice, then got on the phone with Johns Hopkins, and set in motion the wheels that came to collect her within the hour. After that she was never alone, one or the other of us came and went, and we each had time alone with her, and I cried some more with her, and kissed her taut dead flesh.

When Rita A and I dressed her, I could see bruises where she had lain so long the night before, on her thighs and side. But no bedsores. Some places where the diaper of the first night had left her still red, and some other places that would have become bedsores had she stayed much longer and we not turned her several times.

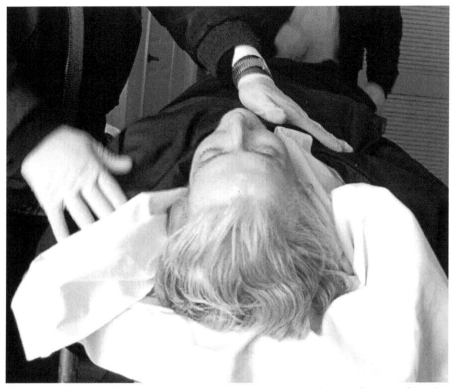

The next to last time I would see my mother, on the gurney for her final exit from her apartment. In death, the burn scar on her forehead became visible again.

Part 3: *After*

November

Saturday, November 13, evening

Now it is late again, my usual time to write, and I feel her absence.

After they took her body away, we all did our separate things. Rita A went through drawers in the bedroom throwing away trash, pills and things so I would not have to do so later, and sorting her jewelry on the table. Who knows what she might have thrown out that wasn't trash in Ali's eyes? Anyway, she spared me the trauma of going over every little thing, and left a neat array of jewelry boxes—had even gone through the drawer. I hadn't intended for her to do that. I sure hope she didn't throw away something worthwhile or valuable. I found a little pincushion in a basket in the top of her trash bag, and I had to keep it.

Jock went to buy groceries for Dad, who I fear will take to drink again and not last long after. I went into her studio and felt completely overwhelmed. The magnitude of the stuff to sort through in that room alone. It's the most cluttered room in the house, and every bit of the clutter meant something special to her. I looked at the itinerary I had sent her for our Utah trip. On a sheet of watercolor paper, I had used watercolor pencils to draw an arch, a cliff, a winding road, the mittens of Monument Valley, the lodge at Torrey, Lake Powell, one sketch for each night including our first and last at my little yellow cabin on Lamborn Mesa. I wrote the name and phone number of the lodging at the bottom of each square, so the Colonel would have it while we were away. She kept it for a dozen years, propped on a shelf. I kept it to take home with me.

I also discovered and gathered up stacks of her drawings. The trees I used to climb at Big Meadows where we vacationed for years, drafts of all her Christmas cats and other Christmas cards, studies I've never seen for paintings I know well from thirty years ago. From simple pencil sketches to intricate ink pictures, every single drawing is a record of a moment of my mother's life. There are dozens, maybe hundreds. I can't bear to keep them all.

There's one that I know the exact moment she took the photograph she drew it from. We were in Yellowstone in 1989, the year after the fires. There is a stand of wind-curved saplings blackened by flames in the foreground, with a little bit of green and yellow grass she colored in on this stark and startling pen and ink. She washed the mountain range in the far background a pale grayish blue. It was before the wolves. She would have loved them. After the fires, before the wolves. We could not stop taking pictures of burned trees. The Colonel required a cane at that point. He remained in the car while we jumped out again and again to photograph the trees, the waterfalls, the bison. We had crested a hill on the south side of the park and the valley stretched before us. Just to our left was this stand of saplings. We crossed the road to get the proper angle.

I left the apartment about three, leaving Jock with the Colonel, and drove to the park to walk the dogs. As I left the complex, I felt her with me. I laughed, thinking, I'm taking my mother for a walk in the park!

I walked along the bay trail. It was bitter and windy, but sunny and lovely. I played the dogs a bit on the beach, where someone had written in the sand. I picked up a stick and wrote in letters taller than she had been, ALI. The tide was coming in in waves, and would soon carry her away. At the end of the trail today, deep through the woods on the far side of the bay, I came upon a flock of tundra swans on the water. I've never seen them there before. "Are you my mother?" I asked. I felt, in a way, that they were.

I remembered the times I brought her out there to sit and watch the boats and birds on the bay. The first time was Memorial Day, the last Sunday in May. A mere five and a half months ago. We went many times after that, but not enough. Each time we drove, she wanted to listen to *Man of La*

Mancha. I tried the last time to substitute *Carmen*, but a few songs into it she wanted Don Quixote.

Last night I asked her if she'd like to listen to a little music, after she'd stopped responding to everything else and responded only to what she really wanted to. She nodded. Do you want *Man of La*—and she nodded again. So we played that. I slipped out at the end for a dog need, but Bob had come in and I'd shushed him so he wouldn't interrupt her hearing the last few tender, triumphant lines of "The Impossible Dream." Later, I put on the CD Beth had sent her in the summer, and played that over now and then throughout the rest of the vigil.

What keeps coming to me in new ways is the realization of how remarkable a feat she really pulled off. She made up her mind, and once decided, she went and did it in short order. She said all along that she was not scared. She was sad, she said, when I asked, but not scared. And then she was gone.

Certainly Tuesday while I was casually dining at Amy's I did not know that Wednesday would be the beginning of her departure. It's amazing how sudden it was once she made up her mind. And how the time flew the past three days. I was so absorbed in the process that hours would fly by and I could not remember: had I just given her morphine, or had that been half an hour or an hour ago? I lost track of time even while watching the clock. At the moment of her death I was mesmerized, and could not look away. She had made me chuckle, and I hope she took that knowledge with her. She gave me a token to hang onto in her last words, though I did not understand that at the time; a knowledge for me that she was conscious and that she was okay. Somehow.

Monday, November 15

I did her ablutions for her the first night. The next day, I smoothed lotion over her arms and legs. But then, I think I lost sight of those physical comforts in the last two days. Once she went to bed after that final embrace, it was as though she had crossed a bridge, and maybe even then left her body behind. I must have washed her face each night though I don't remember. I wish I had smoothed lotion over her poor desiccated limbs several times each day. Wish I had rubbed and touched her tenderly time and again those last several days.

I wish I'd let Wayne and Maryann in to see her on Friday night, when they brought over dinner for me and Jock. I barely emerged from the Dying Room and couldn't eat more than a few bites. But Jock appreciated the good food, and they helped him get through that evening. I kept them from her, thinking that if she hadn't even wanted her *brother* to be there—and that they weren't really family—but I was wrong about that. Wayne has been like a brother to me, and was quite a comfort to her in those last months, especially in their conversation, telling her about his father's death just weeks before, from stopping eating.

As she lay dying I sat beside her and held her hand, spoke with her, prayed with her, and wept in her arms. I lay my head gently on her chest and cried, told her how I would miss her, and how much I loved her. Cried like a baby. She laid one featherweight arm across my back and cupped her other hand over my head, lightly stroked my hair, murmured her love for me.

I crushed ice chips in my teeth and slipped them between her parched lips, moistened her mouth with a swab, dripped morphine into her cheek every hour or half. "Do you want more morphine?" I asked one time. "There's a dearth of morphine," she answered.

I promised her I would tell her story, that her struggle with PSP would not be in vain. I read to her the last chapters of *Eight Cousins* the first night, condensing them to fit the evening, in case there was not another chance. The next night she wanted the room dark, with only the hall light and the light from the living room filtering in. I sang to her the only lines from "Silent Night" I could remember, over and over.

I had intended to be completely present at her death, at her dying. I had intended to give her every comfort she could want, anticipate her needs, hold up and bear her bravely along to her end. I had intended to coddle and caress her, and the truth is, in the intensity of those last days and nights, I fear that I forgot her ablutions.

Would I feel better now if I had shut the door and had more than five minutes alone with my mother's body, after my father and brother had mourned, after Rita A had mourned, if I had just shut the door and sat with her with my full attention on her, would I today feel like I had properly said goodbye?

I remembered, as her agitation seemed to increase, something Wayne had said about giving his father a bit of Ativan. I broke a pill in half, and touched it to the wet swab, and put it in her mouth above her dangling jaw, which snapped shut with the speed and strength of a snapping turtle— to trap her last drop of water? I struggled to turn the swab between her clenched teeth to put the Ativan on her tongue, and then I slowly, gently, pried her teeth apart with the paper stick and removed the swab.

I didn't want her to die with a swab in her mouth. What was that about? Why did I feel compelled to extricate the swab from her mouth? Always taking what she wanted, is that what she was thinking? *She's always taking away what I want!* Maybe all she wanted was to suck as much water out of the swab as she could. I was startled, a little alarmed, by her snapping action—I cannot say why I forced the swab from her mouth, nor what direction that may have turned her dying. It was a part of her dying, of that I'm sure. Did I derail her process, her trajectory toward the divine? Toward whatever tunnel of light or bottomless pit awaited her?

Tuesday, November 16

The memory of those last few minutes, those gasping breaths, will not subside—she was sipping air and then she just stopped. I watched her body go yellow from top to bottom as the life left it. I held her hand and watched and watched. I reached my fingers to her wrist, and held them there for a long moment. Then still holding her fingers in mine I reached my other hand and spread it on her chest, to feel for heartbeat. There was nothing. Literally. There was nothing. No heartbeat, of course, but more nothing than that. She was gone, and there was nothing, no soul or spirit remaining in the room, no lingering. She was utterly gone. Nothing I have read or heard about, none of my limited spiritual training, prepared me for this: Nothing.

Wednesday, November 17

Auntie came yesterday and has been wonderful company, great consolation and a big help sorting things like jewelry. We may get to the closets before she leaves. John and Clara came today, Jock and Caron tomorrow. There was much I wanted to observe on today earlier, but I am just too damn tired to even think, so I'm going to go read.

247

Thursday, November 18

Well, mama, you'd have liked the day today—balmy autumn. It began with a gentle shower and cleared to a beautiful sunny afternoon. You'd have liked your pine box, but I guess you chose that ahead of time. I liked it, very elegant. You'd have liked Father John's service, it was so short it was over before I had a chance to really tune in. I was looking around at all the autumn colors in the trees, which still had lots of leaves, and at the Jewett headstone on the other side of the giant oak, and at your box. Pa was sniffling beside me. Your old friend David showed up! I'm not sure how he knew, because it wasn't in the paper, but there he was just in time to join the procession of two limos, a car, and a van with Dad's scooter.

Dad had originally thought he'd just ride in a limo and wait at the bottom of the hill, so that's what I arranged for on Monday. But this morning he called Everly Funeral Home and arranged for them to take him in a van, and at the time of departure at the circle, he decided to ride in front in the limo with some of us, and let the scooter go alone in the van. It was well worth it. He really needed to be up at the top of the hill. The two limo drivers walked up flanking him to keep the scooter steady as he drove it.

Today during this ritual, and last night when we went to Althea's for drinks, I had this strong sensation of cradling you in my arms as though you were baby size. I held you there at Althea's, and I held you at the cemetery.

In fact, I brought your box down to the Family Sitting Room at the cemetery, and set it in the middle of the coffee table amongst us, thinking everyone else would like it to be there too. But I was wrong. The Colonel grumbled, "Nothing puts a damper on a conversation like that," and Rita got a little weepy. John gritted his teeth. Rita said, "We were talking about toenail clippings," and I said, "There's nothing inappropriate at this point," and John said rather vitriolically, "Have you watched TV lately?" So after a few more minutes of awkward silence I said, "Well, I'll go ahead and take this back upstairs then." I said "this" to spare them. I was thinking, I'll take her back upstairs. I was a little disappointed in them all.

I am still just speechless at how courageous you were and how quickly you took yourself out once you made up your mind. Mom, it was a beautiful and inspiring thing to see. I'm trying not to feel guilty for time I didn't spend with you, for not moistening your lips enough, for interfering in your last words, trying to give you an Ativan to ease what I perceived as distress—trying not to feel guilty, and your note about no guilt trips is helping. But I doubt I am worthy of your death. It was a magnificent thing to watch, and I will see those last breaths of yours for years to come, each time deriving a deeper understanding of you and life and myself. Your ultimate gift was to give me those last few minutes with you. You became all you ever could have wanted to be in your death, dearest. And I am here to attest to it.

I already miss you so much. The hole where you are not grows deeper every day. I hold you inside me with the deepest tenderness, and hope you are well on your journey through the subtle realms. I hope that one day I may hear from you more clearly than I think I already have. I love you dearly.

Saturday, November 20

Dearest Mother,

Well, your memorial service went off beautifully. All kinds of people came. Robin and Freddy were there, and I told Robin that you'd been thinking of calling her all summer but hadn't because you couldn't talk well. She said if anyone had called she'd have rushed right over. Tracy came, you remember, your PT from up at Christy's. Christy couldn't come but sent her best, and Tracy said when she saw the death notice in the paper she told Christy, "I don't care what you've got planned for Friday, I'm not working Friday afternoon." The Morans were there! You know Laura had called while I was reading to you one of those last nights, and I called back and left a message with details about the memorial, and there they were, Emelia, Otis, and Laura.

Elinor Carter played the organ, and everyone was doing great with all the hymns you chose, 'til the last one, "There's a Wideness in God's Mercy." I couldn't figure out why it sounded soft and muddy, and after the first verse Father John walked over to Elinor and she folded up the book, then he turned to us and said, "One of the great things about the Anglican Church is that we try to be accommodating, and so in some cases we have not one, not two, but three versions of the same hymn, and in this case Ali was very specific that she wanted Beecher's version"—he looked at me—"Right? Beecher?" Right, I nodded. So Elinor found it, and we began again, and now the voices were lifted up in hearty worship and sounded as big and solid as all the previous hymns. Also, Father John said at the very beginning of the service, that you had designed the whole service and picked out the hymns in the past two weeks, and so everyone should know they were participating in something you had created, which I thought was a wonderful thing to say. He did a lovely job for you.

But guess what the Colonel did last night? Drank too much I guess. Fortunately, Jock and Caron were still at the apartment. He fell backwards while zipping his pants after peeing, standing up, not holding on. Shot the buzzer off, and the nurse came and said he wasn't seriously hurt, but he's bruised so badly he can't sit up today, can't get into his scooter. He'll need full time care for awhile with toileting, eating, etc. Jock called me this morning at nine thirty to tell me. I thanked him for calling, and for not calling sooner. I spoke with Bob at ten last night! He called to ask me some question I don't even remember, I was already asleep and he woke me up. I wonder—did you push him?

What a crashing end to a great service and a good party celebrating your life. All your girlfriends wept. You may have been right about the scavengers—he may end up remarrying—he's mentioned countless times in just one week how lonely it is there without you. Then he goes and falls, and who knows, this may be the last straw that puts him on the Third Floor for good. And I may end up emptying out that apartment completely by the end of the year. I'm so relieved that Beth is coming tomorrow, though none of it is what we thought it was going to be when she planned her trip.

Was there more I wanted to tell you about the service? Oh, David came to the service and I sat him at the end of the family row next to Rita where there was an empty seat, and I think he helped take the edge off it for her, kept her good company during the rest of the event. Wayne came, and Debbie, Amy and her mom Judy, Dottie and Bill Olin, Bruce Stewart came, Father Frizzell of course. You were surrounded in spirit by many who loved you whom you hadn't seen for years. Melinda and her brothers and their spouses sent the loveliest bouquet, which sat at the altar.

Rita A couldn't come sing, but she told me a dream yesterday that she had about you. Kind of similar to my dream of Grammer after she died, when she said, "I'm fine, I'm just tired, I'm going with the Jewish people next door." In Rita A's dream, you were dead, but you got up to go into the hall, and Rita A tried to tell the Colonel that you were going somewhere, and he couldn't see you and kept saying, "Rita, there's nobody there," but she could see you, and you were fine and you were going somewhere. So I took some comfort from that dream. I just wish it had been mine.

The hole opens ever wider each day. I now have the luxury to miss you that I could not do while I was managing every detail of your care.

Wednesday, November 24, morning

Beth is here at last, arrived Sunday morning, and has been an angel for three days, keeping me smiling, calm, and somewhat focused despite the distraction of getting Bob squared away first in the hospital and now, today, we hope, on the Third Floor.

We went through the closets and dressers, which was edgy at moments. Gaytha came up on Monday and helped in the bedroom and closet, and the three of us took what we thought we could use, and the rest remains for an easy sweep into Goodwill delivery. The hard part begins today with the studio.

I have felt more and more removed from my mother in the effort of managing the Colonel's care. I was feeling her every day, so close, until he crashed in with his nameless pain. Nothing shows anything in hospital tests. I know, the dark side of this is that he is falling apart inside and seeking succor in the physical babying that comes from being helpless in bed. He is asking in a baby voice for *peanny butter and jelly sammiches* and milk, and happily telling me irrelevant stories while I change his poopy diaper. It's all wrong. I want to be clean clear and focused on my mother, and I know she's angry about this too.

Wednesday, November 24, evening

Beth blonded and cut my hair tonight, what fun! Have spoken with Auntie every night, also, and that is good too. We are all very tired.

Bob arrived at the Third Floor this afternoon about three thirty, after Beth and I had set up his room a little bit with his TV and some bath things. Beth again helped with changing his diaper and was very tender and concerned with him. I cannot help but feel a bit disgusted by his babyish demeanor.

We puttered through a few more things in the house, including the book shelf in the living room, where I ran across two photo books I'd made for mom, one from Alaska, which made me break down, and another with poems and photos from where I live, which I didn't quite get through looking at before we got the call that Bob had arrived. So I've felt on the verge of tears ever since then, and may well for a long time to come.

Beth and I discussed my plans for leaving, and now it feels like I might just take all winter to get home, spend some time in Florida on the way, and arrive at the end of March, having been gone one whole year of pilgrimage.

Friday, November 26

Two days after Mom died, I was required to go to the funeral home in my capacity as executor of her estate to identify her body, make final arrangements, and pick out the prayer cards. She had said when the Hospice chaplain sat down with her on the edge of her bed in her darkened room, to help her plan her memorial service, that she wanted "one of those things the Catholics have."

"A prayer card?" he said. She nodded vigorously. I wouldn't have had a clue. I would have probably offered an incense burner.

So I went to the funeral home downtown in Arlington on some hilly side street. In the impersonal lobby, a fisheye view of a faraway receptionist who tells me where to go while I aim for the elevator. Perhaps this is the place where mother transfers to daughter, and daughter takes over management completely, of the family, of the future. Upstairs I met with my "memorial representative," lots of new terms to learn, new rules about dying and what gets done, lots of papers to sign.

Finally I was left alone with the Book of Memories, an encyclopedia of prayer cards: the Virgin Mary, pages 1-4; Jesus with the crown of thorns, page 7; Jesus with stigmata, Jesus and the stations of the cross, all the saints one after another, and then I find St. Francis. I find his prayer and I think of my mother introducing me to birds, her love of the vulnerable precious tiny living things outside. Birds, turtles, squirrels, stray kittens, she treasured their little lives, treating them as tenderly as the good Saint when they came within her range. Though in the astringent safety of her house the Orkin man came often, and I had to sneak spiders and flies outside,

outside all that lived was cherished: the squirrels we fed peanuts out the back door, mockingbirds who came as family year after year, chickadees and goldfinches always a special treat. I learned to love birds from her.

And this may have been the first clear message I got from my mother after her death. There in the sterile, polished hardwood room, surrounded by samples of coffin satin, looking at the Book of Memories, I knew with certainty I'd found the right prayer card out of thousands when I found St. Francis. This was so compelling it felt like she was telling me, "This one." I had no doubt. And so St. Francis, reaching toward birds in the branches of a tree, went out at Ali's memorial service with each program, proclaiming:

> *Lord make me an instrument of Thy peace; where there is hatred, let me sow love; where there is injury, pardon; where there is doubt, faith; where there is despair, hope; where there is darkness, light; and where there is sadness, joy. O Divine Master, grant that I may not so much seek to be consoled, as to console; to be understood, as to understand; to be loved, as to love; for it is in giving that we receive; it is in pardoning that we are pardoned and it is in dying, that we are born to eternal life.*

Then my memorial representative came back into the room, led me out, and deferentially opened the door that led to the cool narrow chamber where the body lay on a gurney, sandwiched between white sheets folded down below her chin. Her head lay on a pillow, hiding the incision from the harvest of her brain. I stood looking and looking, her yellowed flesh waxen and cold to touch, oddly firm, utterly still. I wanted to feel her presence but I didn't. I wanted to sit for hours with her body as I hadn't the day she died. I spoke but I don't know what I said. She both was not there and was. Was she inside me even then, already? Is what I have of her only what's within? Isn't there anything else outside myself that remains of her?

Ali always loved the animals, and taught me to cherish wildlife. I chose a prayer card for her memorial service with St. Francis and his prayer.

Five Years Later

*I*n the grocery store yesterday I encountered in aisle after aisle an elderly woman using a walker, shoulders rounded, her face pointing toward the floor and her neck straining to let her look up toward the items on the shelves. A middle-aged man, burly and patient, accompanied her, reaching for items, discussing them with her.

I remembered coming out of the Safeway in Lorton with my mother when she was still using her walker, standing close with an arm ready to stabilize her if she staggered. A small Mexican man beamed at us.

"Is you mama?" he asked.

"Yes," I said, smiling, tearing up. He was so joyful.

"God will bless you for looking after you mama," he proclaimed, "God will bless you!" And he walked on.

I felt like speaking to this man at the Natural Grocer in Grand Junction, but could not find the words to express the richness of my emotions at seeing him shopping with his ailing mother. I was overcome. "God will bless you," I wanted to say, "for taking care of your mother." But there was so much more to it than that. "Love her now, you will miss her when she's gone," I wanted to say. "Cherish every moment with her." My heart was full, watching them.

For one thing, she looked like she might have PSP. I heard her ask him about some pasta, and in her gravelly, slurred speech I heard PSP. After inadvertently passing them a couple of more times, I discreetly began to follow them. I convinced myself that she did have PSP, and that I could offer some help. I approached them.

"Excuse me," I said, looking first to him, then to her, and spoke to her, "I can see that you have a health challenge, and I can't help but ask you, is it PSP?"

"Celiac sprue," said the son. "I have celiac sprue," said the woman, sweetly.

"Oh!" I said, my flash fantasy of helping caught short, not knowing exactly what to say next. "Oh. I just wondered. I thought you might have the disease my mother had, and maybe I could help—" foundering for words, mild irritation in the eyes of the son, nothing but compassion in the woman's eyes. "Thank you," she said, "but mine is celiac sprue."

Mine. Claiming ownership of her disease. "Well," I said, "good luck with everything." We smiled, and I turned away. Not PSP. Not so different, perhaps, in the end; so many ways our bodies fail us, turn us inside out.

Five years after my mother died, I still miss her every day. Some days more than others. When I see an old person stooped, frail, drooling, on a walker or in a chair, I see my mother, and I want to help. Every Sunday, I see an eighty-year-old neighbor with PSP. I take her to church, then out for a Sunday drive if the weather is fine.

Lily moved in across the canyon from my house last summer. I met her son first, while he was working on the house before she moved in, and I stopped to welcome him to the neighborhood. He told me his mother "has some weird, rare brain disease with some really long name that makes her fall—"

"PSP?" I asked.

"No, it's not some sissy disease," he said, "it's really awful."

I ruffled at his suggestion that PSP is a sissy disease. "Progressive Supranuclear Palsy," I said, "It's not a sissy disease. It makes people fall backwards—"

"—Yeah, that's it," he interrupted, "she just falls straight back!"

I enumerated some of the other symptoms.

"Yeah, that sounds like it," he said. "I know it's got 'super' in it."

Lily arrived a few weeks later. When I went in her lovely new home to meet her, I saw Elizabeth's mother, and my own mother, a little gray-haired

258

lady with frail limbs sitting in a chair, leaning stiffly forward, squinting up at me with one eye shut, her sluggish voice dragging past a drooping, swollen lower lip, her hand slowly coming up to shake mine. I could have met that woman on the street and said she has PSP just by looking at her. It was June, and I had brought flowers from my garden. I trimmed the flowers and arranged them in two glass vases from her cabinet, and put them in two places where she didn't have to raise her eyes to be able to see them.

Her son left me alone with her for about ten minutes while he ran out to check on something. She got nervous when he left, looking around, fluttering her hands anxiously. She looked at me through the other eye with the first eye closed. I said, "Do you see double if you look through both eyes?" and she said, "Yeeess." I asked if her eyes hurt from the brightness and she said, "Yeeess." I brought her sunglasses from the bedroom.

I asked Lily if she had been told what to expect, and she gave me a confused account of where and when she had been diagnosed, but she didn't answer the question. I saw a tear below her dark glasses. She told me she was diagnosed a couple of years ago, and in the past year has been getting worse quickly.

"I have three sons," she told me, and added a little wistfully, "No daughters." Her husband is dead. I wondered if she had anyone to really talk with about her life, her feelings, her physical decline and approaching death. My heart ached for her, and for her family, her sons and her caregivers. None of them had looked into what was coming down the road for her with PSP, how the deterioration would manifest, how bad it could get while she kept on living.

I told her how my mother and I had come to embrace the concept of "the new normal," how things go along for awhile, then some aspect gets worse or a new symptom arises, and that becomes the new normal, and you figure out how to live with the new normal, until there is another new normal. I took her hand again to say goodbye, and she placed her other thin hand on my arm as we looked long at each other.

Within a few months I became part of Lily's caregiving team. I have been able to guide her family and her caregivers as new symptoms arise and old symptoms become worse. We got her into Hospice care, and now she receives weekly visits from her nurse, a highlight of her week. She "progressed" from her walker to a wheelchair. Her speech deteriorates slowly.

"My vision's getting worse every day," she said on the drive to lunch in town one afternoon, riding down the midwinter drab highway. "I don't know what my future holds."

"Well... what do you think it holds?"

"I'm going blind."

This was as far as her thoughts about her future had progressed. Not, as mine would have aeons before now, to thoughts of death. But she is so tired. Every day is a struggle for her to navigate without falling, injuring herself, feeling embarrassed. She has mentioned to me several times concerns about her deterioration. I have told Lily that this disease is like getting older faster.

The will to live is a force more powerful than those of us living in good health can imagine. We often say that we don't want to live if we reach a certain point of incapacitation, but what I have seen women with PSP endure, rather than capitulate to, challenges the notion of checking out when the going gets tough.

I saw it with my mother, with Elizabeth's mother, and I see it now with Lily. She totters when she stands to transfer herself from lift chair to wheelchair. She manages with safety poles installed beside her bed and by the toilet; still, she cannot safely dress or undress with the poles alone, she requires assistance. Her speech is becoming noticeably slurred, and at times incomprehensible. She can still call up articulation when pressed to do so. Frequently her words emerge in less than a whisper, on barely a breath. We can still understand, but we ask her to repeat these whispered comments in order for her to practice articulation while she still can.

She still has not been told the nature of this disease and what is in store for her. But she begins to comprehend that it is not going to get better, and slowly it dawns on her that this accumulation of "not getting better," and "mostly bad days," is leading somewhere beyond blindness. Her son insists that she does not want to know. That she's never been very smart, she doesn't want to think about death. He says I must not tell her anything about her disease. It is excruciating to look at her and know what's in store for her. If I can just sit with her and let her know she's not alone that has to be a comfort.

The other day, coming home after a beautiful spring drive, she told me that she keeps hoping it will get better. I thought hard about what to say. Hope can be a helpful thing, but I think when it is constantly dashed it can be counter-productive. Finally, I told Lily that it might, and I hoped it would, but that it is not in the nature of this disease to get better. I told her that when my mother finally got tired of the symptoms of PSP, she chose to leave it behind. I told her to remember that if she gets sick and tired of being sick, that she has the option of leaving it behind, and asked her to talk with me if she gets to feeling like that.

We all imagine that we will always have all our capacities. We all imagine what we will say in this or that situation to this or that person. What I really want to say to Lily is this: I can't bear that you're sick. I hate that you will have to go through what you're going to have to go through. I don't want you to feel alone. I want you to know that I understand and I hate it and I want it to be different but it's not. Whatever I can do, whoever I can be to you, I want to be.

Currently I am advocating for Hospice to provide a speech therapist for Lily. She is past due for some help with her speech and her swallowing. She is going to ask at some point, "What's happening to me?" and the rest of her team needs to understand that by the time she asks this, she could be incoherent. They need to know what she really wants before she gets that way, they need to be paying attention and communicating, learning what she wants before she can't communicate it to them.

There is this underlying sense of urgency, which I must not transfer from my experience with my mother onto this family's experience with Lily. These people may well be able to handle this shattering decline better than I was able to. But I do know how staggeringly frustrating and painful it was to try to communicate with my mother when she had lost her ability to speak, lost her ability even to write on a notepad; how infuriatingly helpless I felt knowing that she had something to say and she was unable to say it. Her last vestige of communication. Can you imagine what it is to be without that ability?

The relative importance of what a person who cannot articulate wishes to say is not mine or someone else's to evaluate. The important thing is her ability to convey what she feels the need to say. Often my mother struggled for five or ten minutes or more to convey a thought, which when finally comprehended was inconsequential. A punchline far too late, a pleasantry bludgeoned by effort into awkwardness, a question long ago answered. A random thought that a speaking person would have forgotten saying by the time my mother managed to articulate or write it. Yet at the end stages of her disease, these thoughts were all that she had left of herself, her last slip of paper. Uncomfortable as her effort or inconsequential as her thoughts may have been to us, it was of utmost importance to her that they be articulated and understood. And sometimes, it was important, what she struggled to say: "I need morphine." "My bowels are impacted."

This matter of declining communication brings up several things I would say to someone who becomes a caregiver of a person with PSP, and I'll return to the subject of voice later. I'll start with some other important things I learned while caring for my mother in her last year.

Tip #1: Never take at face value the doctors' reports. The importance of a person investigating and pursuing questions on his or her own medical conundrum or that of a loved one, cannot be overstated. Doctors don't know everything, and much of what they do know they neglect to tell patients and caregivers. Ask. Ask. Ask. Look things up. Find people in similar situations and talk with them.

Tip #2: People who tell you that the caregiver must take care of the caregiver are right. You cannot afford to burn out. You must take time off, find pleasure where you can, and share the burden with others, either volunteers, family, or hired help. Most of us simply cannot do this emotionally and physically arduous labor alone. Set up some sort of relief network or system, whether you are caring for your person at home and largely alone, or whether she is in a full-time care facility, or any place on the spectrum between. Arrange visits of friends, family, Hospice, health aides, whoever is called for at the time, to give you respite in your job. If your person is in a care facility, know that you cannot be there all the time and that you need to schedule your visits while leaving time out for your own life.

Each person involved needs to find some way, with others or alone, to ground themselves in the joy of living while being in the presence of such extreme suffering. People suffer in different degrees, which I think has nothing to do with courage and more simply with endurance. As someone said recently about my mother, "She just had to be a burden on you," and I laughed as I tried to explain that she was and she wasn't, and that I would not have had it any other way.

Tip #3: Caregivers must let go of reacting to the accidents that befall their charges, and accept that poor judgment is an unfortunate, inherent part of the disease. Your "person with PSP" is not being willful and disobedient on purpose. Cultivate not reacting to these lapses with anger, disappointment, or aggravation, because reacting causes pain and frustration, and frustration contributes to burnout.

Despite her physical limitations, for a long time my mother wanted to keep doing everything herself, and she never knew when to stop doing it herself. Lily is the same way. She is mentally competent and so she assumes she is physically competent. When her brain says, "Get up and go get the water," her body gets up to go get the water; there is no filter that says, "Oops, I can't do that anymore." The inability to make good judgments is a symptom of the disease. I think that's because the cognizant brain really does stay at a healthy place in general, and it's the functional brain, the neuromuscular control, that fails, and the cognitive brain doesn't get notified. Eventually maybe it does, or the person learns over time, after enough falls and wounds; towards the end, my mother surrendered to having people do things for her. It's a really frightful stage where a person wants to get up and move around but she can't do it herself and she's not capable of admitting it. However unconsciously, it's denial, a misfire perhaps, an electronic denial.

Tip #4: Forgive yourself. There was a little part of me going through that time with my mother with my fingers crossed, hoping my mother would have a catastrophic ending, would fall and crack her skull and die, would get hit by a bus. I thought it would be easier on her for her to go quickly than to go slowly, suffering the way she did. I think that a lot of people who watch their loved ones suffer through something like PSP harbor a secret prayer for a speedy ending. Call it "compassionate ill wishes." Maybe I'm perverse, maybe I'm humane. If our culture would accept the idea of euthanasia, then a person with a terminal disease could have a different outlook: *I'm going to live fully, I'll fight it, but I'll live, knowing that when I really do have to give up, I can be done with it without undue suffering.* Without that option, we cannot help but hope for an easier way out. So forgive yourself if you have compassionate ill wishes for your loved one.

And forgive yourself, too, for your own feelings that you might consider negative: frustration, anger, revulsion, despair, fatigue. Whatever darkness you feel around the work you are doing and the person you love who is suffering, know that this is merely human nature. You do the best you can. Those dark feelings are storm clouds, and inevitable. The sky through which they move remains, behind them, clear and blue. The storm clouds move on through, and the clear blue sky of your love and compassion remains behind and beneath them.

Tip #5: Back to communication, prepare yourself for the possibility that your person may lose the ability to communicate in all but the most rudimentary way, with a finger squeeze, one for yes, two for no, or whatever code you devise. Learn who this person is, and what her likes and dislikes are at this time in her life, so that you may anticipate more accurately and minimize frustration for everyone. Know his wishes for distribution of his belongings when he dies, his funeral arrangements, what hymns and psalms or Irish drinking tunes he wants at his memorial. This necessitates some discussion beforehand of death and dying.

A year and a half after my mother died, one of my dearest friends died of breast cancer. My mother accepted and faced her imminent death, one day at a time, while my friend denied it up until the last few weeks. I learned from these deaths, and others, that dying is a deeply personal process.

Living with PSP or any other terminal disease is also deeply personal. My mother needed to make some choices about how she wanted to live the rest of the days she had left, however many that turned out to be. While she could still talk, we discussed the issue of the feeding tube, which was probably the pivotal choice in her facing her imminent death, and we discussed and experienced and how she could best live out each day. She chose to do that with me, in my company, doing whatever in a day we could manage. It was helpful for us that my mother was my best friend and I hers. It was an honor and a gift to be with her.

Tip #6: No matter what your perceptions of this person, no matter what assumptions your perceptions of this person have caused you to form, do not assume that the person dying before you now is the same person you've watched living all these years.

Lily's son saying, "She's just not smart," is like the Colonel assuming that my mother is not smart, simply because she may be naive or ingenuous, and treating her like she's not smart, and therefore not seeing how smart she really is. Up until her dying moment, my mother continued to astonish

264

me with her deep perceptions and unequivocal grasp of what it meant to be alive. And to die. Lily's son may think that his mother does not want to know that she is dying, and he may be right. But he may be wrong.

My own mother was dying for someone to acknowledge that she was dying. It made her mad that my father wished she would get better when he won the wishbone. Her relief was palpable when I finally asked her if she knew that she was dying. "I know I'm dying, and you know I'm dying, but no one else believes it! I need to be able to talk about it!" The one thing I was able to give my mother, that she wouldn't have had if I hadn't been there, was someone she could talk to about her life, her feelings, and her impending death.

Lily knows on some level that she's dying. Lily's father lived to be one hundred and she thinks she should, too. She's got everything she needs to make it to a hundred, except she also has this disease. She may need to talk about it now, or soon, or later; to assume that she doesn't or won't, cheats her out of a potentially crucial conversation.

Generally, we know only facets of a person gathered from our unique relationship with that person, aspects we've been allowed by them to see, or perhaps insights we've gotten into them they might rather we hadn't, but we don't know the whole of anyone. We don't know their whole story, their inner feelings, the whole life they've painted and created inside themselves. We only know part of it. Given that, when any one person comes to the time of dying, we cannot assume that the end of a person's life will look the same as the way they have lived until now.

A person may have lived his life a certain way, but no matter who he has been all his life, no matter who you have perceived him to be, you need to be wide open at his dying to the possibility that he may be someone completely new, completely different, than you ever thought or expected from him. A person's death is the only thing that she has left, and she's going to do it in her own way. Be receptive and open to whoever she is and however she chooses to do it. Give her a chance to rise to her full human potential. Death is the final opportunity.

People facing death have got nothing left to lose, nothing left to hide, and a side of them that they themselves never even knew may come out. Every person's process of dying and death is unique to themselves, and we do everyone involved, even ourselves, a disservice if we assume that their manner of dying will be consistent with their manner of living, or consistent with what we expect from them. It might be. It might not be. Whatever it is, you can be sure it is not about you.

I saw how my mother's coming to grips with her disease, coming to understand what it was doing to her and what this meant, and through this coming to accept her mortality, was a process that lasted the whole eight months I was with her. The horrors were not clear to her at the beginning. Nor to any of us. Despite reading on the PSP Forum about the symptoms others were learning to manage and live with, until it actually happened to us the magnitude of the changes that overtook her were incomprehensible to me. I watched her cling to life with an unaccountable determination, and I watched her relinquish it with a surprising peace.

More than five years after my mother's death the pieces of the puzzle keep falling into place. Her sister told me recently another new thing: their mother told her, long ago, about my mother, "It's so hard for Ali."

"It's hard for everyone," my aunt said.

"Yes, but it's harder for Ali," said their mother, "because it's so hard for her to forgive."

Equating the difficulty of a life with the inability to forgive was an epiphany for me. In the end, it was my mother's sudden and complete forgiveness of my father that precipitated her final surrender and enabled her to just *let go*.

More than a year after her death, it came to me with painful clarity that what she had been asking me for in those last hours, those gasped, questioning syllables, was the mantra I had tried to teach her the week before. "Hamsa." The one word she could repeat over and over to bring her to a peaceful end. Instead, I gave her "cut the crap." I was not present enough to remember the mantra in her time of need. I have finally managed to forgive myself for that lapse. Maybe "cut the crap" suited her better anyway.

Yet how I wronged my mother even in my best attempts to serve her. Even I did not always see her for her whole entire self, but often as a problem to be managed. I kept my distance from her during much of that time. Kept to my role as caregiver, determined philosophically not to "get caught up in the suffering of the one." Overwhelmed with the crushing amount of need from both my parents, believing I could handle it alone, I ultimately struggled to come to grips with myself as I witnessed my mother saying goodbye to her life.

Where I put so much effort into trying to help her to release herself from her own fears, I must now release myself from mine. My primary fear is gone, that I will die before my mother. And my other great fear is somewhat assuaged from going through this death with her. For as long as I can remember I have been terrified of death. I cannot forget or escape the fact that we meet each day with the foreknowledge of the randomness of our own potential death, and the ultimate death of every one we know.

In every gathering of friends, every mindful visit to the grocery store, every incidental encounter with an acquaintance, I see the specter of death. Looking around at the faces of neighbors, friends, strangers, faces bright with hope, or fellowship, or faith, or liquor, with or without goodwill, I know that each of them will one day face their own death. In the end, perhaps the most valuable lesson I learned from my mother's life, her last years, her dying, is this: Do not come to the end of your life filled with regret and resentment.

I have freedoms now that I never had before. All the judgments that poured from my mother's mouth are mere echoes, and I no longer need to heed them. Now I hear the best of her voice, the clearest, most holy of her voice. The voice that says, "Cover your head when you go out in the wind," "Put on a sweater," the voice that says, "Forgive," the voice that says, "Cut the crap, just be real." Now, I cannot vacuum a rug without hearing my mother's warning, and now instead of making me bristle, her words make me smile. The first time I took a vacuum to a rug after I got home, I stopped cold. I laughed, and then I teared up as I heard her words again: "Don't vacuum the fringe off!"

We continue this dialogue. With her, I helped her to shed her fears and her judgments. I helped her. Now, though wounded and still fearful, as I recover from my grief at losing her, and heal into this deeper, stronger person, I can feel myself flower in the absence of her fears.

I am, however, forever entangled in my mother's disease. It is an integral thread of my life, whether or not I will it. Those days seem long ago now in one way only: The everyday horrors of the new normal have receded into the general haze of memory, perhaps because even at the time, the everyday horrors were mingled with plentiful moments of daily tenderness and connection. Yet I live with a new normal anxiety. I don't know if this disease will come and rob me first of one capacity, then another, until finally all my abilities will be gone. I cannot live my life in wondering, but I can be aware. I can practice rolling my eyes up, and down, and notice if one day they won't go. I can practice yoga and balance, monitoring my muscular coordination. But what can I do if I see a sign of PSP in me?

All I can do for now is share this story of a family coping with a grim disease. If you're one of a lucky few you'll never see anything like it in your life, but most of us will see something similar at least once, in ourselves or in someone we love suffering a terminal disease. Through this experience, the Colonel has become a softer person. He faces his own struggle now with dementia, lost in time and space. I have become a softer person, knowing the power of forgiveness. If our story with PSP can help anyone in any way, can offer insight which will engender compassion, can guide other families who are going through it, can help caregivers to care for themselves, my promise to my mother will be fulfilled: she will not have died in vain.

Near the trailhead of the Great Marsh Trail, setting out through fallen leaves on her last walk, just ten days before she died.

Resources

CurePSP (formerly The Society for PSP)
Foundation for PSP | CBD and Related Brain Diseases
30 E. Padonia Road, Suite 201
Timonium, Maryland 21093
Phone: 410.785.7004
      800.457.4777
Website: www.curepsp.org
       http://www.facebook.com/curepsp.foundation

"Progressive Supranuclear Palsy: Some Answers"
Lawrence I. Golbe, M.D., Professor of Neurology
University of Medicine and Dentistry of New Jersey
Robert Wood Johnson Medical School
New Brunswick, NJAugust 2009 revision
Available on CurePSP website

Compassion & Choices
PO Box 101810
Denver, CO 80250-1810
800.247.7421 (t)
303.639.1224 (f)
http://www.compassionandchoices.org/

Parkinson's Disease: A Guide for Patient and Family
Roger C. Duvoisin, M.D., F.A.C.P., and Jacob Sage, M.D.
2001 Lippincott Williams & Wilkins, Fifth Edition

Made in the USA
San Bernardino, CA
22 September 2013